Cisco

Xiaoying Dong · Yan Yu · Jiali Zhou

Cisco

Integration of Innovation and Operation

北京大学出版社
PEKING UNIVERSITY PRESS

Springer

Xiaoying Dong
Guanghua School of Management
Peking University
Beijing, China

Yan Yu
School of Information
Renmin University of China
Beijing, China

Jiali Zhou
Department of Information Systems, Business Statistics and Operation Management
Hong Kong University of Science and Technology
Kowloon, Hong Kong

ISBN 978-981-19-7869-2 ISBN 978-981-19-7870-8 (eBook)
https://doi.org/10.1007/978-981-19-7870-8

Jointly published with Peking University Press
The print edition is not for sale in China (Mainland). Customers from China (Mainland) please order the print book from: Peking University Press.

Translation from the Chinese language edition: "Cisco's Business Practices" by Xiaoying Dong et al.,

This Springer imprint is published by the registered company Springer Nature Singapore Pte Ltd.
The registered company address is: 152 Beach Road, #21-01/04 Gateway East, Singapore 189721, Singapore

Preface

The improvement of internationalization and innovation is a new challenge and opportunity that Chinese enterprises face in the process of economic globalization. The question of how to build enterprises with global competitiveness, innovative spirit and transformational ability is a subject that scholars, entrepreneurs and policy-makers have considered and explored for a long time. In this process, the continuous study of internationally competitive enterprises is one important way of expanding knowledge in these areas.

In 2008, Guanghua School of Management, Peking University, and Cisco established the Guanghua-Cisco Leadership Institute. Among the institute's educational research activities, SASAC selected senior executives of state-owned enterprises study at Peking University then train leading talent for China's development of world-class enterprises Cisco headquarters. In the four years from 2010 to 2013, the SASAC selected four sessions of nearly 50 senior leaders of state-owned enterprises to participate in this training course. The author had the privilege of participating in these four courses and engaging with the chairman and president of Cisco Corporation, as well as senior leaders in human resources, marketing, operations, information technology, supply chain, risk control, innovation systems, social responsibility, cooperation and strategic alliances. During lecture sessions, leaders of the central enterprises raised many high-level questions about Cisco's practice, and the summit dialog between the two sides fully reflected the insight of the business leaders, conveying their aspirations in management.

The book is derived from a case study that occurred over a four-year period and fully recreates the sessions and refines the essence of the experience, providing a unique opportunity for readers to gain insight into how Cisco has successfully transformed and continued to innovate in a competitive market. The author hopes to provide knowledge of best practices from world-class enterprises to potentially address the real problems faced by Chinese enterprises. Thus, we have written a book. In the process of our research, we adopted a three-tiered pyramid structure: the first part is a study and summary of the Cisco case, which focuses on how Cisco can be both separate and collaborative in innovation and management dual ability; the second part is the main body of the book with nine chapters that explore the specific practices and methods of Cisco's innovation and management activities; the third part is a problem-oriented dialog that complements the second part with more in-depth detail, further presenting questions and solutions on innovation and management in an impromptu question-and-answer session. Each of these three parts has its own focus, providing a step-by-step process for improving innovation and management from practice to theory.

Throughout the writing process, we paid careful attention to three principles. First, we focused our attention on first-hand information. Our project aimed to: (1) record all teaching processes (including Chinese conic interpretation) and relevant videos; (2) simultaneously document all Chinese content in written text to verify English audio recordings or videos of important but uncertain content; (3) integrate text materials from the perspective of practitioners, organizing them by practical problem topic in enterprise innovation and management; (4) refine valuable ideas and practices under the two propositions of innovation and management; and (5) ensure fresh activity and scenario reproduction of the case study. The third part of this book specifically retains high-level dialog between the leadership of the central enterprise and Cisco senior management, whether it is the immediate question of the leadership or the on-site responses by senior Cisco leadership sharing wisdom and management experience. On-site questions and answers are specific and targeted and are closely related to business practice, so they have special value.

The second principle focused on problem orientation. In the process of writing the case study, the basic principle includes organizing the content by problem area at the core and constructing the knowledge system through the internal logic relative to the problem. The author conducts a targeted investigation and analysis of Cisco's case and aims to understand Cisco's experience and methods in practice based on the teaching experience of entrepreneurs and senior managers in Guanghua School of Management of Peking University, the observation and judgment of China's enterprise development, and based on the perspective and needs of Chinese entrepreneurs and senior management. This book focuses on the dual capabilities of innovation and management, and the second part describes Cisco's innovation and management capabilities in nine chapters. The author acknowledges that the length of the book makes it challenging to present a complete and in-depth analysis of the key elements, breadth and depth of information, and the level of analysis may also have limitations. However, the book provides a framework for further discussion of innovation and management strategies.

The third principle involved highlighting areas in need of further attention for research and analysis. Based on systematic combing of the information related to the case, the author tries to excavate the key elements of Cisco's success from the perspective of innovation and management dual capacity-building and paradox management. We chose the perspective of ambidexterity because some internationally renowned successful enterprises have been in decline in recent years, prompting academic institutions and businesses to consider that, in a rapidly changing and uncertain competitive environment, enterprises should have both innovation and management capabilities through investment in technological innovation, market transformation and disruptive business models to build future-oriented capabilities. In addition, bringing stable benefits to enterprises may ensure survival and sustainable innovation and management development. We wanted to determine how Cisco's case study was able to do both. Thus, this book differs from news or other cases in that we hope to summarize and extract from the case study the common topic of enterprise development, that is, how to resolve the issues of dynamic balance of innovation and management, system design and resource allocation in the information age, technological innovation and disruptive business transformation. In the four levels including enterprise learning, belonging, structure and performance, through effective paradox management of dynamic construction of dual capabilities, organizations can better resolve the dynamic balance of innovation and management, system design and resource allocation. The National Natural Science Foundation of China projects (No. 72172155, 71371017) supports the research and translation of this topic.

I would like to thank the Guanghua School of Management of Peking University for the platform and learning opportunities provided to us, the leadership of Guanghua-Cisco Leadership Research Institute and colleagues for their support, the trust of SASAC and the leaders of the central enterprises--your insights into the dialog and discussion have benefited me greatly, the senior leadership of Cisco for their openness and frankness in the course of teaching and dialog, and the project leader for the careful design and organization of the course of this study. All of this support has been invaluable to our case study, and your wisdom and practical experience have provided the foundation and material for this book.

In the course of writing this book, Wang Qixian, Liu Wei, Luo Yinglin and Cui Yanyu from the Department of Information Management of Peking University participated in the data collection and collation work, and Yang Hanyan, Ying Chenguang, Wang Xueying, Liu Rongkun and Huo Haiping from the School of Information at Renming University of China participated in the English translation work, expressing their heartfelt thanks. Finally, I would like to thank my family for their love and care which enabled me to move forward in difficult times.

Beijing, China

Xiaoying Dong

Contents

Chapter 1
Integration of Innovation and Operation: The Way Multinational Companies Survive

Check for updates

1 Background and Motivation

In a rapidly changing environment, the manner in which an enterprise explores and develops new technologies and capabilities while continuing to utilize existing ones in the process of innovation directly affects the short-term survival and long-term sustainable development of the enterprise. This also establishes a positive interactive relationship between the two activities, which is at the core of dual capacity building (Raisch and Birkinshaw 2008; Vera and Crossan 2004). Activities were used to emphasize the optimization, upgrading and improvement of existing systems, with emphasis on "refinement, efficiency selection and realization (March 1991). It focuses on the consistency and incremental innovation of existing capabilities, technology routes and management paradigms (Tushman and O'Reilly III 1996). Exploration activities focus on adaptability to the environment, constantly discovering new markets and technologies, introducing new knowledge, and building new capabilities, including such activities as "search, change, experiment and discover" (Levinthal and March 1993).[1] Enterprises can promote change by exploring and embracing radical innovation (Benner and Tushman 2003; He and Wong 2004). In this process, enterprises are able to escape the existing "system" and enter a new more efficient system (Dong and Zhou 2014).

The dual power theory pointed out that the utilization of enterprises while simultaneously engaged in activities and exploration relates to the present company's survival and development. In practice, high-tech enterprises in the process of innovation ability construction of the dual power theory face three major difficulties: the exploration and utilization of activities in performance, structure, and learning belong to four aspects of existence paradox relations (Tushman and O'reilly III 1996; Andriopoulos and Lewis 2009). The so-called paradox refers to the fact that the two sides of a thing have elements that are both opposite and related, which compete with

[1] In this book, utilization activities refer to organizational operations and incremental innovation activities; Exploration usually refers to innovation or radical innovation.

X. Dong et al., *Cisco*,
https://doi.org/10.1007/978-981-19-7870-8_1

each other, conflict with each other, and depend on and transform each other. Exploration activities focus on long-term goals and sustainable development in terms of performance, focus on acquiring new knowledge in terms of learning, emphasizing diversity, changing in terms of ownership, emphasizing flexibility, authorization and informal relationships in the context of organizational structure. Activities focus on short-term goals and financial indicators related to performance and attach importance to the continuity of old knowledge and technical systems in learning to pursue consistency and stability in terms of affiliation and emphasize overall efficiency and control in terms of structure (Dong and Zhou 2014). Under the circumstance of resource shortages, it is difficult for enterprises to consider the contradiction of these four aspects, and they often pay attention to one and lose the other.

Second, due to the uncertainty and risk of exploration activities, enterprises tend to engage in exploitation activities and avoid exploration activities (Groysberg and Lee 2009). Exploratory activities are the testing and discovery of future potential technologies and new markets with unclear business models and unpredictable returns on investment. Exploration activities require enterprises to change or break away from the existing path and capacity of the organization, and this process is risky. Double risks make enterprises cautious about exploration activities. The higher the uncertainty is, the more cautious the investment. Small and medium-sized high-tech enterprises with scarce resources cannot afford the cost and risk of early exploration activities, so they may choose to imitate, copy or follow an existing strategy to directly enter the market segment (Voss and Voss 2012). However, mature large enterprises are unwilling to give up or subvert the existing advantages, bear the pain of organizational transformation and the loss of short-term gains and are thus silent on exploration activities.

Third, the continuous investment of enterprises in utilizing activities continuously strengthens the existing advantages, improves the efficiency, and ensures the predictability and stability of profits so that enterprises gradually form a self-strengthening mechanism. In the short term, profitable activities are a safe choice, especially in a stable market environment, and help to strengthen the existing core competitiveness. However, in the long run, the self-strengthening mechanism will cause the enterprise to generate path dependence and inertia, attach importance to internal optimization and development, and ignore the transformation changes in the external environment, technology and customers (Gupta et al. 2006). In the context of frequent innovation of radical technology and business models, the self-reinforcement mechanism increases the opportunity cost and conversion cost of exploration activities (Levinthal and March 1993; Gilbert 2005), and it is difficult to respond quickly to the "creative destruction" of competitors, thus missing the opportunity to enter new technologies and new markets. Many prominent large enterprises (such as Nokia, Kodak, etc.) have fallen into a similar predicament (Kaijin and Linjun 2012), and thus the core competitiveness of enterprises has become the core obstacle.

This chapter, with the dual ability of enterprise innovation at its core and the theory of paradox management perspective, tried to implement this in the field of telecommunications equipment and services for more than 30 years. Through the use of Ethan line activities and the separation—integration mechanism as the research center, the five dynasty rival companies sought to resolve three research questions: (1) how can enterprises utilize the paradox of the separation and integration mechanism to realize sustainable development in leading the process of building innovative dual ability? and what are the specific elements and methods of its paradoxical separation-integration mechanism? (2), what is the internal relationship between binary separation and integration from the perspective of paradox management? In particular, how can you make the separated "binary" interact with each other organically through the aggregation mechanism in the construction of innovation capability of enterprises, forming a virtuous circle. (3) what is the important value of the paradoxical separation-integration mechanism in enterprise innovation? That is, how does this mechanism help enterprises solve uncertainty in innovation and return on investment, and how can the continuous success of enterprises in both emerging and mature markets be ensured? The solution to the above three research problems will provide an important reference for the construction of the innovation ambidexterity of high-tech enterprises in China.

2 Explore and Use the Difficulties of Dual Integration and Countermeasures

2.1 Explore and Utilize the Approaches to the Construction of Dual Capabilities

To achieve both long-term development and short-term survival, enterprises must strike a dynamic balance between exploration activities and utilization activities. Especially since 2008, increasing attention has been given to research on this issue in academic circles at home and abroad (Raisch and Birkinshaw 2008; O'Reilly and Tushman 2013; Turner et al. 2013). The research focuses on two dimensions: one is how to promote the parallel ambidexterity; the second is how to establish the integration mechanism between the dual capabilities. The former mainly focuses on three aspects: duality of leadership, duality of structure and duality of situation (Raisch and Birkinshaw 2008). The duality of leadership suggests that leaders with cognitive complexity and complex senior management teams can evenly allocate attention to exploration activities and utilization activities, avoiding the loss of focus due to personal preference or limited energy (Perretti and Negro 2006). The duality of the structure refers to the spatial isolation or parallel design between different departments in the large system of the organization so that each department can lead activities relatively freely according to their own business needs and conduct exploration activities and utilization activities, respectively (Fang et al. 2010). Scene dual sex to solve organizational adaptability to the external environment and internal efficiency is a contradiction to sex; it is no longer by an independent dual structure to solve the problem but pays attention to the subjectivity of the worker to encourage the staff to choose their own according to changes in the environment, since the allocation of time, in conflict with the target to make employees have the ability at the same time engaged in exploration and utilization activities (Gibson and Birkinshaw 2004; Ghoshal and Bartlert 1994).

The limitation of the above research is that although scholars have proposed different forms of integration mechanisms, this integration is mainly embodied in people. The dual approach of leadership places the responsibility for integration on top leaders and senior teams. The structured approach places the responsibility for integration at the top of the exploration and utilization activities. The situational approach places the responsibility for integration on the individual dual capabilities of the average employee. However, construction of a separation and integration mechanism between exploration and utilization activities at the organizational capability level remains a research gap. As stated by Jasen et al. (2009), establishing a well-designed system, process and capability at the organizational level to dynamically correlate exploration activities with utilization activities is the key to establishing dual energy. To date, we do not know what the elements and methods of the separate integration mechanism exist at the organizational level, how they work, and how they form cross-boundary resource combinations, flow, synergy and mutual support of exploration and utilization activities.

2.2 *Explore and Utilize the Thinking Method of Constructing Dual Ability*

To construct exploration and utilization of the dual capabilities at the most basic level, the first step involves completing a shift in thinking, that is, from either/or trade-off thinking to paradoxical thinking (Gresov and Drazin 1997; Lewis 2000; Morgeson and Hofmann 1999; Bouchikhi 1998). The management mode guided by paradoxical thinking is referred to as paradoxical management (Smith and Lewis 2011).

Tradeoff thinking means that people make a choice between exploring activities and using activities. Since the opposite relationship in the paradox often causes emotional anxiety and defensive psychology in people (Schneider and May 1990), the behaviors of negation, suppression and exclusion appear successively (Vince and Broussine 1996). People usually interpret paradoxes with simple, static and separate weighted thinking, emphasizing one side of things, while ignoring or even denying the other side. This may lead to the contradiction relationship of paradoxes being strengthened and the correlation relationship being weakened. People tend to seek conformity with others in cognition, attitude and behavior (Cialdini et al. 1995; Smith and Lewis 2011), which further deepens this contradiction. This consistency helps to reduce the conflicts and contradictions between people's thoughts and behaviors, reduces the cost of coordination and consensus within enterprises, and avoids the uncertainty caused by inconsistent behaviors (Pratt and Foreman 2000). Maintaining the illusion of order by suppressing one of the paradoxes can temporarily relieve anxiety or strengthen one of the paradoxes. Although, it cannot eliminate the tension between the two, after deregulation, the tension will be further intensified, leading to the vicious circle of paradox. Thus, taking balanced thinking or consistency as an organizational defense mechanism will improve organizational consensus and efficiency in the short run, while in the long run, it will lose the other.

A paradox refers to a group of elements that exist simultaneously and continuously and are mutually opposite and interrelated (Lewis 2000; Smith and Lewis 2011). There are essential differences between paradoxical thinking and trade-off thinking (Lewis 2000). First, in contrast to weighted thinking, paradoxical thinking acknowledges the opposition of things and adopts an attitude of "acceptance" rather than "confrontation". Second, the thinking of balance emphasizes the choice of either or the other, while the thinking of paradox emphasizes that both sides of a paradox are opposite and interrelated. If we adopt a positive management mode, it is possible to realize the requirements of both sides of a paradox at the same time. Third, making a choice in the paradox of both sides cannot solve or eliminate the paradox, as both opposite and contact relationships will continue to exist; therefore, the management paradox fully taps the potential of the paradox, uses the method of creating sex development at both ends of the tension simultaneously, and recognizes the possibility of exploration and utilization of coexisting. The theory of the contrast between the two parties establishes the manner and methods of promoting each other's value (Eisenhardt 1989). In this process, people look for management paths and strategies for "simultaneously" rather than "trade-offs" by confronting conflicts and design mechanisms at the long-term and macro levels on this basis (Lewis 2000; Smith and Lewis 2011).

Therefore, helping people transcend the thinking mode of either/or, opposition and solidification through paradoxical thinking, transforming the internal connection between the two ends of the paradox from the perspective, and finding a dynamic balance solution to the problem (Poole and Van DE Ven 1989) provides new ideas for the construction of dual capacity.

2.3 Explore and Utilize the Separation and Integration Mechanism Built by Dual Capabilities

Under the guidance of paradox thinking, it is important to generate a creative method for organically linking the ambidexterity of exploration and exploitation and taking advantage of each element rather than simply making efforts to differentiate exploration from exploitation (Eisenhardt and Martin 2000). The attitude of "acceptance" is the key to making the paradoxes follow each other in a positive way. When people realize that the tension between paradoxes can coexist, they will take the initiative to explore the antagonistic relationship between them and recognize the dynamic transformation of the antagonistic relationship. Through the transformation of the paradox, the effective scope of decision-making is extended to the medium and long term, and the possibility and potential of organizational resources are explored. Under the influence of paradoxical thinking, Poole and Van de Ven (1989) and later Andriopoulos and Lewis (2009) proposed the separate-integration mechanism of paradox management.

Separation mechanism. The separation mechanism focuses on the differences between the two elements of paradox and adopts different methods for dealing with them. The separation helps solve the conflict and competition between the two sides of the paradox. Establishing and developing the separation structure gives them space and time to develop their own uniqueness and creativity so the duality of the organization can be developed simultaneously. The separation can be subdivided into spatial separation and temporal separation (O'Reilly and Tushman 2013). Spatial separation refers to the establishment of separate units within an organization to create noninterfering conditions and environments within subsystems through structural boundaries and spatial isolation (Jasen et al. 2009). Time separation refers to focusing on different aspects of the paradox in different time periods, such as focusing on developing exploration ability in one period and developing utilization ability in another period.

The advantage of separation is that through the separation of time and space, the conflict and competition of paradoxes are avoided so that business activity patterns maintain their independence and consistency and thus one party in the paradox can achieve the best, and the other can avoid the interference of the first party. This is conducive to the development of the organization's professional ability and increases the organization's leadership and differentiation in some fields through a self-strengthening mechanism (Smith and Tushman 2005). Resource-poor enterprises develop exploration and utilization activities simultaneously or alternately according to environmental changes and strategic appeals (Benner and Tushman 2003).

The limitation of separation is that exploration activities and utilization activities must be carried out alone, which leads to high demand for the allocation of organizational resources. Moreover, due to the weakened connection between exploration activities and utilization activities, organizations will face obstacles in knowledge exchange and achievement sharing. In addition, the exploration and use of self-strengthening in their respective systems make it difficult for organizations to evolve into new resource combinations and capabilities. Exploiting units tend to avoid the uncertainty and risk of exploration activities so that enterprises miss the opportunity for transformation. However, the exploratory unit is unable to make full use of the existing assets and capabilities, and it is difficult to realize the commercial value of emerging technologies, which will eventually lead enterprises to pay attention to one and lose the other in the paradox of stability and development. Edmondson et al. (2003) pointed out that the use of separation alone cannot completely solve the organizational paradox, conflict relations in organizations will still exist, and new conflicts will be generated. For example, although polaroid devotes many resources to the research and development of digital cameras, the rejection of this disruptive technology by most senior leaders leads to the marginalization of members related to the new technology (Edmondson et al. 2003).

Integration mechanism. The integration mechanism emphasizes finding the connection point between two seemingly opposite "elements" by establishing the connection between the two, building the binomial capability. An increasing number of scholars have come to realize that exploration activities and utilization activities can form a complementary relationship, and the value of each can be improved through the transformation between the two: exploration activities provide materials for the optimization and expansion of utilization activities, while utilization activities provide a knowledge base for further exploration activities (e.g., Cao et al. 2009; He and Wong 2004). Portfolio capabilities and complementary assets play a key role in this process.

Composition ability is the ability to conduct dynamic interaction and fusion between existing knowledge and new knowledge (Fleming 2001). Schumpeter (1939) pointed out that "innovation is the reorganization of existing resources in new ways". Fleming (2001) mentioned that "in order to cope with the uncertainty and unpredictability of technological transformation, combination is to try to add elements previously not available within the existing vision and knowledge framework. In this process, new elements and new combinations can be considered at the same time so that the creation can continue to develop". These views all suggest that the combination of exploration activities and utilization activities will facilitate the innovation of development organizations, reduce the risk of exploration activities and enhance the value of utilization activities. In addition, portfolio capacity is the basis for organizational absorption capacity, and the creation of new knowledge is the generation of novel applications and new knowledge combinations from existing knowledge (Kristal et al. 2010). Bosch et al. (1995) further subdivided portfolio capabilities into system capabilities, socialization capabilities and coordination capabilities, pointing out that they can occur within organizations, between industries and in industries and environments related to enterprises. Cao et al. (2009) applied the concept of combination to the ambidexterity of product development, thinking that combination focuses on the quantity and proportion of resource allocation of exploration activities and utilization activities but does not further explore the specific means of combination.

In addition to the combined capabilities of exploration and utilization activities, the successful transformation of technologies into business value requires the support of complementary assets of the enterprise. Teece et al. (1997) proposed that the success of core technology commercialization needs to be supported by complementary assets, which will raise the access barriers for imitators to expand the market and improve the commercial value of new technologies. Exploration activities and utilization activities can share the existing assets of the organization (such as manufacturing, channels, services, complementary technologies, outsourcing, marketing, finance, etc.), which can improve the efficiency of utilization activities while reducing the risk of exploration activities. For high-tech enterprises, exploratory innovation and utilization innovation are the core activities of enterprises. Processes, systems and value chains are the auxiliary activities of enterprises. The assets supporting the auxiliary activities are called complementary assets. The optimization and updating of complementary assets play an important role in improving the adaptability of enterprises in the technological transformation period. The existing research results also prove that the success of innovators and new entrants in business is influenced by three factors: investment, technical capability and the exclusivity of complementary assets. In the process of interaction between new entrants and old industry defenders, specialized complementary assets play a crucial role. Innovation performance can be affected if investment and technical capabilities are isolated from each other (Tripsas 1997). Taylor and Helfat (2009) explained the concept of complementary assets in the technical transformation of an organization facing dual challenges through a case study and comparison of IBM and NCR, high-tech enterprises in technological transformation, the core technology and three kinds of connections between complementary assets (linkage): one is the intrinsic connection between complementary assets. The second is the connection between the old complementary assets and new complementary assets. The third is the connection between core technologies and complementary assets. Their case study found that link activities such as communication and collaboration among mid-level managers play a key role in exploring and leveraging the interaction between activities. The study suggests that when new technologies are in the embryonic stage, a separation strategy should be adopted first to enhance the vitality of exploration activities, and that exploration and utilization activities should be purposefully integrated with complementary assets as these assets of the organization continue to mature and perfect (Tushman and O'Reilly III 1996).

Combination ability and the concept of complementary assets to our understanding of the integration mechanism between exploration and utilization activities has inspired much, but the literature failed to reveal the exploration and utilization activities integration mechanism of specific methods and procedures: one failed to reveal how exploration and utilization activities support the dynamic relationship between each other and the mutually beneficial mechanism. Second, it fails to reveal how the dynamic relationship between exploration activities and utilization activities can help reduce the uncertainty and risk of exploration activities. Third, it fails to reveal what value the connection between complementary assets and exploration and utilization activities brings to enterprise innovation. On these issues, there is still a lack of relevant research and large-scale empirical studies at home and abroad (Raisch and Birkinshaw 2008). With a deeper and more comprehensive understanding of portfolio capabilities and complementary assets, we can further explain the approach and integrated mechanism of exploring activities and utilizing activity paradox management in enterprise innovation and open the "black box" of enterprise innovation to achieve success.

On this basis, this chapter puts forth the analysis framework of the separate-integration mechanism in the process of the ambidexterity of enterprise innovation (as shown in Fig. 1.1). We initially proposed the following four propositions:

Proposition 1: Separating and integrating paradoxes in innovation in constructing the dual capabilities of exploration and utilization innovation is an important paradox management mechanism for enterprises to engage in. Under the premise of adopting paradoxical thinking, the enterprise must first separate the "dual element" of innovation, namely, a series of exploration activities and utilization activities.

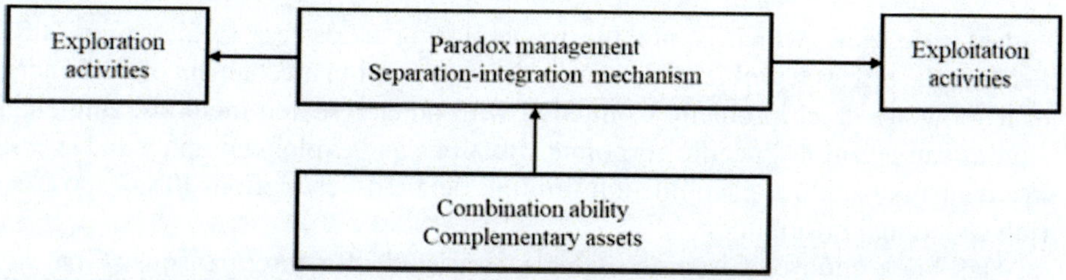

Fig. 1.1 Paradox management mechanism for exploration and exploitation of ambidexterity

Proposition 2: In the process of constructing the innovation ambidexterity of enterprises, the value of separating "duality" (exploration activity and utilization activity) is realized through the integration of paradox management.

Proposition 3: Portfolio capabilities and complementary assets are key elements in the integration mechanism. The combination of exploration activities and utilization activities in enterprise innovation can help enhance the value of each, the support of utilization activities and exploration activities can help reduce innovation risks, and the supplementation of exploration activities to utilization activities can help increase innovation vitality. The integration mechanism with combination capability at the core will play an important role in reducing uncertainty and risk in enterprise innovation.

Proposition 4: The complementary assets of an enterprise are composed of the process, system and value chain of the organization. The complementary assets are logically related and constantly updated. The connection between complementary assets and exploration activities can enhance the efficiency of exploration innovation. The linkage between complementary assets and utilization activities will further reduce the cost of profitable activities. The integration mechanism with complementary assets as the core will play an important role in improving the investment return rate of innovation.

3 Research Method and Process of the Cisco Case

3.1 Research Methods

The nature of the research questions determines the selection of research methods and the design of follow-up studies (Eisenhardt 1989). This chapter attempts to explore how successful enterprises use separation and integration mechanisms to build binary capabilities and proposes a single-case study approach. First, the "integration mechanism" involved in this research problem is a recent emerging research hotspot, and there is no mature theory or accepted conclusion (Jasen et al. 2009). However, the single case study method can grasp the richness of research phenomena through extreme and inspiring cases (Weick 2007) to form a more comprehensive and holistic view, which is suitable for exploring fields less studied (Yin 2003). Second, the research problem focuses on the construction mechanism of dual energy, or a "how" research problem. Compared with other research methods, single case studies can penetrate specific corporate situations and explain complex and specific mechanisms behind a phenomenon through detailed descriptions (Tsui 2007) and rich situational information.

This book chooses Cisco as a single case study for three reasons. First, as a large multinational technology company, Cisco faces many challenges of paradoxical management to maintain a leading position in mature and emerging markets (Xiaoying and Jiali 2014). The book begins with these challenges. Second, as one of the few long-lived high-tech companies, CISCO has a unique practice in building dual capabilities. In its developmental history of more than three decades, Cisco has surpassed five generations of competitors such as Nortel and Linksys. After many technological changes, Cisco has remained the top provider of network equipment and maintained a gross margin of 60–65% in sales. Nearly 80% of the internet traffic passes through Cisco's routers, switches and other devices. The unique practices of Cisco and its successful experience can be used for reference and inspiration for many enterprises. Third, from 2010 to 2013, the main author of this book collected a large number of valuable first-hand interview materials on the research questions of this book. The detailed collection process will be presented in the "Data collection" section. In summary, Cisco's single case study has the characteristics of extreme and difficult to obtain data, which satisfies the sampling principle of a single case study theory.

Eisenhardt and Graebner (2007) pointed out that "interviews are an efficient way to obtain rich data, but interviews can also cause respondents' knee-jerk reactions, i.e., bias in interview data caused by mechanisms such as impression management and 'hindsight'". This book aims to mitigate this bias in two ways: (1) by interviewing multiple subjects to obtain rich information about the same research phenomenon from different perspectives. Because it is very unlikely that a large number of different interviewees will be able to beautify and tamper with their impressions. (2) Multiple data collection methods are connected and used to form triangulation verification between data (Tsui 2007). In addition to first-hand interview data, this book also collects a large volume of second-hand data, including Cisco's annual reports from 1995 to 2012, its enterprise website and news reports, works by domestic and foreign scholars on Cisco's management mode and experience, and Chinese and English literature retrieved in the database.

The analysis process of case data is an "analytic generalization", even though concepts and categories are used to extract facts and refine the conclusion of the problem (Tsui 2007). The data analysis method in this book refers to Miles and Huberman (1994) and adopts the coding steps in grounded theory, including open coding, spindle coding and selective coding.

3.2 *Research Process*

From 2010 to 2013, the main author of this book participated in the relevant projects of state-owned assets supervision and administration commission (SASAC) in bidding for world-class enterprises and participated in the training of Cisco leadership in the United States, with nearly 50 senior leaders of state-owned enterprises selected successively. I had the opportunity to go to the scene, listen to the Cisco Systems experience from chairman and president to human resources, marketing, operations, information technology, supply chain, risk control, innovation system, social responsibility, cooperation and strategic alliance for a total of 49 top leaders. Through peak dialog, I was able to learn the practices of Cisco leadership and how they address the proposed problems. I was also able to obtain valuable resources as I made audio and video recordings of all lectures (including text materials of English speeches, audio materials, video, Chinese simultaneous biographies and on-site dialogs). The English audio or video recordings that were important but contained uncertain content were checked to ensure the accuracy and credibility of the information. On this basis, the research team classified and integrated the text materials, and the sorted text included more than 300,000 words, with 300 on-site questions and answers. The author's book on achieving innovation and management at Cisco has been officially published (Xiaoying and Jiali 2014). The specific steps and processes of data collection are shown in Table 1.1. Table 1.1 shows 2010–2014, where the team collected enterprise information and dialog from interviews, search theory and analysis of the process of perspective. From the high-tech enterprise ability of double drive, two "yuan", the paradox of the dual ability of the management and separation—set into mechanism, the author sought to systematically explore Cisco in fierce market competition, highlighting the key elements of successful transformation. These theoretical perspectives are also revised and deepened in the course of teaching and in the process through which central enterprise leaders seek feedback and confirmation. Therefore, this process includes: (1) practical information acquisition; (2) theoretical induction and analysis; (3) practitioner information acquisition and feedback; and (4) theoretical correction and deepening.

4 Exploring and Utilizing Dual Integration: Cisco's Approach

Through an in-depth case analysis of Cisco, we summarized the separation-integration mechanism of Cisco's ability to build dual innovation under paradoxical thinking, as shown in Fig. 1.2. Following this, we will analyze and elaborate upon this mechanism in detail.

Table 1.1 Case study process

Year Data analysis	2010	2011	2012	2013	2014
Focus and theoretical perspective	Comprehensive understanding and benchmarking of world-class enterprises, focusing on innovation system and information construction	Two-wheel drivers: innovation system and operation system	Ambidexterity in high-tech enterprises	Paradox management of ambidexterity in high-tech enterprises	Paradox management of ambidexterity: separation integration mechanism, complementary assets and combination capabilities
First-hand information	Cisco's innovation system and excellent operation system (14 speakers) On site Q&A:33	Cisco's transformation, transformation, innovation and informatization (12 speakers) On site Q&A: 50	Cisco's transformation, innovation, culture, informatization, human resources, social responsibility, etc. (16 persons) On site Q&A: 68	Cisco's innovation system and operation system (12 persons) On site Q&A: 78	Cisco coach: 15 persons On site Q&A: 70
Data analysis process	Record and collate 35,000 words of the first-hand materials Theme analysis: internationalization, innovation and information construction	The first-hand materials are 60,000 words in total Theme analysis: innovation system, cooperation, strategic alliance, informatization and operation system	The first-hand materials have 105,000 words and the second-hand materials have 120,000 words	The first-hand materials have 125,000 words, and the second-hand materials have 200,000 words Take root in 50 small themes under six major themes of Cisco	The first-hand materials have 25,000 words, and the second-hand materials have 200,000 words

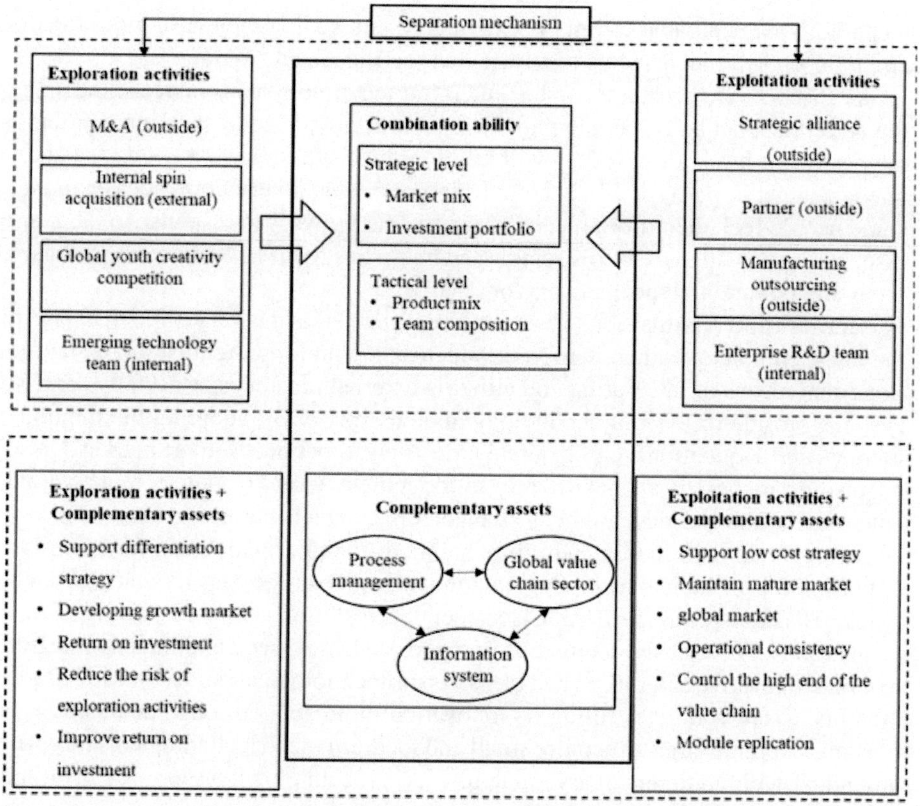

Fig. 1.2 Cisco's ambidexterity in exploration and exploitation: separation integration mechanism

4.1 Explore the Separation Mechanism Between Activities and Utilization Activities

4.1.1 Separate Exploration Activities

The separation mechanism in exploration activities seeks new technologies outside the space of existing technology systems. Large enterprises usually have complete R&D and technology systems. If they focus on self-centered technological innovation for a significant amount of time, they may miss the emergence and opportunities of radical technological development. Faced with this situation, Cisco, as a mature company, "must resist the desire to do all research and development by itself" to avoid losing the opportunity for radical innovation, especially in technologies and products outside Cisco's technological system. To address this problem, Cisco acquired external enterprises and continuously integrated external resources into the internal enterprise. At the same time, the internal research and development team for new technology is "separated" from the existing system so that they have more freedom and independent mechanisms to ensure that their ideas are "unique".

As Cisco's vice president spoke, emerging technology may increase the size of the enterprise, but some people may have natural resistance to such innovation: "in the enterprise has antibody, they will kill your idea, if you have a good idea and no one is against it, perhaps this is not a truly good idea, a very crazy ideas can make some people feel uncomfortable, because it is disruptive." In response to the fear of discovering new ideas, Cisco's senior leadership has focused on fostering a sense of crisis and culture and mechanisms for change.

Mergers and Acquisitions Cisco clearly realized that it is very difficult to provide the latest complete, comprehensive products and solutions. Acquisition is the most important means of integrating and utilizing external resources, especially for Cisco systems outside of existing technology and enterprise. By adopting the method of mergers and acquisitions, Cisco quickly meets customer needs in the market. Cisco's acquisition process is also constantly introducing external resources to activate the enterprise's internal development change force, which helps the enterprise overcome organizational inertia caused by habitual thinking, which can lead to missed opportunities for radical technological innovation. Over the past 15 years, Cisco has made 170 acquisitions. In 2013, Cisco spent $6.1 billion, nearly 13% of its sales, on acquisitions. Through the acquisition of external ideas, Cisco continuously integrates external innovative enterprises and ideas into its technological innovation and product systems. Cisco continues filling its innovation blind spots through acquisition, but may miss opportunities to acquire small and medium-sized technological enterprises and talent with complementary value to Cisco's technology system. Meanwhile, it keeps combining existing technology products and service systems to ensure that they can effectively adapt to market demands.

Internal purchase. Internal acquisition is a way to intervene in an acquired enterprise at the early stages and provides for an active exploration to ensure the success of the acquisition and reduce uncertain risk. In practice, Cisco makes early investments in companies that could be acquired in the future, sharing technology roadmaps with them and sending experienced managers to guide them. Cisco buys a company when its sales reach a predetermined number of customers and milestones.

Global youth creative competition. The creative competition of global youth is another way to internalize external sources of innovation. Cisco obtains its ideas from global youth innovation competition and uses Cisco's learning approach to impact internal action and promote internal entrepreneurship of external ideas. The internet is a young industry and a young people's world. To understand the creativity and needs of young people, Cisco promotes creative competition on social media platforms worldwide and obtains valid ideas from young people in different countries. Across the globe, Cisco has endorsed thousands of projects through competitions aimed at deriving innovative ideas from young people, offering prizes of up to $250,000 to creative winners.

Chambers, in industry executives' exchanges, said: "Cisco as a 10-year-old child looking to the future, keeps the young mentality and provide a range of opportunities to invite young people to the board of directors and understand young people's thinking and pursuit, hope with the young mentality outlook did not come, you will see opportunity and hope."

Emerging technology team. For emerging technology teams, Cisco adopts a separation strategy of internal innovation, supporting them by providing a relatively independent office space, cultural atmosphere, incentive mechanism and independent selection criteria, while keeping distance from the existing mature technology R&D team, maintaining relative independence, and completing innovative projects without interference. At Cisco, the CEO has an innovation fund of 20 million dollars. For strong ideas proposed by employees, there is no need to consult engineers to make plans and discuss the benefits of the new ideas for the company in the future. If the project is approved by the experts and engineers, the staff can form a separate team to conduct the research and development, and the project team will operate like an investment company. Sometimes, creative teams leave Cisco and enjoy more independence and freedom while sharing Cisco's resources and infrastructure free from the constraints of Cisco culture, incentives and working hours, while maintaining time and space separate from Cisco. This type of time and space in isolation allows them to enjoy more freedom to foster a small business innovation team atmosphere from the big enterprise fixed thinking and operation model of interference. Once the product is in the research and development stage and ready to enter the market, companies may seek to buy it back with valuation of the purchase price at market cost. If the creative team was cultivated through Cisco and enters mass manufacturing, through company processes, the team may be integrated into the production system of mature products. Through such cultivation, growth, integration and cycling, Cisco's technology and products continuously enhance the depth and breadth of the product system and enhance the diversity of the whole product and solutions.

4.1.2 Extending the Separation of Activities

Cisco has also adopted a strategy of using external resources for its sales and manufacturing systems for three main reasons. As the technology and product life cycle become shorter, depending on its technical capability, it is challenging for an enterprise to enter the market quickly and occupy a dominant position. Therefore, the ability of an enterprise to ally with external resources becomes more important. The second is to fully meet the needs of customers. With the advancements in internet technology, the needs of customers have become increasingly complex and enterprises must provide a comprehensive solution. Although Cisco expands the complexity and diversity of technology products by constantly acquiring enterprises, for large ones that Cisco cannot acquire, they may be bundled into a community of interests or a complex of common services for customers by means of partners, strategic alliances and outsourcing. The third is the requirement of core competition. In the whole value chain, it is difficult for an enterprise to obtain all resources and capabilities in the whole value chain, so forming a complementary alliance with enterprises having other resources and capabilities is an effective way to achieve multiple wins. There are three main ways for Cisco to make efficient use of the external separation of resources:

Strategic alliances. A strategic alliance is a strategic relationship between one or more organizations that creates continuous high value resource linkages. Cisco uses strategic alliances for businesses that are hard to buy, especially large or well-known ones, or for noncore businesses. The types of alliances are both exploratory and exploitative (Rothaermel and Deeds 2004). The use alliance focuses on the commercialization phase of the product, which generally includes the use of external enterprise sales and promotion channels. Cisco's strategic alliances focus on developing long-term, stable strategic relationships between companies, requiring all parties to share assets, skills and resources, and strong organizational commitment from all participants. This commitment must be passed down from the CEO. Senior management team members should have a sense of ownership and responsibility in strategic alliance relationships. Although different enterprise areas and cultures exist, the process of forming strategic alliances should have common goals and should establish mutual trust relationships and dialog mechanisms to ensure strategic consistency and coordination. There are five main types of strategic alliances: joint ventures, investment alliances, sales alliances, regional alliances, and solution alliances. These alliances are leveraged alliances, mainly used for technology exchange, product comarketing and promotion, marketing, and providing overall solutions. In regard to new core businesses or projects Cisco cannot accomplish this on its own, thus, Cisco uses a buying strategy. From the perspective of capital and control, mergers and acquisitions are overall controls, while strategic alliances are partial controls. Companies such as Cambridge Technology partners, Ernst & Young and KPMG serve as strategic alliances with Cisco.

Partnership. The difference between a strategic alliance and a partnership is that a strategic alliance is a long-term, stable, strategic relationship based on mutual recognition of the value of the other party, while a partnership is a special project or sales system based on mutual benefit formed according to market and customer needs. Cisco's partners mainly focus on its sales system. Fourteen percent of Cisco's products are sold directly by the company, and the other 86% are booked by nearly 30,000 partners (54% through primary dealers, 15% through secondary dealers to address needs, and 17% through service providers). Cisco will consider seeking partners before entering new markets because this can greatly reduce its cost of entering new markets, reducing barriers to entry, and quickly seizing new markets. Cisco employs more than 15,000 salespeople across the globe through its partners, 20 times as many as Cisco's direct sellers, if 55,000 channel partners are included. Partners influence Cisco's value chain in three ways. First, expanding Cisco's sales and service channels (expanding geographical areas, providing integrated solutions and vertical experience); second, mutual support of hardware and software with partners. The third is to provide mutual technical support with partners.

The relationship management between strategic alliances and partners is an important part of the enterprise's ability to extract resources. Cisco is famous for its technical engineering ability, but market ability is also important for technology enterprises. The speed of technology development is so fast that if the technical products cannot be quickly marketed, the market opportunities may be lost in a relatively short time. As a result, Cisco outsources 80% of its market capabilities. Through partners, Cisco can bypass mergers and acquisitions, quickly enter markets with high barriers, or through partners, reach customers it cannot reach and possibly reduce the cost and risk of entering a new market.

Manufacturing outsourcing. Cisco makes more than 95% of its products through outsourcing, many of them to developing countries. Before the rapid growth in wealth, Cisco built and manufactured its own products using a build-to-order business model, but this model was too complex to manage, and rapid expansion required so much capital that the company began to consider outsourcing. In deciding whether to outsource manufacturing, many worry that outsourcing could deprive Cisco of effective control over supply and transparency in its management. For manufacturers to produce high quality, low cost, and fast demand products, Cisco looks at continuous supply, inventory management, agile production, and the overall management of manufacturing. Based on a comprehensive review of manufacturing enterprises, it is common that the demands of manufacturing are met by means of contracts through independent third-party companies who brush printed circuit board testing, assemble and repair products. More importantly, Cisco chips are developed with knowledge of software and are used to control products and the manufacturing process, including the product configuration to meet customer demand and ensure quality and safety.

4.2 *Explore the Integration Mechanism of Activities and Utilization Activities*

4.2.1 Elements of Combined Ability

Combination ability is part of exploration and utilization activities, which build a bridge between the exploration and use of combinations between the activities, information sharing and personnel flow. Activities in the accumulation of experience, knowledge and ability to explore activities, reduces uncertainty and risk and improves relevance, which is the specific aim and purpose of exploration. On the other hand, new technologies and new capabilities of search, discovery and creation in exploration activities will be enriched in utilization activities to avoid the inertia of utilization activities and the aging of knowledge. Cisco's portfolio capabilities are strategic and tactical: strategic focus outside the enterprise, portfolio and investment for different types of markets. The tactical level focuses on the internal part of the enterprise, combining the high-quality resources between exploration activities and utilization activities through the sharing of technical routes and matching team members.

Strategic level—market mix. At the core of exploration activities is to constantly discover new needs of growth markets and customers, create or introduce new technologies, build new capabilities, and form new requirements to meet the growing market. When enterprises constantly find space for rapid growth in growth markets, the sustainable ability of enterprises will be guaranteed. Cisco's exploration of continuous traction by growth markets, such as attention and cloud computing, 2010, 2011, focused on smart grids; in 2012, injection into the video and data center field, focused on all connected areas such as in 2013. It is the market and the exploration of the new technology that ensures Cisco will not lose new development opportunities in the market transition and growth will find a new engine for the enterprise. When evaluating and selecting M&A companies, building strategic alliances and developing partnerships, Cisco combines mature markets with growth markets. Mature markets bring stable cash flow to enterprises, while growth markets bring new opportunities and space for the subsequent development of enterprises, helping Cisco quickly enter new market segments. To quickly occupy the growth market, Cisco constantly conducts forward-looking research and prediction on future market development and customer demand. Meanwhile, it integrates resources to enter emerging markets rapidly when opportunities arise and continually expands and deepens enterprise market capacity through the integration of new and existing products. Cisco, in mergers and acquisitions or choosing a strategic alliance objective, has little homogeneity in choosing a new enterprise. Thus, despite the value chain, complementary businesses and technical mastery of Cisco, its impact may not be as strong in terms of technology and resources for a newly acquired enterprise. The formation of an effective goal driven win–win alliance may address the market gap and expand market. In addition, Cisco examines the speed of market transformation to determine the intensity and timing of combined exploration and utilization activities. When the market enters the low-speed development period, enterprises have enough time to carry out the research and development of new technologies and new products. However, when the market accelerates, it is difficult for an enterprise to keep up with the development needs of customers and the market only by relying on internal forces. If competitors launch new products at a faster speed, it is difficult for the enterprise to gain the position of market leaders. In this case, companies quickly acquire the latest technology from externally through mergers and acquisitions.

Strategic portfolio. Cisco's R&D portfolio uses a multiproject horizontal portfolio rather than a continuous vertical investment strategy in just a few technologies to reduce the chance of missing out on new technology development opportunities. In other words, Cisco allocates aggressive or incremental technology innovation projects by adopting a portfolio approach similar to that of the financial sector. Before investment, the prospects, expansibility, profitability, risk and other factors of each project are considered, and the technology and products are evaluated and screened on the basis of systematic analysis to determine the best product for the portfolio. Of course, the market outlook for technology is also a factor that must be examined. In 2013, R&D accounted for 12.2% of Cisco's sales, or $5.2 billion. In the technological innovation portfolio, radical technological innovation, especially the high-end R&D costs of technology, was approximately 3%; only a few professionals are involved in the project, and the project develops approximately 15 items per year. Seventy-five percent of research and development costs are invested in future market technology, especially 20 emerging technologies with great market potential over the next one to two years, and 22% will be used to strengthen and enhance the diversity of the existing technology system. By continually optimizing its portfolio and incubating projects with market potential in a variety of technological possibilities, Cisco ensures that the enterprise not only generates short-term profits, but that it also has enough radical innovative products to maintain its market position and sustainable development. Cisco keeps its portfolio of research and development projects from overexpanding and diversifying, adopting a "lean strategy" when necessary. This includes the following: (1) closing R&D projects of limited commercial value when investing in new projects; and (2) when market fluctuations occur and shareholders question the profitability of exploration activities, focus on the most critical business areas.

Chambers indicated, "High-level enterprise is easy to fall into the trap of doing too many things, such as have five major issues and twenty second-emphasis issues". If the enterprise can focus more on one investment, as opposed to blindly seeking many, the outcome may serve to reduce the total amount of investment for each key project and may therefore reduce exploration and the consumption of resources. "Cisco has been through some of the worst times in its 25-year history, but it has been through some of the worst times and has been through some of the best time. In a bad economic environment, companies should adopt a focused strategy and focus on their core technologies and products by 'slimming down'. More is not always better," he said, citing his experiences at GM and Cisco. "A lot of great companies die of indigestion, not starvation."

Tactical—technical combination. Cisco attaches great importance to the combination of new technology and mature technology, integrates the innovation activities that are highly related to Cisco's existing technology system into the company's internal R&D activities, and achieves continuous upgrade and optimization through gradual innovation, for purposes of enhancing the consistency, continuity, unity and integration of the whole technology system. Therefore, utilization activities are the most important foundation and represent the core strengths of the company. New technologies that differ from the original technology systems of Cisco, or technology fields that Cisco is not familiar with, are classified as innovation exploration activities. External resources are internalized through mergers and acquisitions and external creativity. The new technology team is then able to carry out independent research and development to achieve partial separation, but overall collaboration.

In combining exploration and utilization activities in technology development, Cisco uses the enterprise's complex system architecture as a guide for selecting and judging new technologies. A complex architecture system provides comprehensive and personalized solutions to meet the complex needs of a large number of customers. A complex architecture system is built around the needs of target customers.

From its activities in innovation, Cisco also converts knowledge and experience into analytical tools that help judge the value of new ideas and technologies. For example, in the process of evaluating external ideas, senior professionals at Cisco have created an analytical framework to evaluate the market potential and business value of new technologies. This framework includes an opportunity concept diagram and an internal venture capital function diagram. The opportunity concept map shows the semantic network of the company's technology and products in a visual way. This allows leadership to view internal correlations of the new technology product system and the potential correlations between new ideas and the original technology system through concepts, links and connectives. The concept map of opportunities includes collaboration, video, data centers, virtualization, and energy, which Cisco currently considers very important market opportunities. On the basis of identifying the core areas, the internal VC function chart helps Cisco concentrate resources on a few high-potential projects. These tools help Cisco effectively evaluate and select the business value of ideas so that the enterprise can broaden the source of ideas, expand the space and quantity of ideas, and form a comprehensive view of the innovation field in the early stage of exploration activities. In middle and later periods, according to the accumulation of knowledge and methodology, Cisco utilizes exploration activity to pressure test and screen ideas, eliminate 98% of proposed ideas, select the most valuable ideas for development and, within 2 to 3 years, develop the market product, fully implementing the creative idea to gain business value.

Tactical level—team composition. To ensure the success of the exploration activity, Cisco adopts two ways of team combination: new and old employee combination and technology and market combination. In particular, in the case of a spin-off acquisition, Cisco sends in people with experience in sales, customer support, engineering and manufacturing to bring their existing knowledge and capabilities into the small business. These Cisco employees share their technology, experience, and product roadmap with small business employees to develop integrated products in a collaborative manner. At the same time, senior employees have the right to supervise management when necessary. To this end, Cisco has created special incentive systems to encourage older employees to work in spinoff acquisitions. At the same time, Cisco also has requirements for future acquisitions of technology products in the market, such as when the company reaches preset customer numbers and sales milestones to buy the new company. The correlations between the acquisition price and the company's marketization ability makes the acquired company take note of the market value of the technology, thus reducing the market uncertainty in technology R&D. Those engaged in radical innovation in emerging technology teams are a carefully selected group of passionate, unconventional, independent, free-thinking and reliable employees. Cisco considers age factors in external idea production. In terms of commercialization, Cisco derives ideas from global youth and will obtain thousands of creative ideas through competitions for prizes. Sixty senior leaders with a variety of viewpoints and angles evaluate ideas, cultivating a measure for creative screening prior to selecting an idea for development. Cisco's internal action learning team will then develop the ideas into products.

4.2.2 Contribution of Combination Ability to Enhancing the Mutual Value of Exploration Activities and Exploitation Activities

A strategic level of combination ability is to make Cisco simultaneously focus on growth markets and fulfill mature market needs, through strategic layout and investment transverse combination. The company constantly seeks for the new technology and new market growth to ensure that it is not lagged during the technology and market transition. The company should balance between the growth markets and mature markets by dynamic combination.

Reduce uncertainty in exploration activities. By combining capabilities, accumulation of knowledge activities are used to help reduce the uncertainty and risk of exploration activities. As a high-tech enterprise, Cisco transfers the knowledge and talent from the utilization activities to the exploration activities through the combination of technology and teamwork at the tactical level so that exploration activities can be separated yet still connected to the utilization activities simultaneously. To some extent, this correlation serves to function as the filtering mechanism for selection and risk assessment and to ensure that exploration activities are not aimless. Over the years, Cisco's accumulation of knowledge in research and development and the market has evolved into a complex technical architecture system. This architecture has been used to judge the value of exploratory technology ideas, guiding the direction of exploration, resources input and value, and helping enterprises identify the correlation of new technology to existing technology, the new technology and now has a combination and locking relationship between the technical architecture. This helps improve Cisco's ability to meet the diverse needs of its customers and solve problems comprehensively. The composition of the team can timely supplement the lack of personnel and experience of the small business and help them experience fewer detours, while still satisfying mature markets. Enterprises can thus quickly enter emerging markets and form new market advantages.

Enhance the differentiation of technology systems in utilization activities. By combining capabilities, new technologies acquired from exploration activities can continuously enrich the category of activities and meet the new requirements of market development. The new technologies of exploration activities are constantly integrated into existing technology systems to enhance the differentiation and diversification of those systems. The systematization and serialization of the technology systems may ensure technological and product advantages for enterprises and widen the gap between the enterprise and competitors. The integration of old and new technologies gained through discovery activities also supported Cisco's transformation from equipment provider to comprehensive solutions provider, laying a solid foundation for its move into more profitable services. According to the 2013 annual report, the gross profit of Cisco in product sales reached 59.1%, and the gross profit of Cisco in service delivery reached 64%, which also reflects the foundation created by its technology portfolio for enterprise transformation.

4.2.3 Complementary Asset Elements and Internal Connections

Complementary asset elements. Cisco's complementary assets include GVCS, information systems and flows, which are critical to Cisco's success. As Cisco's vice president of enterprise positioning puts it:

Companies often look for one or two strategies to be successful, and one of Cisco's strategies is operational excellence, scaling up, global reach, and having a global brand. If either operational excellence or innovation is more effective, research shows that companies with operational excellence often surpass innovative companies in the long run.

Global value chain operation system. Cisco has more than 60,000 employees in 32 countries or regions and more than 1000 suppliers with a global production and logistics infrastructure that includes 5 manufacturer partners, 5 original design manufacturers, more than 30 manufacturing bases, 4 logistics partners and 17 logistics bases. To connect all stakeholders, Cisco has built an end-to-end interorganizational value chain operation system that integrates customer service, architecture, strategic planning, global supply chain, operations and value chain to provide integrated solutions for the customer experience from delivery to use. To better deal with the complex challenges of global value chains (GVCS), Cisco has developed strategies from six aspects. To integrate supply and demand and achieve balance, the information of sales, business and finance departments needs to be integrated. The second is to establish a multidimensional global department to analyze and solve problems from a global perspective in an effort to support the sustainable growth of enterprises. In this process, Cisco adopts a vertical perspective to design the operation system from the regional dimension and a horizontal perspective to conduct the overall layout of the operation process. The third is to manage volatility. Cisco continues to build a more agile and flexible supply chain and, at a strategic level, to achieve product flexibility by using common platforms and reusable components to minimize the number of specialized components. At the same time, less than 20% of the space meets the needs of customization and personalization. The fourth is to realize the transfer from a single value chain to a synchronous value chain. Today, Cisco has multiple value chain models, including "order to order", "order to order quickly" and "inventory to stock quickly". Fifth, the way of work should be simplified. Cisco simplifies business processes through extensive process reengineering and encourages employees to advise on workflow simplification. The sixth is personnel localization. Since 2010, Cisco has adopted a strategy of localizing people, imposing as much authority as possible on regional executives to give more decision-making power to local management.

Information management. The information system of Cisco takes the global value chain operation system as the object of realizing efficient support for its operation system. Because Cisco's customer value chain is longer, a unified operating system and information system is very complex. Logistical questions exist around Cisco's endeavors such as how will the information in the supply chain system standardize and optimize the supply chain service system? Additionally, how will the financial management system support enterprises collaboratively and in coordination with external manufacturers and partners for the business within the information system? To meet business goals, Cisco's information division employs more than 7,000 people, or 10% of its workforce. The annual input of informatization accounts for 3% of its sales revenue. The value of the information system to the company is mainly measured by eight indicators: support for performance growth; customers' and employees' experience of using information systems; the contribution of information systems to improving work efficiency; the time saved by information systems in enhancing Cisco's business capabilities; replicability of system application; flexibility of the system; contributions to the expansion of the business scale of the enterprise; and the rate at which new technologies are adopted.

Process management. Cisco's M&A is successful because the integration of external resources associated with high-level ability is strong. The merger and acquisitions process utilizes a comprehensive target analysis, process management, monitoring system and talent team. Once a merger is in process, the M&A from external objects, function of employment services, market and multifaceted cooperation begin immediately, ensuring that the external knowledge and resources are integrated and orderly. In a large number of merger cases, Cisco quickly accumulated and extracted various aspects of experience to optimize the existing process, which is a strong indicator for the merger process to improve in terms of execution. In Cisco's high number of M&A cases, key factors include digestion, integration and absorption.

Internal connection of the three elements. The global value chain department plays a leading role in information systems, process management and optimization by being highly relevant to customer needs and business activities in the architecture design and overall planning of the three elements. The value chain bears the main responsibility for the design of and development direction of the information system. The strategic intention of the value chain department is clearly reflected in the information system construction roadmap, and the information system supports the value chain. When there is a conflict between customer needs and value chain arrangements, the initial solution is to listen to and understand the customer's problems. Based on this, teams are able to optimize the existing value chain and information system. Within the connection of information systems and processes, information systems play a role in the infrastructure and supporting systems for business processes.

The connection between complementary assets and exploration activities. The value of the connection between complementary assets and exploration activities is mainly reflected in improving the integrated management ability of external resources, increasing the successful proportion of exploration activities, and realizing the commercial value of exploration activities. Its supporting role is mainly reflected in the following two aspects:

One involves increasing the return on investment of exploration activities. Through the combination of complementary assets and exploration activities, Cisco is able to quickly bring new technologies obtained externally and internally to the global market, as well as its own efficient production and sales system, which will help solve the problem of investment return after the development of new technologies. Through the global value chain, the benefits to the acquired companies are obvious.

On the Cisco platform, the product positioning and development direction of the acquired enterprises will not change significantly, but the sales market and channels will be greatly expanded. The products are not only sold to small businesses but also to large enterprises through Cisco's partners and channels and can then enter the global market quickly. At the same time, it can take three to four years or more to form a market model, which is a challenge for small businesses.

The other option is to reduce the risk in the process of acquiring external enterprises. The risks facing Cisco in the acquisition process include the integration of operating systems, especially for enterprises that have comprehensive and complex large operating systems. Managers monitor the risks of complexity, especially the challenges of managing more complex operating systems brought about by mergers and acquisitions. Cisco's outstanding GVCS, information systems and process management capabilities ensure that the integration of its acquisitions is highly efficient. Cisco has strong integration ability in the process of mergers and acquisitions, and the success rate is as high as 75% thanks to Cisco's information system. The functional departments of the acquired enterprise (such as financial affairs, human resources management, office automation systems, etc.) are directly integrated by Cisco's information system so that the enterprise's resource management capabilities can be unified in a short time. For young enterprises that lack experience in acquisition, the loss of key employees, customers and dealers poses an assortment of risks, thus giving competitors stronger positioning. To reduce risks in M&A process management, Cisco sends a set of complete screening criteria, strategies for acquisition and integration of process and methodology, and a professional team of more than 400 people to assist in successful integration.

The linkage between complementary assets and utilization activities. To create a virtual value chain that integrates external resources, Cisco's integration of complementary assets and utilization activities gives it the ability to dynamically monitor external manufacturing and sales systems in real time. This results in efficient virtual operations. Cisco's information management, ability to outsource manufacturing, and efficiency in overall management and control can produce a virtual information system in the context of a networked virtual supply chain. This serves to realize remote real-time management and quality control, reduces the risk of divisive thinking, produces outsourcing management, and improves the ability of headquarters to control the manufacturing enterprise. More than 90% of the company's global transactions are done online.

Achieve low-cost manufacturing. Cisco's management of manufacturing processes through information systems gives it the ability to tailor hardware and software configurations to the differentiated needs of its customers, ensuring manufacturing agility. Cisco's software systems manage factory production processes and global supply chains in a virtual manner, providing comprehensive inspection, testing and statistical process control to ensure product quality and reliability, while outsourcing manufacturing significantly reduces Cisco's costs. Manufacturing costs accounted for 1.7% of Cisco's total revenue, according to its 2012 annual report. Due to market changes and other considerations, Cisco does not sign long-term cooperation agreements with partner manufacturers but rather enters into short-term contracts as needed.

Collaborative R&D and knowledge sharing system. Cisco's information systems strongly support its global R&D synergies and speed. Its applications include (1) solving global R&D problems through information systems. Cisco uses a product lifecycle management system developed by Parametric Technology Corporation (PTC) to synchronize product development globally, manage the consistency of global innovation processes, and support rapid retrieval of innovation results and effective management of R&D data; (2) management and improvement of the visualization of new global product R&D through a distributed R&D system that enables engineers in global design centers and remote R&D centers to work efficiently through rapid data transfers; (3) use of robust media to promote communication among innovation teams. In an interconnected business environment, innovation teams bring together people with diverse backgrounds, skills, and experience to find the best solutions, solve problems, and make decisions. Through effective collaboration and mutual support through the use of rich media, innovation teams can work together quickly and effectively, ensuring the achievement of goals across borders, regardless of geography or time constraints; (4) virtual collaboration. Cisco's IT department focuses on providing a service manual and virtual desktop infrastructure that allows Cisco employees to log in from any office or terminal and access customized information about their work. At the same time, effective system management methods and rules should be developed to deal with emergencies.

Business model development and replication capabilities. According to Cisco, the operation and management capability of the global value chain is most important to the core competitiveness of Cisco. The construction and optimization of Cisco's operation system always pursues the goal of providing replicable and expandable resource management platforms and value chain systems for the globalization of enterprises. Standardized templates, global replication of systems, and global collaboration and integration are critical. Information technology plays a central role in achieving efficient, flexible and responsive global management.

5 Case Study Findings: From Dual Integration to Dual Strategy Implementation

For high-tech enterprises, the key ability to ensure sustainable development is to simultaneously engage in exploration and utilization activities and to meet a dynamic balance between radical innovation and gradual innovation. The case of Cisco gives us a better understanding of how to establish a separation and integration mechanism between exploration and utilization activities through paradox management in enterprise innovation activities to make enterprises participate in radical innovation while employing incremental innovation. Through the case analysis, we found that the key to the management of exploration activities and utilization activities is to find the

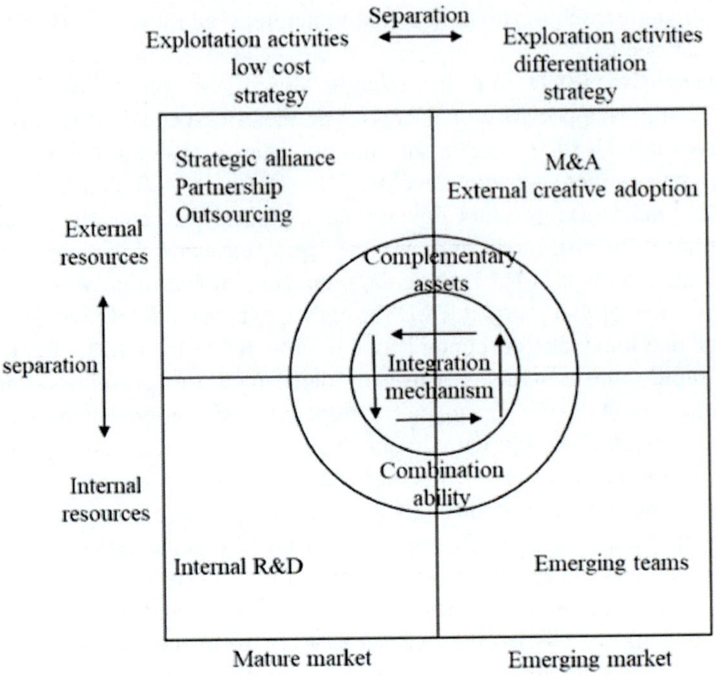

Fig. 1.3 Constructing the paradoxical management model of innovation ambidexterity

appropriate separation-integration mechanism in the opposition and connection of the two. Based on this, we condensed and constructed the innovative "dual" paradox management model, as shown in Figs. 1.3.

Theoretical contribution. Different from the duality of leadership, the duality of organizational structure and the duality of situation, this book, under the guidance of paradoxical thinking, reveals through case studies that exploring the separation-integration mechanism between activities and beneficial activities is an important way to construct dual ability. The separation determines whether high-tech enterprises can continue to attain innovative resources in sustainable development and achieve full development in exploring and utilizing the two activity spaces. Integration determines the ability and efficiency of the enterprise to integrate and manage resources after acquiring them. As a set of paradoxes, separation and integration are both valuable and interdependent and need to be used together (Poole and Van DE Ven 1989).

The separation of exploration activities solves the externalities, diversities and dynamics of the sources of enterprise innovation resources. Externalities lie in the fact that enterprises can seek to expand the sources of innovation resources on a global scale and expand the development space of enterprises beyond the boundaries of enterprises. By accessing external diversity (such as resources and purchases) and scarce resources, (such as creativity), high-tech enterprises are seeking dynamic resource bottleneck breakthroughs in the development, growth process and boundary limits. This diversity can help enterprises expand their search for new technologies, explore, and integrate the source and scope of meeting the needs of emerging markets, to avoid missing an opportunity to harness emerging technologies. Diversity is reflected in the fact that while maintaining the existing product and technology system, the enterprise focuses on emerging markets and emerging technologies so that technical products of the enterprise have a wide coverage of various types of markets and can meet the needs of various customers to the greatest extent possible. The diversity of resources maintains a certain distance between exploration activities and utilization activities to ensure that enterprises have the ability to constantly differentiate technology systems and enhance the complementarity between innovation systems. Dynamic capability is also reflected in the fact that large enterprises constantly acquire and merge small enterprises with new technologies to absorb young people's ideas and continually activate their vitality. The internal separator system (the new entrepreneurial team) in exploration activities can help break the path dependence and system inertia of large enterprises and enhance the flexibility of the innovation system of large enterprises.

The separation of activities enables enterprises to outsource lower value-added links (such as manufacturing and sales) in their activities or seek common development opportunities with partners and strategic alliances to maximize the use of external resources to serve enterprises. The enterprise can focus on core strategy, core business and core technology by developing and establishing a business ecosystem with leading enterprises at the center to ensure high-end positioning in the whole value chain network and, at the same time, to achieve a low-cost strategy by utilizing activity separation.

The integration mechanism determines the enterprise's ability to integrate external resources, including the scope and efficiency of integration, to ensure the consistency and efficiency of internal and external resource operations. There are two main approaches to the integration mechanism revealed in this book, namely, the effective invocation of combined capabilities and complementary assets, which solve the difficulties in binary capacity building from different levels. Through the combination of exploration activities and utilization activities at the strategic level, the combination has realized the duality of the market, making the enterprise pay attention to the growth of the expanding market while maintaining the profit of the mature market. The combination at the tactical level allows for exploration and utilization activities to complement each other with technology, which not only reduces the uncertainty and risk of technology exploration but also continuously enhances the richness of utilization technology.

The connection between complementary assets and exploration activities enables external resources to be efficiently integrated into the enterprise and improves the return on investment of exploration technologies. The connection between complementary assets and utilization activities enables the enterprise to engage in additional noncore business with external resources while reducing costs, thus ensuring that the enterprise focuses on the core business with high added value in the value chain. The internal connections and continuous updates among complementary assets enable

Cisco to systematically strengthen its core competitiveness, achieve efficient internalization and integration of external resources, and ensure its leading position in the value chain by building a global value chain system, information system and process management system. Cisco has the ability to implement the business model with standard, modular consistency, which can be replicated, to manage its ability to compete in global markets. This plays an important role, as Cisco executives place particular emphasis on its main focus. This theory should be tested operationally to confirm this.

Another important contribution of the combination capabilities and complementary assets in the integration mechanism to Cisco's dual capacity building is the realization of strategic duality. The combination capabilities of internal and external exploration activities enable Cisco to continuously enhance differentiation in the market, technology and product system and perfect a differentiation strategy. At the same time, complementary assets enable exploration activities and the use of manufacturing and marketing activities through strategic alliances, partnerships and outsourcing to achieve low-cost strategies. Complementary assets provide a solid base on which to build dragon enterprise development. Their application in value chain control and management plays an important role and continuously strengthens the research and development and engineering knowledge-intensive link at the core of enterprise value. They also allow enterprises outsourcing manufacturing and marketing activities to developing countries or partners at the same time to have a certain ability to control them.

Practical significance. What does the book's case study of Cisco tell us? The authors summarized the implications from the following three aspects.

First, the key to ensuring that radical innovation and progressive innovation go hand in hand is to explore the dual integration mode of activities and utilization activities.

Through the study of Cisco, we can see that innovation and management are a dual combination of enterprise future and present, new and old, change and stability, incremental and stock. When companies settle for stability and do nothing, the consequences of this stagnation and rest will manifest themselves in the foreseeable future because markets, customers and competitors will not. One approach to management behavior may be to build capacity over time. Innovation, which is full of risk, uncertainty and trial and error, can negate mainstream endeavors and stand out from the crowd. This can delay rewards and is often an option that people are happy to avoid. When innovation itself is under pressure, if incentives are not inclusive and do not encourage these behaviors, innovation may remain to be empty talk. In addition, a business without innovation means missed opportunity and a lost future. However, innovation also needs to be balanced and coordinated by management. Through the construction of a management system, the risk of innovation will be reduced, and the benefits will increase. Therefore, innovation and management are similar to a pair of conjoined twins, which are independent, interrelated, and supportive and need to grow in a healthy manner within a symbiotic system.

Second, operational excellence is a key foundation for building multinationals.

In this book, we incorporate superior operational management capabilities into the concept of complementary assets, which are important assets for gaining competitive advantage of leading or large enterprises. In the market environment of rapid technological innovation, new high-tech enterprises can quickly subvert the leading enterprises in technology through radical technological innovation. However, if leading enterprises also acquire radical innovative technologies, they can rapidly expand the scale of complementary assets and gain a large market share. Therefore, complementary assets are an important mechanism through which enterprises can build competition barriers. For small and medium-sized high-tech enterprises, it is not enough to only own new technologies. They also need to build and acquire complementary assets to quickly bring new technologies to the market to realize the strategic goal of expanding market share and obtaining investment returns.

In the process of promoting the development strategy of "One Belt and One Road" in China, the operation model of Cisco's multinational companies has a reference role for Chinese enterprises to go out and realize the internationalization strategy. On the one hand, multinational companies should respond quickly to the demand and development of global markets and formulate sales and innovation strategies for markets worldover. On the other hand, multinational corporations need to have a unified control system, resource allocation system and operation system at the group level. The construction and optimization of Cisco's management and operation system always pursue the same goal, that is, to provide replicable and expandable resource management platforms and value chain systems for the globalization of enterprises to realize efficiency, flexibility and quick response in globalization management. In this process, information construction plays a key role. America's global companies firmly grasp the value of decision-making, technology, knowledge, innovation, an organization system and information management to push intellectual resources into development, leading to high returns for companies. Cisco's margins in the past 15 years have remained at high levels of 64 and 66%. At the same time, they have also outsourced manufacturing to developing countries. Cisco USES memory chips, which are electronically programmed, to automatically set up configurations, automatically detect equipment, and automate quality control and statistics. Cisco's total system accounts for 1.7% of its sales, and it has the world's largest internet business site, where more than 90% of transactions in the company's global business are done online, greatly reducing the total cost of production. In the process of promoting the globalization of Chinese enterprises, the key aspects to be cultivated include the global thinking of leaders, the cross-cultural ability of enterprises, an in-depth understanding of the market of each country, global operation management ability and global resource integration ability.

Third, identifying opportunities for external transformation and promoting internal changes are the core driving forces for the sustainable development of enterprises.

The Cisco case to our inspiration is as follows: an entrepreneur's strategic insight and forward-looking approach may make them avoid external markets, technology development and new growth points. However, Cisco has led in new market spaces by embracing the cognition of internal dynamic organizational change and strategic resource configuration, mobilizing enterprise resources to continuously build a differential products and service systems, and continuing to meet the customer's new demand. This is the core driving force for the spiral development and growth of an enterprise. In this process, the openness of the enterprise, the ability to transform and change, and the speed and effectiveness of adapting to the development of new technologies are the keys to ensuring the survival of the enterprise. Companies can never afford to confine themselves to a self-enclosed system. In a fully competitive market environment, the competitive mechanism of survival of the fittest urges enterprises to continuously invest in their future capabilities. Enterprises will evaluate which resources and capabilities are most valuable for their future survival and development. Enterprises that can survive are those with a strong sense of crisis and development momentum. Therefore, to return an enterprise to the enterprise owner, the entrepreneur who struggles out of the market is a true market expert.

References

Andriopoulos C, Lewis MW (2009) Exploitation-exploration tensions and organizational ambidexterity: managing paradoxes of innovation. Organ Sci 20(4):696–717

Benner MJ, Tushman ML (2003) Exploitation, exploration, and process management: the productivity dilemma revisited. Acad Manag Rev 28(2):238–256

van den Bosch FAJ, Volberda HW, Boer MD (1995) Coevolution of firm absorptive capacity and knowledge environment: organizational for ms and combinative capabilities. Organ Sci 10(4):551–568

Bouchikhi H (1998) Living with and building on complexity: a constructivist perspective on organizations. Organization 5(2):217–232

Cao Q, Gedajlovic E, Zhang H (2009) Unpacking organizational ambidexterity: dimensions, contingencies, and synergistic effects. Organ Sci 20(4):781–796

Cialdini RB, Trost MR, Newsom JT (1995) Preference for consistency: the development of a valid measure and the discovery of surprising behavioral implications. J Pers Soc Psychol 69(2):318

Edmondson AC, Roberto MA, Watkins MD (2003) A dynamic model of top management team effectiveness: managing unstructured task streams. Leadersh Q 14(3):297–325

Eisenhardt KM (1989) Building theory from case study research. Acad Manag Rev 14:532–550

Eisenhardt KM, Graebner ME (2007) Theory building from cases: opportunities and challenges. Acad Manag J 50(1):25–62

Eisenhardt KM, Martin JA (2000) Dynamic capabilities: what are they? Strateg Manag J 21(10–11):1105–1121

Fang C, Lee J, Schilling MA (2010) Balancing exploration and exploitation through structural design: the isolation of subgroups and organizational learning. Organ Sci 21(3):625–642

Fleming L (2001) Recombinant uncertainty in technological search. Manage Sci 47(1):117–132

Ghoshal S, Bartlett CA (1994) Linking organizational context and managerial action: the dimensions of quality of management. Strateg Manag J 15(S2):91–112

Gibson CB, Birkinshaw J (2004) The antecedents, consequences, and mediating role of organizational ambidexterity. Acad Manag J 47(2):209–226

Gilbert CG (2005) Unbundling the structure of inertia: resource versus routine rigidity. Acad Manag J 48(5):741–763

Gresov C, Drazin R (1997) Equifinality: functional equivalence in organization design. Acad Manag Rev 22(2):403–428

Groysberg B, Lee LE (2009) Hiring stars and their colleagues. Exploration and exploitation in professional service firms. Organ Sci 20(4):740–758
Gupta AK, Smith KG, Shalley CE (2006) The interplay between exploration and exploitation. Acad Manag J 49(4):693–706
He Z-L, Wong P-K (2004) Exploration vs. exploitation: an empirical test of the ambidexterity hypothesis. Organ Sci 15(4):481–494
Jasen JJP, Templaar MP, Bosch FAGV, Volberda, H. W. Structural differentiation and ambidexterity: the mediating role of integration mechanisms. Organ Sci 20(4):797–811 (2009)
Kaijin N, Linjun L (2012) Should I start a new business. Harvard Bus Rev (9)
Kristal MM, Huang X, Roth AV (2010) The effect of an ambidextrous supply chain strategy on combinative competitive capabilities and business performance. J Oper Manag 28(5):415–429
Levinthal DA, March JG (1993) The myopia of learning. Strateg Manag J 14(S2):95–112
Lewis MW (2000) Exploring paradox: Toward a more comprehensive guide. Acad Manag Rev 25(4):760–776
March JG (1991) Exploration and exploitation in organizational learning. Organ Sci 2:71–87
Miles MB, Huberman AM (1994) Qualitative data analysis: a sourcebook of new methods, 2nd edn. Sage Publications, Thousand Oaks, CA
Morgeson FP, Hofmann DA (1999) The structure and function of collective constructs: implications for multilevel research and theory development. Acad Manag Rev 24(2):249–265
O'Reilly C, Tushman M (2013) Organizational ambidexterity: past, present, and future. Acad Manage Perspect 27(4):324–338
Perretti F, Negro G (2006) Filling empty seats: how status and organizational hierarchies affect exploration versus exploitation in team design. Acad Manag J 49(4):759–777
Poole MS, Van de Ven AH (1989) Using paradox to build management and organization theories. Acad Manag Rev 14(4):562–578
Pratt MG, Foreman PO (2000) Classifying managerial responses to multiple organizational identities. Acad Manag Rev 25(1):18–42
Raisch S, Birkinshaw J (2008) Organizational ambidexterity: antecedents, outcomes, and moderators. J Manag 34(3):375–409
Rothaermel FT, Deeds DL (2004) Exploration and exploitation alliances in biotechnology: a system of new product development. Strateg Manag J 25(3):201–221
Schneider KJ, May R (1990) The paradoxical self: toward an understanding of our contradictory nature. Insight Books New York
Schumpeter JA (1939) Business cycle. A theoretical, historical and statistical analysis of the capitalist process. McGraw-Hill Book Company, New York, Toronto and London
Smith WK, Lewis MW (2011) Toward a theory of paradox: a dynamic equilibrium model of organizing. Acad Manag Rev 36(2):381–403
Smith WK, Tushman ML (2005) Managing strategic contradictions: a top management model for managing innovation streams. Organ Sci 16(5):522–536
Taylor A, Helfat CE (2009) Organizational linkages for surviving technological change: complementary assets, middle management, and ambidexterity. Organ Sci 20(4):718–739
Teece DJ, Pisano G, Shuen A (1997) Dynamic capabilities and strategic management. Strateg Manag J 18(7):509–533
Tripsas M (1997) Unraveling the process of creative destruction: complementary assets and incumbent survival in the typesetter industry. Strateg Manag J 18(S1):119–142
Tsui AS (2007) Taking stock and looking ahead: MOR and Chinese management research. Manag Organ Rev 3(3):327–334
Turner N, Swart J, Maylor H (2013) Mechanisms for managing ambidexterity: a review and research agenda. Int J Manag Rev 15:317–332
Tushman ML, O'Reilly III CA (1996) Managing evolutionary and revolutionary change. Calif Manage Rev 38(4):8–28
Vera D, Crossan M (2004) Strategic leadership and organizational learning. Acad Manag Rev 29(2):222–240

Vince R, Broussine M (1996) Paradox, defense and attachment: accessing and working with emotions and relations underlying organizational change. Organ Stud 17(1):1–21
Voss GB, Voss ZG (2012) Strategic ambidexterity in small and medium-sized enterprises: implementing exploration and exploitation in product and market domains. Organ Sci 24(5):1459–1477
Weick KE (2007) The generative properties of richness. Acad Manag J 50(1):14–19
Dong XY, Zhou JL (2014) Innovation and management in the information age: cisco apocalypse. Peking University Press, Beijing
Yin RK (2003) Case study research: design and methods. Sage Publications, Thousand Oaks, CA

Chapter 2
Strategic Leadership

1 Introduction

Strategic leadership mainly includes three aspects: First, absorptive capacity, which is related to the learning of leaders and their perception of the business environment. Specifically, leaders emphasize experiments and exploration in the learning process and are willing to take risks, make diversified choices, update the existing learning processes, and promote strategic change and innovation. Through this process, leaders not only lead by example but also actively lead the organization to acquire new capabilities by identifying, absorbing and applying new knowledge. The second is the ability to lead the change, which means that the strategic leader has foresight and crisis consciousness for the future and cognitive complexity. Under the guidance of far-seeing insight and crisis awareness, leaders try to steer the organization to carry out transformation and change, overcome various resistances to change and move forward, introduce new systems and structures, change the understanding of institutions, and focus on differentiated thinking. The behavioral complexity of strategic leaders means they question assumptions, seek substance, take appropriate risks, and observe new phenomena. Strategic leaders communicate effectively, are approachable and value the opinions of others. They may require contributions from multiple sources of knowledge, openly discuss mistakes and encourage the management of information sharing. Effective managers are able to instill meaning, challenge, be charismatic and encourage communication within and between teams. The third is management wisdom, which includes the vision and insight to seize opportunities, the keen and timely perception of changes in the environment, and an understanding of changes in the internal relationships with changes in social environment and roles.

The strategic ability of leaders is mainly reflected in two aspects: First, the cognitive analysis ability, which is reflected in the grasp of strategic content and reflects the cognitive complexity of leaders. The second is interpersonal ability, which mainly shows that leaders need to lead employees to learn quickly, change their minds and dare to challenge the status quo, showing the complexity of leaders' behaviors. For leaders, balancing these two aspects and allocating time to them influences their

X. Dong et al., *Cisco*,
https://doi.org/10.1007/978-981-19-7870-8_2

leadership style. The following questions also reflect the roles and characteristics of the leaders: What are the core responsibilities of the key strategy makers? Is it the architecture that focuses on the content of the strategy or the architecture of the strategic process? The former mainly reflects the importance leaders attach to strategic results and the important contributions of foresight, crisis awareness and insight to the content of strategic decisions; the latter reflects the importance that leaders place on the decision-making process, emphasizing the process of making transparent and rational decisions and allowing those involved to leverage their intelligence and combine it into a systematic problem-solving force. What are their main jobs in the current strategy development process? What type of decision-making team is involved in strategy development?

According to a 2009 study of more than 2,000 leaders in three countries by the Center for Creative Leadership Research (CCL), the capabilities of existing organizational leaders are inadequate to meet organizations' future needs. There are seven main areas of focus for leadership today and in the future: Leadership, strategic planning, management change, accountability, resources, the ability to face reality in a difficult environment, and the ability to learn quickly. The results show that leadership, strategic planning, managing change and inspiring a sense of responsibility are among the weakest skills of existing leaders but are important for the future development of the organization.

2 The Leadership of Cisco

John Chambers was born in Cleveland, Ohio, in 1949 and graduated from West Virginia University and Indiana University. He grew up in Charleston, West Virginia. His father was a wealthy obstetrician, his mother was a psychologist, and his parents later opened a restaurant in Charleston. It was there that Mr. Chambers had the idea of running his own business one day. As a child, Chambers suffered from dyslexia. However, his parents had full confidence in him and provided him with all kinds of support. According to Walters, a reading expert, Chambers was always optimistic and determined to succeed. Later, he even turned dyslexia into an advantage. "I cannot explain why, but I can do things differently," Chambers says. "It is easy to get out of the routine."

In 1976, Chambers became a computer salesman for IBM. He was indomitable, had the good temper of a southerner, and did well. In his pitch, Mr. Chambers recognized IBM's shortcomings, such as its focus on business computers and typewriters, at a time when the personal computer era had arrived. This experience gave him the most important asset of his life—valuing his clients. "A lot of [IBM's] managers are moving away from their customers," he says. "They always tell their clients that they know what they want. However, that is wrong." In a recent interview, Mr. Chambers again emphasized the importance of clients. He says Cisco wants to be the "No. 1 IT company," which means important to its customers. "Whoever is the most important partner that the client thinks of is going to be number one." In the executive suite of high-tech companies, Mr. Chambers is something of a rarity. He does not have the technical background of people like Bill Gates at Microsoft. In fact, when he left IBM, he lacked an engineering degree. Chambers' genius is in managing people.

In 1983, after listening to a speech by Wang, the founder of Wang computer, he became interested in Wang's business thinking and quickly convinced him that he was the right person to lead its Asian sales team. His easy-going personality once again made him a success in the Asian market. Chambers also held Wang in high regard. After his father, he said, Wang was the person who had most influenced him. "I will never forget his trust in me," he said.

Chambers also learned how to hire and fire at the company. When Mr. Wang died of cancer in 1990 and the company went from boom to bust, he followed the Chinese tradition of appointing his son as the heir, but investors did not buy it. The company's stock quickly fell in value, and Chambers, an executive vice president, had to cut 5,000 jobs before the Christmas holiday. It was a painful memory for him. "Layoffs were the hardest decision a leader could make," he later recalled. "But if we do not, the company will not survive."

Chambers joined Cisco as CEO in 1991 after John Morgridge. At a restaurant in San Jose, California in January 1995, Cisco created one of the most brilliant performances in the history of the internet under Chambers' leadership. Internet companies were among the fortune 500 in the U.S. 1997 (in 332), with a market value of more than $1 billion (1998), a significant milestone given that the world's most valuable company is worth approximately $5.50 billion. In the wake of the September 11, 2001 terrorist attacks on the United States, he led the company through the crisis by laying off 85% of its market value for the first time in Cisco's history and cutting his salary to $1 a year. Since then, the development of the new economy has varied in performance, and Cisco's stock price has fluctuated, but Chambers has not been phased by this. As CEO, he says, he reads analysts' reports but does not make decisions based on them. "The best is yet to come. There are peaks and valleys, but I'm an optimist."

Chambers is good at leading companies through transformation and change. He is a tough and tough leader in the process, during which 30 percent of the leadership changes. "I realized that at the CEO level and at the business execution level, most people have a hard time reinventing themselves. Therefore, it is hard for me when companies are transforming and changing, but we have to execute painfully. I tell people in human resources to figure out how to develop leaders. We have a huge human resources development program to figure out how to develop the next generation of leaders, including the next CEO."

In 2012, Chambers said he would retire in two to four years and named the candidates to succeed him: Rob Lloyd, head of development and sales, Chuck Robbins, senior vice President of field operations, and Edzard Overbeek, senior vice President of services. Chambers, 66 officially announced his retirement as CEO in 2015 and will no longer lead the board in 2017. Rodrik officially succeeded Chambers.

When Chambers was 66 years old, he was respected as "Mr. Internet" by Business Week. He spent 24 years at Cisco and 20 as its CEO. Today, two-thirds of the key devices that power the internet come from Cisco. With operations in 165 countries and

74,000 employees, Cisco is trying to get ahead of the internet's next big opportunity, the Internet of everything. As a visionary, risk-conscious leader, Chambers saw the Internet of Everything as "the internet that connects people, data, processes and objects in an intelligent way. This is an exciting new phase for the internet. Its impact on society will be five to ten times greater than it was before."

As an outspoken Silicon Valley CEO, Chambers made a surprising prediction that of the five largest technology giants—Cisco, IBM, Whipple, Microsoft and Oracle—two of them would fail in the near future. Chambers charts the last 14 quarters of the five companies. Only Microsoft has had 14 straight quarters of revenue growth of more than 3%, and Cisco, which has had 12 straight quarters of growth, has had trouble recently. Chambers did not specify which companies would be eliminated, other than to talk about the difficulties facing Cisco's rivals IBM and HP: "When you look at the five players, HP and I.B.M. have not had revenue growth in two or three years." Chambers also referred to his "subversion". He thinks that in an era of huge technological change driven by the Internet of things, perhaps only 40% of tech companies will survive a decade from now.

It is said that before Huawei formally entered the us market in 2002, Zhengfei Ren had contact with Chambers and expressed his desire to cooperate with him. However, Chambers felt that Huawei was too small and even proposed to buy the company. Later, the rise of Huawei also made Chambers feel slightly nervous. At a network equipment exhibition in the United States, he personally formulated the "plan against Huawei" and took the "aggressive" Huawei to court. However, in the end he chose to bury the hatchet.

In the book of "The World of Huawei", there is a description about Mr. Chambers' visit to Zhengfei Ren in China: "One day in December 2005, in Huawei's headquarters office in Bantian, Shenzhen, Zhengfei Ren, adjusted his tie in front of a mirror. This Huawei president, who usually does not care much about his clothes, was dressed in neat clothes. Because today he will have a guest—Cisco CEO, John Chambers, a longtime enemy but a future partner." Unfortunately, 10 years later, Cisco and Huawei are not future partners. Chambers said of Huawei in 2015: "Zhengfei Ren is a good leader. He leads a successful company that is growing and maturing. I have been following his remarks. Our understanding of bringing digitalization to China and the benefits of digitalization is the same. We are competitors here, and we will continue to compete here. Many of the transformations Huawei is undergoing are good for the company. I'm personally interested in Huawei's mobile business, and it looks like they're doing quite well." Mr. Chambers is adept at studying the personal circumstances and decision-making habits of rival executives. He said he could give details about the life and decision-making of Zhengfei Ren, Huawei's founder and CEO, even without any hints. "I can also guess what other competitors' executives think," said Mr. Chambers.

Chuck Robbins joined Cisco in 1997 and was quickly promoted from account managers to regional managers and directors of operations. Prior to that, he was senior vice president of global sales at Cisco, where he led the company's global sales and global partner divisions and helped drive a number of investment initiatives and operational strategy changes. Chuck Robbins provided a great support to the company's safety and collaborative business development t, and was also an important impeller of acquisition business of the Sourcefire and Meraki. Chuck Robbins had more than 20 years of leadership experience. During his 17 years at Cisco, he held a series of senior management positions, including senior vice president for Cisco's largest business division, the Americas, and senior vice president for U.S. enterprise, business and Canada. During his tenure as vice president of Cisco's U.S. and Canadian channels, he helped build Cisco's most powerful partner program in the industry, which contributed more than $40 billion a year to the company's revenue. He gained the honors of "Best Channel Leader" in 2008 from CRN magazine and". Top 100 Channel Executives" in 2005 and 2006 from VAR Business magazine.

Since taking over at Cisco, Mr. Chuck Robbins has assembled a 10-member executive team, three fewer than his predecessor's 13-member team: CTO Padmasree Warrior, director of globalization Wim Elfrink, and senior vice President of services Edzard Overbeek. Second, Mr. Chuck Robbins set out to restructure Cisco, trying to shift the company's focus to four key areas: Security, the Internet of Things, networking and cloud computing. To meet that goal, Cisco laid off 5,500 employees, or 7% of its work force, in August 2015, and many of its top executives' positions have changed in response, with some beginning to make new career choices. For example, Gary Moore, a strong candidate for President at the time, is now an executive at Ohio State University and teaches at the business school. Rob Lloyd became CEO of startup Hyperloop One, which recently raised $50 million and resolved a lawsuit filed by a former executive. Padmasree Warrior has joined the board of Microsoft and become CEO of Chinese electric vehicle startup Next EV. After leaving Cisco, Wim Elfrink founded and became President of WPE Ventures Digitized Solutions, which focuses on security and the Internet of things. Edzard Overbeek became CEO of HERE, a cloud platform company, focusing on digital maps, autonomous driving, and the Internet of things.

3 The Core Responsibilities of Global Business Leaders

Leadership is the ability to motivate and influence others to work hard to accomplish important tasks. Great leadership goes hand in hand with vision, and we need leaders who can translate that vision into reality, who can communicate their vision of the future vividly and powerfully to everyone, and who can bring the team together. The core role of a leader is embodied in the following four aspects: The ability to inspire, motivate, communicate effectively and maintain enthusiasm when leading others; Ability to map out the future, set direction and formulate plans for building consensus and formulating strategies; In terms of the organizational system, it has the ability to create and optimize the organizational structure, use the platform, improve the management efficiency and establish the organizational culture and performance system; In terms of risk control, it has the ability to build a balance mechanism, establish a security system, ensure the achievement of goals and achieve the sustainable development of the enterprise.

At Cisco, we had a chance to hear Chambers' dialogue with Robert A. McDonald, former President of Procter & Gamble; Jeffery R. Immelt, former President of general motors; and Mike Duke, former President of Wal-Mart, as well as with the leaders of central enterprises from China. The atmosphere of the dialog was equal and frank, filled with insights. Many ideas were put forward on leadership vision, decision-making, team-building, leading change, working style, self-motivation and self-management. The author recorded what she heard and shared with you.

Chambers believes that the CEO should have three main responsibilities to ensure that the company has the ability to grow steadily. First, he should set the vision and strategy for the company and allocate relevant resources according to the development strategy of the company. Second, to recruit talent and build leading bodies. He especially talked about the appointment of people in Wang a company, which was mainly promoted from within and lacked the mechanism of absorbing external excellent talent, which made the thinking of the whole team converge, reduced the chance of ideological exchange and new thinking, and weakened the vitality of the enterprise. Third, cultivate enterprises. In both Europe and the US, he argues, culture is embedded in all the activities of a company and is linked to its capabilities. Corporate culture is the fundamental force for the formation of differences among different enterprises, whose formation and shaping are driven by the CEO.

In a speech in 2012, Chambers pinpointed, especially in regard to facing fierce competition, the enterprise must maintain sustainable development, corporate leaders and senior teams shall have the ability to continue learning, to force yourself to learn, even those who do not want to learn something, force yourself to face the complicated problem but also learn from the mistakes of others; only in this way can we constantly improve ourselves. If business leaders refuse to accept new things and to learn, the business will go downhill, so learning is the top priority. One thing, which Chambers often did, was to invite those global executives who worked for the company for more than 20 years to have the meeting together, at the same time invited young people from 18 to 20 years old to attend the meeting together. In the meetings, young people could share their favorite work, communication, even some grumbling, and older people could understand young people's ideas and accept their challenges. For Chambers, the key to growth is the ability to continue learning. Young people often complain that old people's minds are fixed, and continuous learning is becoming increasingly difficult, which requires special attention and prevention. A leader who loves learning must create an organization full of learners, an organization that cannot adapt to a new environment without learning.

As for CEO's role, Chambers said it is also important for leaders to promote innovation, ensuring operational excellence while promoting technological innovation and balancing innovation with operational excellence. The source of Cisco's innovation is listening to its customers. Cisco entered China in 1995, when the U.S. did not take China seriously, but Chambers says it is important to understand what your customers want, to understand the market, to build trust, to build confidence in innovation. In a very fast changing environment, every two years there is a market transformation, one step slower will be left behind, so innovation is key. "People joke that I love change," he says, "You truly have to create a culture that encourages change, even if it makes you sweat or uncomfortable."

Leaders also have an inescapable mission in spreading corporate culture. Cisco's cultural communication involves various regions and countries around the world. Chambers has repeatedly said that maintaining Cisco's culture is the core source of ensuring the sustainable development of the enterprise. Cisco's every employee has a small card, carry with employee's national language to write the Cisco's 12 core values: Customer success, high-quality team, authorization, extension target, no technology worship, open communication, teamwork, market transition, trust, fairness, integrity, culture, thrift and enjoy it, which is the important foundation of sustainable development to ensure Cisco.

According to Robert McDonald, former President of Procter & Gamble, the core responsibility of a CEO is mainly in four aspects. In this process, leaders need to be good communicators, listen carefully to the feedback from customers, employees, shareholders, partners and the media, and assume the social responsibility of the enterprise. In particular, he said, CEOs should consider the relationship between stakeholders and balance between long-term goals and short-term goals. To ensure balance, he often sits down with aides to review the agenda, analyzing how much time is spent on strategic issues and how many key issues have been resolved. Otherwise, by focusing on the specifics or day-to-day business, the CEO loosens his grasp on the big picture, resulting in an imbalance between long-term and short-term goals. The second is to focus on the enterprise goals and maintain the sustainable development of the enterprise. The third is to deliver the company's strategy, vision and goals. When the CEO is promoting the development goal of the company, he should not only focus on the next year but also focus on the strategic goal and vision of 3–5 years. "CEOs need to be good storytellers and send their own signals through storytelling," Robert McDonald said. The fourth is that the success of the president is not only a personal success but also the success of the whole team. Therefore, the president needs to stimulate the wisdom of the whole team, pool the wisdom of the team, maintain the stability of the team, and absorb more talent and talent to join the team. 'the core of P&G's success is its culture and values,' he said of P&G with a history of 175 years. P&G is not a perfect company, but it has a very good culture, the core of which is to make everyone's life better, and it has long-term meaning. The leader of a large enterprise should set an example in cultural communication.

When talking about the main responsibilities of a CEO, the former head of general electric emphasized that the core responsibilities of a business leader are focused on six aspects. The second is to allocate resources and capital in different ways according to different markets and establish different market positions. The third is to communicate and discuss with employees about the corporate culture to make it a greater culture. Fourth, regular staff meetings should be held to promote the dissemination and practice of culture. Fifth, the leaders of each region should be carefully selected so that they can promote the development of each regional business. Sixth, leadership talent should be identified, developed and used to help implement the corporate strategy.

----- Video conversation with Immelt, the former CEO of General Electric -----

4 CEO's Forward Thinking and Decision-Making

How can global business leaders navigate the complex economic, political and social environment to ensure the right direction for innovation and make forward-looking strategic decisions? Chambers believes that the predictions and decisions of leaders are not always correct, but the decisions must be the combination of decisions. When the practice proves that the decisions of enterprises are correct, leaders will find which decisions have more long-term significance. At the same time, customer feedback is also a litmus test to determine whether the decision is correct. In judging the trend of market transformation, the combination of decisions is more important, and to determine whether the right decision should be based on the response of the customer, the customer will tell us the product development direction and the direction of market transformation because what the customer requires to do must contain its value. Mr. Chambers says they spend 50% of their time listening to their clients, and when Mr. Wang succeeds, he stops listening to them, only to see the business decline.

Vision—strategy—execution timing. For Cisco, the first step is to capture the big trends in the industry and then develop the company's vision. Cisco's strategic vision—to transform the way people work, study and live through the Internet—has not changed much in 28 years. The vision will determine the development status of the enterprise in 10 years. After the target of 10 years is determined, it will take 3–4 years to realize the differentiation of the enterprise and another 14–18 months to implement the differentiation strategy. The specific implementation of the strategy should be carried out on a weekly basis in various regions to forecast, prioritize and implement and to select future development. In this process, the key is not to forget the balance and to follow the right path forward.

Decision combination. As a high-tech enterprise, many investment decisions of Cisco are forward-looking, and in the process of making decisions, there will inevitably be various risks. Chambers believes that Cisco's forward-looking insights and decisions are tested by practice, time and customers and that decision-making is an important way to guard against risk. In the process of making decisions, Cisco is very careful not only to refer to the direction of market transformation but also to conduct research and actively seek feedback from different customers. Almost all of his decisions are driven by the needs of his clients, so he spends about half his time listening to them and talking to the 150 CEOs of fortune 500 companies twice a year.

Data-based forecasting. Explaining how Cisco predicts the future of the economy, Mr. Chambers said the company can typically determine the future market three months in advance and know what's going on two quarters ahead of its competitors because 80% of its business is known within 120 days. "Listening to customers and looking at order rates are good ways to predict the future,' he says. He himself looks at the 12th five-year plan as a basis for his forecasts.

The importance of a young mind. In particular, Mr. Chambers talked about how leaders develop a strategic vision for the future. At a networking evening for information industry executives, a Microsoft executive told him to 'look to the future like a 10-year-old and stay young'. For example, although IBM is a century-old company, it still keeps a young mind. Looking into the future with a young mind, it will see opportunities and hope.

5 How Does the CEO Shape the Corporate Culture

The culture is shaped by the leader's past experience. As a third-generation leader, Chambers placed great emphasis on strategic development and cultural development. He argues that culture is shaped by leaders, not by human resources departments. The leader's past successes and failures are at the heart of the corporate culture. Chambers himself worked for both IBM and An Wang, where he was Wang's tennis buddy and very good friend. IBM ran into trouble in the 1970s when it ignored the needs of its customers and opted for cheap, open computer standards. In the early 1990s, Wang's technocratic leadership team insisted it was better than its customers, leading to the company's bankruptcy. Mr. Wang ignored the shift to personal computers, and many software companies missed out on the technology and market transition that led to the loss of 37,000 jobsin related industries. This painful experience was an important background for Chambers to establish Cisco's core culture. As a result, as CEO of Cisco, Mr. Chambers has made it important to listen to customers, not worship technology, in shaping the company's culture. In contrast, many successful businesses tend to decline after alienating customers.

A customer-oriented culture. In practice, especially in Cisco's culture and performance system, customer demand and customer satisfaction are very important, and customer-oriented culture permeates daily decision-making and operational systems. At Cisco, the concept of "customer-driven" takes on a whole new meaning: Let the market take you where it wants you to go. If you enter the market with the idea of serving the market, you will find customers you can trust. When customers ask for something and companies listen to them, accept their suggestions, and follow their ideas, opportunities for transformation and innovation are found. The Cisco customer advisory committee meeting is held on a regular basis to support the work of each business committee. Appointed top managers attend the meeting and deep communication with each customer committee member occurs based on the results of the communication action list. These results are then released at the next meeting according to the action table. Following this, concrete steps can be taken as the Cisco customer was driven into the deeper aspects of corporate strategy and execution.

Create a culture of self-change. How can the enterprises have the ability of sustainable development? According to Chambers, in today's world, industry changes very rapidly. In the past, the cycle of technology transformation was approximately 10 years. Now, 2–3 years will usher in a new wave of transformation, and enterprises with slow transformation speed will fall behind. In this process, not everyone likes change and innovation, so a culture that encourages change and innovation needs to be created. The key to transformation is innovation, thus companies must continue to innovate. Robert McDonald, former CEO of Procter & Gamble, explained the importance of corporate transformation with the story of the boiling frog. He said that as a cold-blooded animal, a frog's body temperature gradually increases with a change in water temperature. He points to the example of Kodak, once one of the greatest companies in the world, whose one-square-mile park in New York state once symbolized its heyday. Kodak is a vertically integrated company that generates its own electricity and makes its own chemicals for photographic paper and rolls, but it is this type of stability that may lead to inertia in the film industry. They are aware of the challenges and changes of the digital age, but they are slow to take action and end up as metaphorical boiled frogs. Compared with traditional century-old stores, the survival rate of modern enterprises is much lower than in the past, which is yet another challenge of leadership.

6 Cultivation and Character of the CEO

Self-motivation through corporate vision. When Mr. Chambers talks about his continued passion for his work over the years, he makes several references to the motivational effect of corporate vision. For more than 30 years, Cisco has always taken "the Internet changes people's work, study and life" as its corporate vision. When the vision is achieved through the efforts of employees, the top management of the company feels a great sense of achievement and develops it into a driving force for change. This vision has also become an important principle for enterprises to promote, appoint or replace core leaders in times of change.

Know yourself clearly. 'As a leader of a large business, you need to have a clear understanding of your strengths and weaknesses,' says Mr. Chambers. Once you've identified your strengths and weaknesses, be open to them. You don't have to share them with your team, but you do have to be aware of them. After understanding clearly, although sometimes the development speed of the enterprise is relatively slow, and mistakes will be made along the way, the enterprise can choose the right direction for reform and development and always insist on not giving up. Leaders should realize that the night before success is often the darkest. Cisco used to act slowly, perform poorly in a short period of time, and often made mistakes. However, mistakes are not terrible.

Indomitable will. Chambers believes that in times of stress and failure, people who create miracles, find and seize business opportunities demonstrate real leadership. The key role of a leader is to be able to lead an enterprise from scratch, from small to large, from weak to strong, and from loss to gain. Therefore, it is very important for leaders to be visionary, persistent, adaptable and guiding. As Cisco is in an Internet industry with rapidly developing technologies, its leaders need to be more alert to the environment, more willing to explore the uncertainty of the future, and more patient and persistent in strategy. Leading the change is the key factor for enterprise leaders to ensure that enterprise carriers are not subverted.

Master of strategic balance. Mr. McDonald, a former boss of Procter & Gamble, spoke in particular about the importance of balance for business leaders. He believes that, first of all, business leaders should be able to effectively balance the relationship between relevant stakeholders, form a good communication with all stakeholders, and reach a full understanding; second, to establish a balance between the daily work and system construction, leaders cannot let the daily tedious business work bury the important system construction of the enterprise; finally, the balance between strategic goals and development opportunities is important. Every enterprise has its own strategic intention and strategic plan, but when people pay too much attention to their own strategic intentions, they may ignore unexpected opportunities.

Match words with deeds. How do CEOs deal with tough decisions? The new leader should keep pace with the development goals of the company. When asked how to deal with difficult circumstances and decisions, such as how to cope when a long term colleague moves on or the act of firing an employee, Chambers said it is important for leaders to be consistent in what they say and what they do. Predictability of behavior. In the field of management, a primary concern has always been the study of leaders' characteristics. In a 1998 study of more than 3,400 managers, the vast majority of respected leaders were described as honest, competent, visionary, charismatic and credible. Such positive traits may enhance a leader's ability to lead, especially in terms of vision and delegation. The key attributes of successful leadership include drive, willingness to lead, motivation, honesty and integrity, self-confidence, intelligence, and adaptability.[1] When asked as an industry leader what the most

---

[1] "Women and Men, Work and Power", Fast Company, 1998, 13:71.

important source of success is and what the biggest challenge is, Chambers replied: "as a leader, the key is how you treat others, will you be able to respect and trust of others, the way of human behavior decides your letter can establish with others, also reflects the nature of a man is kind." A leader's ability to build trust with others, to respect others, to walk the walk, to be consistent and predictable in his or her words, and to maintain balance are very important qualities. "Leaders also need to put themselves in perspective, have a correct view of themselves, and at the same time look at themselves objectively. One who feels good about oneself also makes others feel good. When I get home, my wife can make me feel like I'm not a CEO anymore, so I can relax and balance is established," Chambers said. Just as important, leaders must make employees feel that their leader's behavior is consistent and predictable.

The ability to focus. An easy trap for top executives, says Mr. Chambers, is to do too much: Five priorities, 20 priorities. In the United States, the information industry is highly competitive, and the leading enterprises that can survive and develop have their core technologies and products, which are hard for competitors to surpass. Hosts and services, for example, IBM, HP servers, Microsoft's operating system, etc. Cisco has 12 leading products in the industry, the 12 product category, internal connection to the enhanced combination system of product differentiation ability, Cisco through continuous input for the research and development of these products to ensure its leading edge.

A sense of humor. A sense of humor is important, and the Chinese have a sense of humor, especially when discussing difficult issues,' Mr. Chambers said. Dare to take on social responsibilities. Messrs. Chambers of Cisco and McDonald of Procter & Gamble both talk about corporate social responsibility as an integral part of corporate culture, and the responsibility of a company to give back, even though many companies around the world do not necessarily believe that. After the terrible earthquake in Sichuan, China fared better than any other country. Because Sichuan is in the mountains, Cisco understood the difficulties of mountain transportation and donated $90 million to rebuild health and education, the largest donation the company had ever made.

7 How Does a CEO Lead a Global Company?

Cisco wants to be a Chinese company in China and a German company in Germany,' Mr. Chambers said in a 2011 lecture to central government executives on how to lead in a global company. At the same time, as a global enterprise, its operating system should be consistent regardless of the country. If an enterprise wants to succeed in the global scale, it needs to establish a common discourse system and communication platform in all branches of the world, so each branch has a clear strategic goal. Cisco expects its investments in each country to become successful within 5–10 years and has the patience to localize in each country and to differentiate itself from its competitors through continuous efforts to achieve common goals cooperatively.

Promote the globalization of corporate culture. As a global enterprise, Cisco strives to promote the globalization of corporate culture. Cisco transmits its core cultural values in different languages around the world, in the form of small CARDS that all employees can carry with them. As a channel to promote corporate cultural identity and communication around the world, this investment of more than US $10,000 has been very effective and far-reaching. How to integrate the culture dominated by Cisco in the United States with that of Cisco in other countries is a challenging prospect. In the interview, the top management of Cisco replied that the culture of Cisco is like the main course, the culture of the world is like the dessert, and the mainstream system of culture is based on the headquarters of the United States. The unified core values of the formation of a unified discourse system, the company's internal multinational ditch platform and mechanism, helps form the common understanding and practice of corporate core values and culture and cross-cultural differences. This mutual understanding will help enterprises identify Cisco's core values and common knowledge, thus enhancing cohesion of the enterprise.

Common pitfalls of global corporate failure. For a global enterprise in a highly competitive environment, where technological innovation and substitution emerge one after another, how can corporations avoid mistakes and potential risks? In his report, Mr. Chen Shiwei, President of Cisco greater China, often talked about how big companies can avoid failure. Cisco's experience is: (1) listen to the needs of customers, ask more questions, and fully consider the needs of customers when making major strategic decisions and transformation; (2) initiate the change, avoid the feeling of complacency, and promote the transformation and change of the enterprise by constantly learning new technologies and understanding the new needs of customers to prevent complacency; (3) avoid greed. Cisco has endured several downturns in its 34-year history but has bounced back from the worst circumstances. When the economic environment is bad, enterprises adopt the strategy of focus, by "slimming down" to focus on their own core technology and core products. More is not always better, says Mr. Chambers, citing his experiences at GM and Cisco. Many great companies die of indigestion, not starvation; (4) develop the right leaders. In the process of development, some enterprises have no way to breed excellent leadership or find remarkable talent, so they develop processes. The processes are increasingly complicated, and the management team is continues to grow, leading to a vicious cycle. The important thing for Cisco is to find the right people, give them responsibility, build a solid culture with core values, and continue to develop great leaders through incremental change.

Build a transparent company. Company culture is based on how to ensure customer success. Make everything public and demonstrate that Cisco is a transparent company. Companies with fear will survive, or they will be replaced in 3–5 years.

Act quickly to seize global market opportunities. For Cisco, where 70 percent of opportunities come from outside the US and 90 percent of revenues come from outside the US, it is crucial to develop a replicable business model quickly and flexibly. "I still feel that Cisco is moving too slowly, but sometimes react too fast without support, so it's important to restructure the organization and innovate the operating system," Chambers said.

Building complementary teams. 'The best combination of a leader and a deputy is complementary,' says Mr. Chambers, referring to team building at the top and coordination between the President and his deputy. The training of a successor is very important and the leader should see both growth and learning experiences. American business leaders used to come from the east, but more will eventually come from the west.

8 How Do Leaders Promote Corporate Change?

See corporate change as a religion. Chambers believes that the speed and scale of enterprise change is especially important. In the future, Cisco strives to develop from a $40 billion high-tech enterprise to an $80 billion enterprise. The most important thing is to conduct continuous innovation and change. However, innovation and competent operation are both indispensable wheels for balanced development of enterprises.. Only focusing on innovation and ignoring strong operation, or only focusing on strong operation and ignoring innovation will leave hidden trouble for the long-term sustainable development of enterprises.

Faced with the expansion of enterprise scale, how to deal with the relationship between innovation and enterprise inertia has become a major challenge for the leaders of large enterprises because the excessive maturity, stable environment and operation of enterprises will bring many obstacles to innovation. Chambers believes that in a period of rapid change, leaders must first define the future direction of the industry before they can lead their companies into the future. If the strategic vision is unclear or incorrect, keep looking for opportunities and redirection and get the team moving quickly. Companies should view change as a belief that if they don't change as others do, they will be surpassed by others. The reality is that the most successful companies tend to be the ones that change more slowly, because the most successful people find it hard to adapt to change, and may view people and organizations as lazy. In the face of seeking the driving force and direction of future change, people's understanding is often inconsistent. In the process of change, if there is resistance, the management team needs to constantly adjust and update. Asked if people who did not support change would be replaced, Mr. Chambers replied decisively: "Yes, but not the President." In Chambers' view, leaders cannot stay only four or five years. He has remained in his current job for 15 years, and corporate strategies often take three to five years to show results. For executives or subordinates who are still unable to adapt to the pressure and environment of change after 3–5 years, they should be rotated or transferred. In the past, many information technology companies in the United States had their headquarters in Boston. However, now there are only three left in Boston and the rest have moved to the Silicon Valley, indicating that the fierce competitive environment has accelerated the rate of elimination of enterprises.

The predictability of leaders. The predictability of leaders determines whether companies can seize the opportunity for change. Strategies for seizing the opportunity of market changes to drive organizational change and making changes when others do not expect them are the main challenges faced by many leaders of large enterprises. The way Cisco operates is to look at the world market. Cisco does not care who its competitors are. It only CARES about rapid transformation and building market scale quickly by working with partners. During the Asian fiscal crisis, many multinational companies decided to leave Asia and exit the Chinese market, but Cisco did the opposite and ultimately did well in the Asian market. For example, in the automobile industry, Cisco has established a close relationship with General Motors and Ford. At the beginning, Cisco invested a great deal, but its sales performance was poor. However, Cisco persevered and became a supplier of General Motors. In the process of entering the Chinese market, Cisco transferred manufacturing here by outsourcing, which now seems to have been a wise decision.

Establish a culture and path for change. There are usually two ways to change an enterprise. The first is continuous change through regular procedures, and the second is major irregular changes, also known as "transformation". In Cisco's view, companies generally go through the following stages to change: thinking about why they want to change (change awareness), participating in change (change desire), knowing how to change (change knowledge), implementing new skills, taking new actions (change capacity), and maintaining change momentum (change consolidation). To make a successful transition, leaders must urge people not to be complacent about the status quo and to offer good wishes for the future. In other words, if the enterprise wants to make successful change and satisfy employees following the change, it must facilitate methods for making employees dissatisfied with the status quo. If any of the stages mentioned above are not done well, change will fail, and these failures will all be attributed to the failure of the leadership.

Fear and resistance to change often stem from a fear of losing familiar circumstances and systems. There are numerous reasons why people resist change. Increased workload without increased rewards; loss of an established position or identity due to change; loss of power, control, or resources in the process of change; loss of due interest; change in encountering new competitors and so on. If we do not support resistance to change, change can take various forms such as the spread of gossip, increased work, inability to finish tasks on time, complaining, physical discomfort, listlessness, silence, perseverating on the worst things, being distracted, harboring anger, reduced customer satisfaction, and so on.

Cisco describes employees who resist change as the "zoo of resistance" of different animals: ostriches, snails, dogs, moles and tigers. The ostrich buries its head in the sand, immerses itself in its own world and ignores change. The snail clearly knows that change is happening, but it is happening very slowly. The courage of the dog is not enough, only knowing the slogan, but lacking action. The mole never explicitly reveals his true feelings, but sabotages them. The tiger, on the other hand, is blatantly resistant to change. "Zoos" can become more harmonious and receptive to change if they can understand the inner needs of these animals and the real reasons for their resistance to change and take corresponding measures. However, if they cannot find the source of resistance, the animals will surely continue to engage in discord. Therefore, senior leaders should pay more attention to the reasons why employees resist change and take the following measures to overcome the resistance to change:

(1) urge people not to be satisfied with the status quo; (2) draw an achievable vision that enables employees to understand the value of change; (3) make the core steps explicit; (4) reduce the psychological cost and provide constant guidance and help; (5) minimize the economic cost and cost to be paid by the cooperator.

It's easy to make changes objectively or just think about them in your head, but it's hard to accept them subjectively. "Change creates a sense of loss," says Grashow in the "Practice of Adaptive Leadership".[2] The learning process is often painful. One person's innovation can make others feel inferior, betrayed, or irrelevant. Few people like to start over. It takes time to get used to. Thus, leaders need to recognize that change will cost them some people. An example of the importance of change is the ice industry in the United States. In New York in 1850, ice was collected from a lake, polished and transported elsewhere. In 1900, it was thought of opening ice-making factories in big cities, where the ice would be frozen and kept fresh, so that women would not have to buy food every day. The move was so successful that ice-making became the ninth-largest industry in the United States in 1920, and businesses that had previously collected ice disappeared. In 1927, the refrigerator enterprise emerged and flourished, while the previous ice-making enterprise completely vanished. In more than 70 years, these market leaders had failed to make the transition to the next generation of technology. The leader of ice mining failed to become the leader of ice making and was replaced by others. Likewise, the leader of the ice maker did not become the leader of the home refrigeration business. This shows that transformation is difficult, but it is also important.

Resisting change means losing leadership. One leader may always push for change, and after four or five years, the momentum for change will dissipate, and leadership change will be needed. In this process, a person's future position, the key to whether his personal goals and the enterprise's goals are still consistent, will require more contemplation. The change in subordinates is designed to make the enterprise more progressive. In the changing environment of the Internet industry, it is dangerous for leaders to be complacent. People should never dwell on the past.

9 Summary

In the process of leading global enterprises to participate in the fierce international competition, the key leaders need to solve three core problems.

First, the external environment and external relations. The global vision of strategic leaders is important and can transform this vision into strategic capabilities of the enterprise. Leaders can perceive and grasp the changing trends of the global market, customers, technology and competitive environment early on, quickly and accurately, transmit their foresight and crisis awareness to the organization, and form a core driving force of enterprise transformation and change. In this process,

---

[2] Ronald A. Heifets, Marty Linsky and Alexande Grashow, The Practice of Adaptive Leadership[M]. Harvard Business School Press, 2009.

the perception and judgment of the leader may also have errors, but can be corrected by means of a high-level team decision-making combination, listening to the voice of customers and timely error correction. In fierce international competition, leaders need to determine the enterprise's strategy and positioning, develop an effective dynamic adjustment mechanism in interacting with the market, allocate resources efficiently according to the needs of the enterprise's strategic development, and establish a highly adaptive organization through fast learning. Second, the leader should be a master of balance. Senior leaders should establish contact with all stakeholders of the enterprise, develop a balance mechanism, coordinate the conflict between different stakeholders, and establish close communication and a trust relationship with customers, especially key customers. At the same time, balance should be found between external and internal interests, short-term and long-term goals, strategic and tactical issues, innovation and management efficiency.

The second is to treat the internal development of enterprises. In the process of leading the development of enterprises, the key challenge for leaders is to solve the problem of personnel. Selection and use of leading talent are of great significance to the development of enterprises, and building a strong leading group and complementary team are critical to the implementation of enterprise strategy. At the same time, the top leader of the enterprise is the core builder of the enterprise culture. The values, core concepts and past experiences of the leaders, especially the hardships and frustrations they have experienced, determine their expectations and requirements for the most critical elements and behaviors of the enterprise culture. Management of their own behavior is an important benchmark of enterprise culture; leaders shape, build and play a key role in the enterprise culture. The decision to transform the enterprise through energy and courage can lead to the development of a new spirit of quality.

The third is to treat oneself. The success, failure, prosperity and decline of an enterprise are highly related to the leader. The vision, learning ability and courage of leaders directly affect the enterprise's ability to foresee and adapt to the future. Thus, the mindset of the leader, the ability to absorb new knowledge, introspection and self-awareness determine the company's ability to invest and focus on the future. Building trust, predictability, consistency, and a sense of humor are all important characteristics of a leader in dealing with others. At the same time, leaders' self-management ability, including the balance between work, life and health, social responsibility and moral awareness, are also necessary elements of the sustainable and healthy development of enterprises.

Chapter 3
Enterprise Transformation and Change Management

1 Introduction

Enterprise transformation is a process of dynamic selection, adjustment and change of strategy in response to changes in the external environment. Change refers to the process that an organization constantly undergoes within its internal organizational system, process, technology and management system in order to effectively respond to challenges and opportunities brought about by the external environment. Enterprise transformation and change originates from the high-level leadership team's cognition, response or guidance to the new trends and patterns evolved from the environment, market, customers, technology and service. The first is the fundamental change of thinking. An organization and its members unleash their potential by developing innovations, architectures, processes, and systems that are conducive to competition through the intellectual exploration of leaders. To meet challenges from the future, leaders need to prepare their organizations at the individual, team and organizational levels to embrace, adapt and embrace new opportunities and challenges. Transformation is an efficient interactive and strain mechanism between enterprises and the external environment. Through transformation and change, organizations abandon old concepts, technologies, methods, knowledge and capabilities, and constantly build new systems of technologies, management, products, services and capabilities. Through transformation and change, enterprises are constantly expanding their horizons and have the ability to solve more complex problems, provide more sophisticated products and services or market demand. Organizational change is not only a forced change by means of restructuring or process reengineering, but also includes the attitude and ability to actively respond to environmental opportunities and challenges. It is not easy for enterprises to face uncertain environments and fierce competition in transformation and reform. Many enterprises with long-term accumulation, mature and successful enterprise, inherent thinking, methods, processing and behavior have become stable. Meanwhile other organizations may lead a path of dependence, in a

X. Dong et al., *Cisco*,
https://doi.org/10.1007/978-981-19-7870-8_3

state of selfish departmentalism, face transformation challenges, change and restructuring, and the formation of stubborn resistance. The innovation of the fierce market competition requires flexibility, agility, and rapid response.

Enterprise transformation is an arduous challenge that the leadership must deal with. There is no simple path or method for the transformation process. It requires a series of factors, including: (1) Broader thinking and vision. Leaders' foresight should match the change rate of the environment, even ahead of the identification of problems in the industry. If they can foresee the change and development trend of the environment, they will bring opportunities for the transformation and change of the organization. (2) Transformation and change are not just change of skills, but change of the entire thinking and mental model, and the change of the integrated organizational assets such as the organizational system, architecture and process. (3) In the process of promoting organizational transformation, it is necessary to reveal the potential ideas that hinder and oppose the enterprise. It is the management system, status, rights, interests and control system that have been lurking in the organization for many years that secretly hinder the advancement of the transformation. (4) The transformation and change of an organization are first and foremost the change of leaders, especially the change in thinking, culture and behavior. The personal responsibility of leaders in the process of change is a key element in ensuring the success of reform. (5) Decision-making is the core of transformation and change. The initial behavior of transformation and change is unknown, but its value is known. The process of transformation and change is hard to crack. It is not enough to rely only on soft skills. Such leaders need to have a broad vision, not be satisfied with the status quo, stand firm, not give in under pressure, have their own judgment in the face of different views, have enough patience and courage to push for change, and constantly examine the costs and results, which shows the importance of culture.

The timing of enterprise transformation is particularly important. Some enterprises choose to transform in the period of rapid growth, while others choose to transform in periods of downturn. Some enterprises choose active transformation; some enterprises choose passive transformation; some enterprises choose a comprehensive transformation; some enterprises are partial transformation. The core driving force of corporate transformation is the foresight and crisis awareness of the leadership, as well as pressure from the market and stakeholders. There are usually two ways to change a company: the first is to use regular procedures for continuous change, and the second is a major irregular change, that is, "transformation". Continuous transformation, transformation and evolution are important genes of longevity enterprises. In 1937, the life expectancy of an S&P 500 company was 75 years. In 1983, it was 40 years. Cisco is now 34 years old. The key to Cisco's survival in the competitive Internet industry is its ability to transform, change and innovate, a key lesson of its 34-year history of staying young.

2 Outstanding Enterprise Is the Result of Continuous Transformation

The Internet industry is known for its rapid changes and fierce competition. The capital market has high requirements for the update speed and profitability of products and services, so enterprises often face the dual pressure of sustainable development and profitability. Enterprises must constantly meet challenges, embrace change and promote transformation. Since Chambers took over, Cisco has undergone nine major transformations that have relied on sharp market observation and effective decision making. In these transformations, the focus of Cisco's core competitiveness is also changing. If we look at the history of Cisco's transformation, we can divide it into three periods.

Lecture about Cisco's transformation

From 1984 to 1999, Internet equipment provider. Cisco entered the Internet business in the 1990s and has since moved into adjacent technology areas through acquisitions. At this stage, countries all over the world are accelerating investment in information infrastructure construction, so the Internet industry is growing rapidly. Cisco took this opportunity to grow rapidly, with $24 billion in sales. As it grew, Cisco focused on building core enterprise capabilities to meet the rapidly growing market demand and on expanding its product portfolio and enhancing its R&D capabilities, with a view to continuously launch new products and surpass its competitors. With the bursting of the dotcom bubble in 2000, global Internet demand fell sharply, and Cisco's sales fell from $24 billion to $18 billion. In the meantime, many of its competitors left the market, and Cisco has sought new space by adjusting its business model.

From 2000 to 2008, Cisco optimized the overall operation system. Learning from the lessons of the bursting of the dotcom bubble, Cisco is actively developing leading technologies while improving its operational capabilities and supply chain management capabilities in markets, technologies and business models. During this period, Cisco actively developed leading technologies, continuously expanded its business in the Internet, and improved its operational capabilities in the market, technology and business model through acquisitions, thus optimizing and enhancing its internal capabilities.

From 2008 to 2012, total solution provider. Cisco seeks to transform itself from a product provider to a comprehensive solution provider. Cisco has built more than $10 billion worth of businesses in the Internet industry through leading technologies, with hardware accounting for 70% of its revenue. At the same time, the company is still facing considerable pressure to transform from product seller to service and consulting provider to better meet customer needs. In the process, Cisco tries to make changes by executing strategy, adjusting its core business and product portfolio, and investing in advanced technology to enter new markets. Modern technologies and new markets, especially the spread of video technology and the use of cloud computing, have pushed enterprises into new growth Spaces.

From 2013 to 2018, Cisco enabled digital transformation. During this period, Cisco took the Internet of everything as the core, further utilized its comprehensive technical system advantages, and intended to make great achievements in the Internet of everything. According to Cisco's projections, the number of connections to the global Internet of things will grow from 5.8 billion in 2016 to 13.7 billion in 2021, leaving plenty of room for growth. At the same time, Cisco has accelerated its presence in manufacturing, healthcare and education, promoting deeper integration and connectivity between the next generation of information technology and professional industries. In the manufacturing sector, Cisco provides interconnected factory suites that integrate network expertise and knowledge with enterprise networks to help manufacturing companies improve management performance in optimizing operations management, leveraging data to support management decisions, accurately recording and predicting equipment operational efficiencies and insight into potential failures. Cisco is also building a fully digital connectivity factory with cloud computing as its core through manufacturing enterprise interactive network architecture. In the medical field, Cisco's technology is used in telemedicine. By establishing a safe and reliable connection between patients, doctors and medical processes, Cisco can improve the visit rate, improve the quality of medical treatment and improve the medical effect. Cisco provides services in the form of digital medical innovation solutions and telemedicine selection diagrams. In the field of education, Cisco's information technology enables students to use any device on campus anytime and anywhere, breaking the limitation of time and space, and building a smart campus.

Cisco judges the timing of change and transformation from four perspectives: first, to seize the development trend of global corporate change; second, to seize the opportunity of technological transformation; third, to seize the opportunity of market transformation; fourth, to realize transformation when the enterprise is healthy. When the company's stock was undervalued by the financial market, Cisco took building internal business capabilities and product development as its core activities, and took advantage of the downturn to improve the efficiency of R&D. When the economy recovered, Cisco quickly formed sales scale through global sales network as it strives to expand market shares in emerging industries. After a new product is confirmed by the market, the core strategy of the enterprise is to ensure the rapid growth of the market.

3 External Driving Forces of Strategic Transformation

The company should identify recent changes in the external environment as early as possible. Cisco is focused on information technology and the Internet, and the rapid growth of this area means that Cisco has to constantly adapt to change. While continuously promoting its own transformation, Cisco has found that the external environment has changed significantly in the following eight aspects. These new changes have also continuously pushed Cisco to change.

The rapid development and application of information technology. Information technology is the core force leading scientific and technological innovation in the past 50 years. From basic research and development to market application, the development of information technology has experienced one cycle after another. New technologies are first developed in universities, research institutes or enterprises, then gradually adopted by enterprises and applied in practice, with a period of about 15 years. In turn, consumers will enjoy the benefits of modern technologies such as personal computers, laptops, the Internet, mail systems, and IP telephony. But that has changed a lot since 2000. The latest adopters of technology are no longer corporations but consumers. If companies are sensitive to new technologies and are quick to learn, they may be able to catch up with consumers within 15 years. Web 2.0 technologies such as instant messaging, Wikipedia, blogs, Twitter and other social networks catch on with consumers before they are adopted and used by businesses. This shift means that the time has passed when consumers learned from companies to apply new technologies. Consumers are now leading the way as the main adopters of new technologies. Consumers are more advanced and effective than enterprises in communication and collaboration. In this process, emerging Internet enterprises have become leaders in the application of innovative technologies, which places pressure on enterprises (especially those already successful or those in traditional industries). For enterprise information in charge (CIO), they bear pressure from the superior, to ensure that the enterprise information system is safe, reliable and efficient. Companies are also under pressure from consumers as they once educated consumers on new technologies. Now consumers are leading the way. Companies need to learn from consumers and adopt new technologies, or they will be abandoned by consumers.

The Internet is reinventing every aspect of social life. There have been four revolutions in media and technology over the centuries. The second revolution,

200 years ago, included the telephone and the telegraph. The third, 150 years ago, was recording technology when people began to record sound films, records, etc. The fourth, 100 years ago, occurred when television and radio appeared. These technologies are widely used in the premise of covering the world's infrastructure construction, and in these processes, countries have invested a lot of money and other resources. Although the above four media technologies can be fully utilized in their respective fields, they are independent of each other. The reason the Internet is called "Internet" is because it can connect all people and things, connect all media, and set reception and transmission functions in one. At the same time, the Internet has greatly reduced the cost of communication, which not only supports one-to-one communication between people, but also supports one-to-many and many-to-many communication. On the Internet penetration measure, North America is over 66% and Asia 20%, which means that one in five people use the Internet. But in terms of the total number of users, almost half of the world's Internet users are in Asia. The Internet has reinvented every field of the world, and this process has penetrated into every field of international politics, economy, society and culture. Although many people feel the changes brought by the Internet, they do not see the deep impact and structural changes brought by it. Among them, the most obvious is the transformation of the industrial economic system, and the traditional business model has been challenged unprecedentedly. The emerging Internet enterprises are constantly using the network to optimize and innovate the business model and enter the influence scope of the traditional industry with lower cost, faster speed and wider scope. In this environment, strategic challenges and opportunities coexist. How leaders face such profound changes, how they challenge their own thinking habits and existing organizational systems, will mean whether enterprises can seize opportunities in the next wave of development to achieve growth and prosperity.

The power of the people has grown stronger. In the 1990s, the development of the Internet mainly focused on the technical aspects of information infrastructure. By 2012, the development of the Internet has focused on "interaction", "community" and "co-construction". The Internet connects people, forming virtual communities based on common interests and hobbies to quickly share information on a large scale. The Internet has become the most important platform for arousing public opinion and promoting social movements. An example in Colombia in 2007 illustrates the power of the Internet. After nearly being abducted in the mountains of Colombia by a group that carried out a series of crimes including kidnapping, torture and murder, a Facebook user posted a complaint online, triggering an immediate global response. On July 6, a million Colombians took to the streets in a mass demonstration demanding that the government punish the group severely and release the hostages unconditionally. This action quickly spread around the world, and over the next 30 days, 12 million people in 120 countries marched around the world to denounce the violence. In the past, an ordinary citizen who knew about this incident could hardly take any direct action, but in the age of the Internet, one can call on tens of millions of people to protest. The Internet gives everyone a voice, and ordinary people are likely to replace authoritative media as the source of most information.

The growth of the digital generation. People born between 1980 and 1999 live in a global multi-cultural information environment. They have a vast amount of information, an open mind, active thinking, strong communication skills, and the ability to cooperate and organize. They are called the "digital generation". The Internet provides them with the technical environment and cultural atmosphere for communication anytime and anywhere. Compared with their parents, they are more receptive to information, learn faster, are more tolerant and receptive to global multiculturalism, and are often indifferent to geographical and linguistic boundaries. Therefore, the generation gap between them and their parents is evident.

Information explosion. According to Cisco, two-thirds of the world's mobile data traffic will be self-viewing. The explosion of information will have a profound impact on the future of the Internet. Another development trend of the information explosion is the impact of information on enterprises. The number of global companies is growing rapidly. Unlike a decade ago, many of the world's top 500 companies are now headquartered outside the U.S. In 2012, for example, China accounted for 50 of the top 500 companies. Enterprises, thus, need to constantly adjust, make full use of market trends and network technology, to achieve innovation in the field of business model, to not only survive in the market, but also to succeed within it.

The Internet has become a disruptor of business models. The proliferation of the Internet in social and economic life is changing the supply chain, operation system and business model of industries and enterprises. Many intermediate links are replaced by the Internet, and enterprises that have adopted new business models are growing rapidly. In the music industry just 5 years ago, companies began to master all elements of the industry for an act to be successful. From development of the music, album cover design, production of the record, club and theatre tours, video production, special performances and other elements, record companies that dominated the entire process reaped the biggest benefits. But today, bands and singers are taking advantage of social media to take the initiative, uploading songs to video sites, signing deals with sponsors and hosting special shows once they gain a broad audience. Another example of this is in the media. When the sea roar happened in Japan, the information from the tsunami disaster area came from the ordinary people first, and then from news media outlets. These examples show that the Internet has given more people the power to change traditional industries, and that many industries that have not adapted to these changes are at a loss.

The Internet has greatly improved the efficiency of business processes. In the Internet era, information content is no longer loaded to specific media, but can be spread through the network through a variety of channels–virtual and Internet downloads, instead of having to rely on a tape recorder, DVD player, vinyl records or electronic readers. In the paper age, it took a long time for a book to reach the reader: the author wrote it, the publisher reviewed and edited it, the book was printed and distributed, the retailer stocked and sold it. Now, authors write, publishers receive and edit manuscripts, then store them on a server for readers to download. The process is much simpler, and readers can purchase books at a lower price than in the past. In addition, electronic supply chains have cut the cost of shipping, forestry, paper, book shelving and store sales. Thus, e-books have become increasingly more popular.

Paper books have been around for hundreds of years, but within the next decade, e-books are likely to replace them. This is an example of the disruptive impact of business model innovation on the market.

The development of networks has led to an increase in the complexity of decision-making. IBM's survey of thousands of CEOs shows that 60% of companies believe they are facing extremely high levels of complexity and 79% believe the world will become even more complex in the next five years, however, only 49% of CEOs believe they are ready for a complex environment.

4 Internal Driving Force of Strategic Transformation

The internal driving force of Cisco's transformation is shown in four aspects: improving experience, accelerating growth, improving efficiency and improving revenue. The specific model is shown in Fig. 1.

Improve the experience. The main goal of improving the experience is to make the business more convenient, and there are two main ways to do so: first, making the work of employees easier and providing a better working environment and experience in the enterprise, such as the experience of information system application and internal collaboration, and the experience of interacting with customers. The second is to let customers have a better experience, customers as partners and end customers. The partner experience is demonstrated through the partnership with Cisco, resulting in a seamless workflow and good return on investment. The end-customer experience is where Cisco provides end-to-end value chain integration and one-stop service.

Cisco sees customer demand as the most important force driving market transformation. The direction of the company's transformation is to achieve seamless

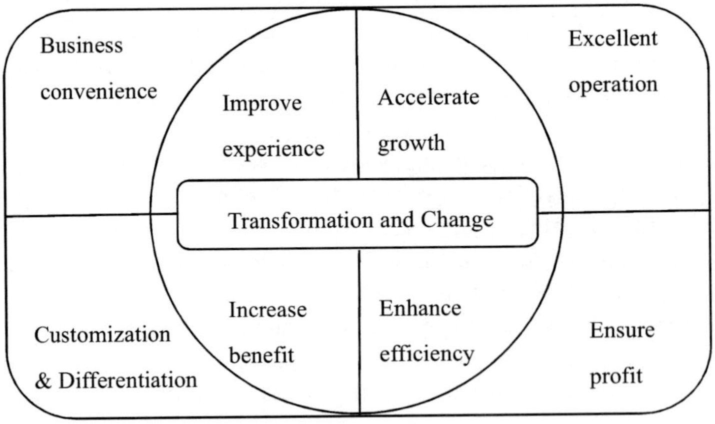

Fig. 1 Drivers of Cisco's transformation

connection between products, enhance the complementary and combined capabilities of products and technologies, provide a customer experience, and provide new profit space for the company's partners while the market grows. In this process, man–machine interconnection technology will bring great influence and change to the cooperation between enterprises and will lead the innovation direction in the future. Moreover, through social media and Web 2.0 technology, it can ensure efficient connection within the organization, so people can obtain the right information and knowledge through the right media at the right time. Man–machine interconnection is also a fast business processing method, which can help people overcome barriers in information transmission and sharing, eliminate the delays caused by various obstacles in information processing and decision-making communication, and connect more people to form a borderless network. Therefore, man–machine interconnection technology has a strong influence and a vast space for potential development.

In addition to the Internet, Cisco sees opportunities on the smart grid as well. Take the smart grid, for example. In the United States and European countries, the grid infrastructure is aging rapidly. Generally speaking, the average life of the grid transmission system is 45 years, but in Europe and the United States, the grid transmission system has only 40 years of use and is now in an extended state of service. At the same time, traditional grid infrastructure cannot support new applications, such as charging electric cars, which are already popular in China. In Europe and the United States, most employees entered the power industry in the 1960s and 1970s and will soon retire. Thus the knowledge and experience of these old employees may be lost with their retirement, which may present obstacles for the safe operation of the power industry. From Cisco's perspective, the more problems the power industry has to solve, the more pain its customers have, and the greater the market opportunity. The current state of the American and European power grids is like a person with a musculoskeletal system but no nervous system and no way to sense information. Therefore, for the innovation team of Cisco, they need to install the digital nervous system for the power grid, enhance the communication function between the power grids, collect the information and distribution of power resources comprehensively, and use the power resources reasonably and intelligently based on this. Recharging cars at a time when electricity consumption is low, allowing smart batteries to interact with the grid and making the best use of electricity at the most opportune times have rejuvenated an ancient industry. With this understanding, in 2012 Cisco entered the line of strategic adjustment, the core competitiveness of focusing on five strategic areas: core business leadership (network routers, switches and related services, such as network security and mobile solutions), collaborative technology (fixed and mobile network integrated language, video and data), virtualization and cloud computing data centers, video systems, and the structure of the business transformation. Cisco's focus on enterprise customers, service providers and business users as the focus of enterprise strategic development and innovation points the way for the company's technological innovation and acquisitions.

Accelerate growth. Cisco has focused its growth on providing customers with new solutions and consumption patterns through the continued discovery of transformational opportunities in emerging markets and emerging technologies and the integration of disruptive technologies into existing technology and product systems. For this reason, Cisco attaches great importance to the forward-looking discovery of new technology applications and customer demand based on the Internet platform. This includes acquisition and other means of SMEs into the new technology, optimizing the original product structure, and finding rapid growth in emerging markets.

Cisco's strategic transformation is driven by the development direction of the market. To identify the development direction of the market, the leader should have broad strategic vision and forward-looking vision. The formation of this strategic vision requires the high-level decision-making team to have a clear understanding of the future human survival mode, the development trend and potential impact of existing technologies, the transformation direction of traditional industries, and the problems that people need to face and solve. On the basis of this understanding, the decision-making team is required to further seek solutions to the problem. On top of the big platform of the Internet, Cisco sees human–computer interconnection as the most important innovation space of the future. The innovation of man–machine interconnection is mainly reflected in the global impact of information technology on human communication and interaction. As a huge platform, the Internet brings people from all levels of society together, and its technology diffusion and penetration become wider and deeper, which is mainly reflected in the development of social media. The sector has already shown robust business opportunities and has been a major driver of innovation and change at Facebook, Twitter, YouTube, Apple and others. Social media accelerates social innovation and promotes interconnection of innovative industries. On the contrary, in large traditional enterprises, innovation is still slow, there are many islands of information, and it is difficult to recognize connections between each other. In an environment where executives need to constantly explore and determine which new technologies will ensure that employees sell products differently or how to use new technologies to gain market intelligence, Cisco sees plenty of opportunities for growth.

In 2013, Cisco sought three emerging markets: smart connectivity, cloud computing, big data and video. In the future, Cisco will have 46 equipment connections to the Internet, while only 1% of world systems are connected to the Internet. In the transportation system, intelligent buildings, intelligent energy-saving power grids, water supplies, food value chains, medical care, smart cities, and smart homes, there are numerous objects connected with opportunity, meaning the Internet of things encompasses huge market space. In addition to the huge market for technology and equipment, there is also room for growth in services that provide integrated solutions. After clearly positioning the new market space, Cisco will first consider what incremental development space exists in the existing market and what new technologies and products need to be added. At the same time, Cisco will analyze what new elements should be added to the existing technology and product system to meet the needs of the future market and how to expand the depth and breadth of the system. In terms of technical equipment, Cisco has positioned itself to develop high-end technology. There's a huge market for this kind of technology, and it's hard for small businesses to participate. Technical equipment can be sold at high prices, although not necessarily in large quantities. Having an advanced understanding of the market and technology, the next step is to quickly create a new market. Second, Cisco constantly looks for gaps in markets, such as emerging markets, as well as gaps in business categories, such as smart services, a strategic focus of Cisco's development in recent years. Intelligent services are automated software analysis functions, network data diagnosis, deep knowledge base comparison and analysis provided on the basis of network infrastructure construction. After the establishment of this new business category, we will explore ways and means to deepen the service system and realize the development from passive service and active service to predictive service and forward-looking service.

In market and technology transformation, Cisco also analyzes its impact on organizations as well as people and their decisions. For the Internet of things, people are building an environment that continuously connects people, things and processes, and are making better decisions through efficient information exchange, data integration and data analysis. In the Internet environment, people at the grassroots level have more data and real situations and have the ability to respond quickly. Organizations and countries that connect people to people, things to things, and people to things will have the opportunity and capacity to innovate, to create deeper relationships, to gain insight into the underlying laws of business development, and to discover the interconnections between things that cross borders, such as weather and agriculture, humidity and nutrition. After mastering the inner relationship between people and things, people have the ability to make more intelligent decisions and allocate resources scientifically and rationally. It is in the fast growth markets of the future, with an understanding of development trends, that Cisco finds the direction of enterprise transformation and the development of space, providing integrated products, services, software platforms of intelligent network architecture and technology, the rapid integration of technology and partners, and the drive to achieve leading in the industry.

Through transformation, Cisco constantly evolves to ensure the growth of enterprises. Investors are usually bullish with regards to fast-growing companies and their future potential. As a company matures and grows slowly, the stock market will abandon its support. Cisco has undergone nine transformations in the past 34 years. The main motivation for the transformation in 2011 was that the enterprise was fledgling. Cisco lost the trust of investors due to Wall Street's doubts about Cisco's ability to execute its strategy, especially its ability to maintain its promised growth target of 12% to 13%. Under the circumstances, Mr. Chambers and Mr. Moore, the chief operating officers, were determined to push for a transformation, one of the main ways of which is to contain costs. What strategies did Cisco use to cut costs? Cisco's approach has been to "downsize", divesting itself of some businesses while adjusting the limits and allocation of resources that inevitably lead to layoffs.

Increase efficiency. Cisco has excellent operation systems, manufacturing process outsourcing, quality management and process monitoring for outsourcing factories through information management. Its supply chain management level is in the leading position among US state-owned enterprises. Through this operating system, Cisco has made high profits. Its development goal is to increase profits more quickly than revenue. At the same time, its unique approach to problem solving and experience have prompted Cisco to develop consulting services with cost controls to achieve optimal results.

Cisco's transformation is also driven by its unique perspective on the industry. In the conventional view, the Internet is just a computer network. Cisco sees the Internet as a big platform on which to build products, services and business models. Guided by this perspective, Cisco found plenty of room to expand. In the past few years, Cisco has been trying to realize the transformation of body, from the enterprise product guide (routers and switches) to the service guide (cloud computing, data center overall solutions and blade server technology), and the consumer guide (interconnected netvision frequency and video conference system) transformation; the transformation process has not easy. On the basis of traditional network technology equipment, Cisco added nearly 30 new industries and new businesses through independent research and acquisition. In 2006, it bought WebEx, a maker of webcams, for $3.2 billion. The same year, it bought Scientific Atlanta, a maker of set-top boxes, for $6.9 billion. In 2009, it bought Flip, a video camera company, for $590 million. Through these decisions, Cisco has as many as 30 consumer businesses, covering video, digital home, fiber optic networks, wireless, IP telephony and more. Now Cisco strives to be a solution provider like IBM and HP. Just like cloud computing, users only need to care about the answer and result of the problem, while the combination of process and solution is left to the vendor. For example, even though 90% of electricity comes from natural gas and the remaining 10% comes from solar and wind, consumers don't have to worry about how the electricity is combined.

Increase efficiency. Cisco's high profits and benefits come from the best combination of economies of scale and customization. Facing the global market, Cisco's strategy is global unity: the higher the unity, the more obvious the economies of scale. But at the same time, different countries and regions have varied market development levels, and customers have customized demands. Under the general premise of global consistency, Cisco proposed that the customized and differentiated demands should be kept below 20%. This combination of consistency (80%) and customization (20%) enables Cisco to achieve the benefits of economies of scale while meeting personalized needs, thus achieving the compatibility of efficiency and flexibility.

As a telecom equipment and service provider, Cisco has maintained a sales share of 64% to 66% for 15 years. Its core business model is designed to achieve global unity through product scalability, while achieving local relevance through product flexibility. The former is the replication of its solutions in the global market. Although the market size of each country is different, the integrity and systematisms of the product series is not affected but are only adjusted in scale. In this way, the replication cost of the solutions is minimized, and the benefits are maximized. Of course, different countries have different needs, and Cisco keeps its portfolio reasonably flexible, with less than 20% of the variation. This business model replicates successful solutions in a low cost, highly efficient way, with the highest efficiency in terms of growth speed and cost.

In the transformation process, Cisco has attached great importance to markets outside the United States. In terms of geography, China, India and other emerging countries are the focus. The key businesses of Cisco are smart grid, cloud computing and so on. Cisco is bullish and wants to enter the physical security market. For example, there are more cameras in the city of London than in any other city in the world. These cameras are connected to the Internet to monitor crime. In any particular situation, the police will be able to view the video in real time and react quickly. This physical security business market is worth twice as much as the routing/switching business that Cisco is currently skilled in and needs to be valued and developed. The video system has many other features: if a person falls when there is no one around, the video system automatically recognizes this and sends an alert for help. When a group of people are in line, the video system can help determine the number of people in line. The video system can also quickly determine the license plate number of a moving vehicle. Cisco hopes to break into this new business and become number one or two.

5 How to Grasp the Opportunity of Strategic Transformation?

In the process of strategic transformation, the company should grasp the development demand and transformation trend of global enterprises. Nowadays, many enterprises need video networks to support the collaborative work of R&D personnel from all over the world, and internal companies need to share and collaborate tacit knowledge through this means of video communication. Cisco actively expands its business in the video field as a result of this development trend.

Customer demand is the traction of enterprise transformation. Over the past 34 years, many tech or Internet companies have been knocked out of business, and one of the most important lessons Cisco has learned in surviving and becoming an industry leader is that being "customer-oriented" reaps tremendous rewards. The customer-centered concept is embodied in all aspects of enterprise development strategy, industrial transformation, R&D innovation and employee performance appraisal. The research and development department of the enterprise focuses on collecting national intelligence, scanning the global competitive situation and customer demand, in order to find the concept of innovation, generate ideas and launch innovation activities, giving Cisco's products global advantages. Cisco listens to its customers every time it makes a market transition, paying close attention to what they want to purchase. With forward-looking insights from its customers, Cisco is likely to take advantage of every market transition and enter three to five years ahead of its competitors. For example, customers may have demand for things like video and the Internet of things, and they need a smarter, more efficient, more productive Internet. In this way, through in-depth communication with customers, Cisco can better grasp the context of market development and make continuous investment to quickly seize opportunities and form market capacity when a new wave of technology application emerges.

Seize the opportunity of market transformation. In the process of strategic transformation, the company should see the opportunity of market transformation. Nowadays "energy-saving" has become a topic of global concern, therefore, Cisco's smart grid is an important area of development when trying to achieve diversity in this area. Disruptive technology research and development in the process of market transition sales of scale and expanding market share keep the company growing. Chambers believes that the most favorable development period is often the worst period for the entire industry, and Cisco is seizing this opportunity to expand market share during the transition period to realize the organic combination of technology and business models.

Seize the opportunity of technological transformation. Technology can often be a major driver of strategic transformation, with virtualized servers, computing centers, and communications networks bringing together the various components of an enterprise. Collaboration and communication technologies help companies connect with their business partners. Through the advancement of technology, the company can establish the competitive advantage, obtain a profit, and continuously expand its own competitive advantage.

Make the transition when the business is healthy. As Cisco's operations become more complex, the company as a whole will slow down. Cisco engaged in major "downsizing" and adjustments in 2012. In the July 2011 corporate fiscal year, Cisco's sales had reached $40 billion, growing 8% in the first quarter and 11% in the final quarter, a strong pace for the company. Routers grew 76% and switches 62%, approaching $12 billion. At this time, Cisco provided video technology services for local governments in the southern European market and achieved a strong sales performance. By contrast, HP and IBM announced problems in their markets, where Cisco has gained an edge by identifying and solving them two quarters ahead of its rivals. Regardless of market success, Cisco once again began to make changes. Why choose this time to adjust and make changes? The answer is to continually get ahead of the competition.

6 Guiding Enterprise Transformation and Reform with Strategic Direction

Clear the strategic positioning of the enterprise. Cisco's strategic goal is to become one of the few companies in the world with product portfolios that might otherwise not enter the business. Cisco will abandon a product once it is overtaken by a competitor. A case in point is the small video camera: Cisco acquired the product, but the technology moved too fast, and Apple released the camera-powered iPhone two weeks before Cisco was ready to market its wireless camera. Given that Apple's products are not only of high quality, but are also produced in large quantities, effectively reducing production costs, Cisco cannot become a global leader in this field. Therefore, it had to announce its withdrawal from this market and invest R&D funds in other technology fields. The consistency of strategy is also an important guarantee for defining the goal of change. In the process of studying changes in external environments and customer needs, Cisco found that the greatest challenge facing companies is how to help customer enterprises improve labor productivity and operational efficiency to ensure competitiveness in the market as the Internet becomes increasingly intelligent and an asset owned and used by all other enterprises. **Objectively judge the current situation of the enterprise**. What will the future of Cisco look like? What is the goal to achieve? Cisco wants to be the trusted IT technology business partner of its customers and to realize the return on investment and help them succeed. To do this, Cisco needs to reallocate existing resources to do business more intensively and with greater focus on related industries. This may also ensure that the company has enough capital for research and acquisition and the ability to lead the development of network technology. Cisco is profitable, cash-rich and has bought back some of its equity. However, in order to further raise profits, Cisco needs to make products faster and streamline operations, production systems, and internal decision-making processes. More importantly, it is important to cultivate employees' sense of belonging within the company. With the continuous development of other enterprises in the field of IT, Cisco has lost some talented young employees to such companies as Google and Apple and will need to reflect on this. At the same time, the small business enterprise growth speed can earn the favor of market investors and, by contrast, Cisco has become a very large scale company, which has thus affected the company's share price. The industry's market share relative to the yield is better than that of SME appeal but is still not big enough. Therefore, the transformation is necessary for the future development of Cisco.

Make clear the direction of future development. In 2011, Cisco's senior leadership team of 12 members met to prepare for deployment of the next strategic plan. There, they put forth a new strategy for Cisco's business direction which included five main points: (1) lead network technology transformation, focusing on the previous 54 strategic elements of the five core technology products while also paying close attention to market transition direction the process of transformation. (2) promote the construction of business and technical architecture by optimizing the business architecture and operational system to clearly grasp various products, services and software, and to quickly enter the market through the integration strategy. (3) take a leading position in emerging countries and regions; to achieve this goal, the company should increase investment in emerging countries, develop partnership models and understand access channels permitted by laws in different countries. (4) accelerate the transformation and simplification of Cisco; by simplifying the entire organizational system, the operation system will also be simplified and the actions will be faster so responsibilities can be implemented in each subsidiary. (5) build a software platform, not just develop software. Given how well the product line is already placed, companies need to build software platforms to increase profitability at a faster pace.

The above goals can be achieved through communication with employees and with the market.

After several meetings, the 12 members of Cisco's senior leadership team reached a consensus that the team needed to make efforts in four areas to achieve its strategic goals: first, optimize the cost structure and greatly reduce costs. Second, instead of fostering 54 strategic areas, Cisco was going to reduce them to five, cutting out companies or businesses that were not performing well thus increasing profitability. The third was to control every market Cisco entered. It could take months to get customer orders, the decision-making process was slow, and hundreds of decisions were pending. Therefore, the company sought a better way to effectively measure the status quo. Fourth, Cisco put an accountability system in place. The company is acutely aware that it has to change the way it does things to make a difference.

Accelerate the transformation through strategic focus. In 2011, the global financial crisis led to the market decline. Cisco encountered great pressure in the capital market and failed to realize the growth rate of 17%. In August of that year, Cisco announced 7,000 job cuts and approximately 3,000 early retirements, accounting for 14% of its workforce. The cuts involved both consumer and core businesses. This was a big change for a company that is normally reluctant to lay off workers. The 12 members of Cisco's senior leadership team often sit together and discuss every step of the enterprise and every business maneuver.

It is through this discussion that Cisco ensures that its 12 members are fully aware of the company's current situation. Before 2012, Cisco had a total of 54 key businesses, and it was difficult for the 12 core members to focus on all of these businesses simultaneously. Therefore, Chambers suggested the enterprise focus on five core areas, including:

(1) Core business, namely router and switch business. These are an important source of corporate profits. In addition, the service sector is also an area of focus for Cisco.
(2) Collaboration. Collaboration plays a strong role for Cisco. It covers a wide range of fields, from desktop phones to mobile phones and videos and also hardware and software.
(3) Data center, virtualization, cloud computing and new business model. In the current market revolution, this is an area of high focus. In 2006, Cisco began investing in a new technology that could change the way data centers are run. It entered the market in 2009 with an 11% share of the global market and is expected to expand further.
(4) Video service. Cisco's goal is to provide the best video equipment in the industry, including telepresence and other products, which is the company's strength.
(5) Infrastructure. Cisco CARES about how customers buy technology and products, how they can collaborate effectively with their goals, or how they can combine video or desktop devices to implement critical communications technology.

Chambers said Cisco would adopt a streamlined business structure to build internal relationships in all five areas—routers and switches have been the cornerstone of Cisco's growth; at the level of enterprise application, collaboration becomes the driving force of various organizations to improve productivity and cooperative communication. Data center, virtualization and cloud computing are internet-centric architectures. Architecture is an abstract model that combines multiple applications to help people combine multiple products when using information technology. Video represents the next generation of voice over the Internet services, the Internet will move increasingly toward the road of visualization. The changes have made Cisco's own strategic path and business systems clearer, while it has also led to the sale of non-core businesses, such as its top-box to Foxconn.

Gary Moore, senior vice President of operations, was hired by Chambers to lead the effort to slim down Cisco. In this process, he first spent a lot of time reading the technology portfolio and reviewing data to understand the situation in various departments of the enterprise. He then spent eight weeks identifying potentially fatal problems facing the enterprise and more than a month deciding how to approach these problems. At the same time, a team of 7–9 members spent 6 weeks in intensive discussions on the company's transformation plan, focusing on 5 development priorities instead of 54. The attrition plan, which includes retirement (18 months' salary plus bonus) and project reductions, resulted in a 10% reduction in personnel costs and a 19% reduction in top management costs. Corporate slimming reduced staff costs by $1 billion. The slimming project took two quarters. In the process, Cisco invested the savings in five strategic core areas. In terms of the organizational system structure, the global sales pattern was centralized from emerging regions to three continents, reducing unnecessary personnel redundancy and coordination costs. The results of the changes are assessed on a quarterly basis, and if they fail to meet expectations, solutions are found. In the process of change, Cisco has about 300 people to participate and cooperate and put forward thousands of innovation ideas. The slimming program increased Cisco's profits and gained recognition in the capital markets, while basically achieving six goals: reducing its cost structure, optimizing its product portfolio, improving the efficiency of its organization, ensuring the reliability of its operating model, revising its evaluation metrics, and improving its processes and policies.

Cisco's strategic focus and transformation are also reflected at the market level. Before 2011, Cisco had nine sales regions around the world, then three in the Americas, Europe and Asia Pacific to reduce costs and improve efficiency. This approach helps clarify leaders' decision-making and accountability, while significantly reducing unnecessary administrative expenses.

Reduce business costs. In terms of cost reduction, Cisco's approach is to reduce labor costs by early retirement according to the laws of different countries. In countries that allow early retirement, generous pensions give workers incentives; for employees who leave early, Cisco gives them up to 18 months of regular pay and two months of dividends, while allowing them to retain equity. A total of 12,000 people left Cisco in the last two quarters of 2011, several thousand of them Mexican factory workers. Cisco outsources manufacturing and, through repeated acquisitions, many of its employees go on to work in manufacturing plants. At the same time, Cisco signed an agreement with employees to outsource for Cisco, so that employees could continue to work for the company.

Optimize product mix. On the product portfolio, Cisco's strategy is to look at product priorities and analyze the cost structure of the portfolio to integrate or cut out unprofitable, low-margin products. In the process, some project teams may be eliminated altogether, and Cisco has reshuffled more than 20,000 employees after their supervisors or team leaders were replaced.

Business transformation. Cisco entered the services business about a decade ago, and the business has grown from $2.6 billion to $5.6 billion today with an estimated $10 billion in future growth. Mr. Gary Moore was in charge of the transition into this new field. His strategy was to actively communicate with Cisco's big customers and understand their needs. Also, he engaged in one-on-one conversations with Cisco executives to get a sense of the state of the company's business. The process, which took about six weeks, was designed to identify areas where the company needed to transform, to carefully consider how to drive the transformation and to develop an implementation plan. The key is for senior executives to report to Moore, who then reports directly to Chambers, ensuring that each layer of management is truly accountable. Based on the clear direction of the business transformation, Mr. Moore set about building a team, inviting six or seven of his youngest and brightest employees to join the team. One of them is an experienced employee from the Internet solutions business who helped IBM reorganize its business. In addition, Moore invited consultants from large international consulting firms to work together as an integrated team. Team members began to explore the future business development goals, mainly thinking about the service team's portfolio and product portfolio, analyzing the rate of return on investment, and figuring out the source of profits. Through extensive, comprehensive and in-depth research, as well as referring to the suggestions of external consulting experts, the service team has made market strategies in six areas and proposed effective strategies to enable the product and service to successfully cover the target market.

Realize the transformation of market growth. Mr. Rob Lloyd is in charge of sales for Cisco. He started in Canada, then Europe, and now is in charge of global sales for Cisco. When he started selling in Canada, neither he nor his team expected sales to grow from $300 million to $2 billion. When the sales volume was only $300 million, he led the team to draw up an action plan and proposed to achieve the target from $300 million to $700 million. At that time, the team members expressed doubts about this goal. After listening to everyone's ideas, he adopted the sales model used in the European market and achieved the goal through the innovation of the business model. Lloyd has always believed that the market is so big that if you don't fear hardship, you can achieve your goals. After sales reached $700 million, he predicted that sales may reach $1.4 billion. He stated, "When I share the idea with the whole team, they all think I'm crazy, think it is impossible to achieve. Some even think that the core members, according to this goal, the company will team."

Faced with this challenge, Lloyd's approach was to take a step back and think about how to free team members from their mental limitations. In his view, the GDP

Numbers themselves reflect market opportunities, and since many competitors have already met this sales target, he believes Cisco can do the same. Cisco was mainly making mid- and high-end enterprise equipment, but customers also needed some low-end equipment, so he catered to this demographic. To boost morale, he invited a special guest at a large sales conference, Erik Weihenmayer, who, though blind, climbed mount Everest with great will and courage. Mr. Weihenmayer explained to all members of the sales team how he had climbed Mount Everest and how he had overcome the difficulties, including how to reach the camp, how long he rested, how he continued the climb, what difficulties he encountered and how he adapted to the local height. Weihenmayer said at times he doubted he would make it to the top, but he did not give up and made it to the summit of Everest.

After listening to the report, Lloyd broke down its target of $1.4 billion in sales, as if Weihenmayer had climbed to the top, from base camp and onward. Lloyd suggested that the company could continue to grow its sales by 10 or 20%, while the team thought a 20% increase was feasible in light of the GDP figures. "When we step up, as the English saying goes, we eat the elephant one by one. If the goal is too big and too grand, people will feel that it is out of reach psychologically. But after hearing Mr. Weihenmayer's story, we know that the key to getting the market from $700 million to $1.4 billion is to break down the goals and the process," Lloyd said. He then had an in-depth discussion with his team members about this goal and the difficulties they might encounter in the future. In this way, the team members reached an agreement with him. Lloyd believes that if the team believes they can do it, they have a chance. In the end, enabling teams to see into the future, set reasonable goals, and gradually achieve growth is the key to ensuring market leapfrogging.

7 Stages and Methods of Transformation

Cisco's transformation process can be divided into four stages.

7.1 Define the Transformation Objectives

At this stage, on the basis of a lot of research, the senior management team of Cisco should rank the importance of the business and adjust the priority of the project according to the needs of customers. To accelerate the transformation, we need to achieve four objectives. First, we need to optimize the operation model, including further clarifying the decision-making rights, increasing the transparency of the organization and involving more employees in the transformation process. Second, ensure profitable growth. Third, improve the execution and efficiency of world-class enterprises. In order to improve performance, three main approaches have been taken: the rationalization and simplification of processes, strategies, transformation mechanisms and tools, the identification of key performance indicators, and the follow-up and continuous optimization of the results of their implementation. Fourth, enhance the convenience of business.

During this period, Cisco executives met regularly to rethink and revise its internal and external business and operating models to find areas for improvement. In the external business model, to find the market closest to the company and change the path to enter the market; for the internal operation model, the accountability system should be clarified and simplified, performance indicators should be clarified for the market in different geographical regions, and indicators and data should be included in the information system, so that the entire company can have accurate statistics on performance objectives and structures. Before that, the company did not have a clear income statement. Through this reform and statistical procedures, the report was improved with the full participation of employees.

Transformation is also a process of internal resource reconfiguration. In innovation, Cisco uses a "kind of flower weed" (refers to an end in which there is no future for research and development projects or money for new projects) in the configuration of its R&D costs of $6 billion. These are prioritized in terms of research and development and used to audit the configuration of the investment pool. Some market prospects are lost unless concentrated resources have important strategic value to the company at the core of the project. In terms of operational excellence, Cisco seeks to build a world-class management system that objectively shows which departments are doing well by optimizing processes, simplifying operations, and building key performance indicator dashboards, while also making it easier for the company to work with customers and suppliers.

7.2 Diagnostic Stage

Through external benchmarking and internal audits, Cisco identified its major shortcomings and problems, obtained the actual data of the company's development status in the industry, held global conferences through video conferencing, explained the company's strategic decisions, and explained the need for transformation to senior management and employees. The transformation will take place in a comprehensive and open manner. The survey results of the top management in the early stage of the transformation show that some of the top management hold negative opinions and are unwilling to participate in the transformation. Cisco reflects the attitude of top management and encourages all to participate in the transformation project by "turning enemies into friends" in various ways. In the process of transformation diagnosis, the company established a product service and quality diagnosis team, an excellent operation team and a financial market team under the operation committee. It then incorporated employees into the transformation process through the matrix responsibility system. The finance department pays close attention to all details to ensure a return on investment. Human resource departments also play an important role in recruiting talent in different geographical areas, seeking solutions to multidimensional problems, and determining whether opportunities are feasible. All departments work closely during transformation, encouraging cross-functional thinking, linking benefits to performance, and focusing on gross margins.

In the diagnostic stage, the enterprise needs to release new energy through the audit. Cisco designs a "card-off" process to manage this stage. First, it is creative in finding new development opportunities. Employees come up with thousands of suggestions, and on this basis, funnel the ideas to match the market value. The ideas that are supported enter the business implementation stage. The second is analysis of which market opportunities to seize then choose a method and path. The third is the independent research and development of plans and cases, to find the measures to translate ideas into market actions, financial models and stakeholders' demands, and methods to balance these demands, and to make plans for emergencies. In this process, the management of Cisco conducts quantitative and qualitative analysis on creativity from the perspectives of methodology, expectation, opportunity and quality. The financial department will analyze and track opportunities, conduct quantitative indicator monitoring and strict evaluation by the review department. Fourth, sorting, according to the value and potential of the project to determine the allocation of resources.

7.3 Implementation Phase

During the implementation phase, each team will develop a more detailed action plan, define the bottom line of commitment, and deploy tasks and goals to the relevant team with clear accountability and delivery of results.

7.4 Evaluation Phase

Cisco's turnaround has seen its stock rise 56% from \$13 to \$15 in the fourth quarter of 2011 to \$23 to \$25 in 2013. In addition to ensuring shareholder value, Cisco believes that the transformation also contributes to the intangible asset indicators of the enterprise, such as the evaluation of partners, the improvement of enterprise transparency, and the growth of innovation and operational capacity. The transformation goal of enterprises in the trough period focuses on finding out what went wrong in the operation system and then investing money to improve the basic capacity of enterprises, such as whether to obtain accurate data of enterprise operation through the implementation of ERP system. If the basic capacity is weak, it will be difficult for enterprises to follow in the new wave of innovation. The transformation goal of the peak period is to find ways and methods to push technology into the hands of customers, to convert technology and products into market revenue, and to accelerate the operation of the enterprise. From the perspective of Cisco's transformation, its focus is more on improving operational excellence, expanding and deepening established markets, building a solid foundation for future innovation, and making internal processes run efficiently. To this end, Cisco has a permanent transition organization and team, a dedicated vice President in charge of transition, and consultants who are responsible for the transition budget and process management.

8 Cisco's Digital Transformation

What is digital transformation? Digital transformation is an important global leaders can use to promote the development of the digital economy. What is digitization? What are the differences between digitization and informatization in terms of technology, society and enterprise? From the perspective of academic research, and in technology, digital (digitization) refers to the analog signals into digital signals, the physical simulation process, the content or objects using digital signal encoding.[1,2] Digitizing refers to the process of converting analog signals into digital ones. Digitalization has two core characteristics, namely homogenization of data and programmability. Among them, data homogeneity means that the digital signal adopts the form of 0/1 discrete binary coding, which makes the data free from the bondage of storage, transmission, processing, display and other technologies. Reset ability means that the separation of digital signals from physical devices makes reprogramming possible. On this basis, digital technology has programmable, accessible, communicable, memorable, perceptible, traceable, and cooperative attributes.[3]

At the social level, digital transformation refers to the process in which digital technology is adopted and used by organizations and society. The attributes of digital technology not only extend the boundaries of products and services, enterprises and industries, but even make these boundaries permeable and changeable. More and more organizations use digital technology for innovation.[4] Digital technology represented by the form of 0s and 1s language, signal, image, sound and objects has the greatest impact of industries including media, banking and finance, telecommunications, medical treatment and health care, retail, manufacturing, etc. Some emerging

[1] Loebbecke, C. and Picot, A. Reflections on Societal and Business Model Transformation Arising from Digitization and Big Data Analytics [M]. Butterworth-Heinemann, 2015.

[2] Gölzer, P. and Fritzsche, A. Data-driven operations management: organisational implications of the digital transformation in industrial practice [J]. Production Planning & Control, 2017, 28(16): 1332–1343.

[3] Yoo, Y. Computing in everyday life: A call for research on experiential computing [J]. MIS Quarterly, 2010, 34(2): 213–231.

[4] Yoo, Y., Henfridsson, O. and Lyytinen, K. Research commentary—the new organizing logic of digital innovation: an agenda for information systems research [J]. Information Systems Research, 2010, 21(4): 724–735. Nambisan, S. Digital entrepreneurship: toward a digital technology perspective of entrepreneurship [J]. Entrepreneurship Theory & Practice, 2016, 41(6): 1029–1055.

industries, such as the Internet, the Internet industry 4.0, big data, artificial intelligence, machine communication, and chain blocks, such as monetary encryption, continue to arise.

At the organizational level, digital transformation includes innovation driven by or embedded in digital technology, which is widely permeated into product services, business processes and business model innovation. Digital innovation of products and services refers to embedding and applying digital technology into products and services to produce new products and services, such as smart phones. The digital innovation of business process refers to the embedding and application of digital technology in the organizational workflow, which changes the organization's production process, decision-making process and transaction process. The digital innovation of business model means that the use of digital technology produces a new way of value creation, which is often accompanied by the innovation of products and services, so is often discussed together with the digital innovation of products and services. At the organizational level, there may be multiple patterns of digital innovation in an organization.

Cisco's strategy and methods for promoting the digital transformation. For its part, Cisco, a former networking giant, has a strong sense of crisis and a drive to transform itself. In 2015, the New York times reported that Chambers, the chairman and CEO of Cisco, wanted to make a major transformation of the company before he retired, fearing that Cisco would be destroyed in the technological upheaval. In an interview, Chambers said Microsoft, IBM, SAP, oracle and Cisco have been hit hard by the changes brought about by the Internet of things in mobile devices and sensors. "In the next five years, two or three of these tech companies will drop out of the list because the rate of change is faster than ever before." Mr. Rodrik took over at Cisco and began a major restructuring of the company, trying to shift the company's focus to four key areas: security, the Internet of things, networking and cloud computing.

At this time, Cisco's transformation pressure mainly comes from three aspects. First, with the development and popularization of cloud computing, Cisco's days of manufacturing network equipment (accounting for nearly 70% of sales revenue) have passed. How should Cisco transform itself into a software and service solution provider? Second, as the network infrastructure construction tends to mature and stabilize, Cisco's traditional business growth declines, but the emerging industry development, the rapid development of cloud computing, Internet of things and, big data may allow Cisco to quickly enter these emerging fields, especially for the government, big companies that provide effective services, such as transportation, digital cities, the Internet of things, and other fields. Third, in the great transformation period of industry and enterprise, Cisco is faced with the problem of changing leadership. Chambers resigned as CEO in 2015 and chairman in 2017. How will Cisco achieve a new round of transformation in the context of frequent internal and external changes?

For Cisco, which has a tradition of technological optimism, although there are multiple reform challenges inside and out, Cisco has also gone through the battle of transformation and has been tested for a long time. They also see hope and prospect in the face of pressure and challenges. As Cisco's chief marketing officer Karen Walker said, Cisco is adhering to the technological optimism that makes it see "fully digital subversion" technology a huge application prospect. The Internet's application to people's work, life, entertainment and learning will bring about change. Cisco has reason to believe that the massive value-added market still exists, but if the transition speed is too slow, "fully digital reversal" will make four of the nearly ten big industry leaders obsolete.

In the process, Cisco struggled to find the direction for future transformation. As an enterprise with more than 30 years of experience in the ICT field, Cisco tries to play a leading role in the process of promoting the digital transformation of traditional enterprises through a series of acquisition strategies and initiatives using its own technical strength. In the process of promoting the digital transformation, Cisco believes that its technology and service system has four capabilities: first, data and connection capability. The network connects millions of terminals in the whole value chain and collects data. The second is ensuring the security of network and data and providing continuous threat defense based on policy. The third is the automation capability to help customers realize the automation of the entire process from the network edge to the data center to the cloud. Fourth, big data analysis ability and collecting data around equipment, network, users, applications and security risks, and analysis of the data to provide feasible business insights for senior managers. To further strengthen these four capabilities, Cisco has adopted a series of acquisition strategies to integrate emerging technologies related to the digital transformation to enhance the diversity of its technology system and its competitive advantage.

How does Cisco deploy digital technology systems through acquisitions? After missing the opportunity to develop big data in cloud computing, Cisco recently proposed the concept of the Internet of everything and set out to make breakthroughs in the Internet of things. In order to obtain a larger market in the process of global digital transformation, Cisco has carried out a series of strategic layouts, one of the important measures being to acquire enterprises related to its strategic objectives and quickly combine the technical capabilities of digital transformation and enhance the internal synergy of the service system. Cisco makes an acquisition almost every six weeks, with many of its acquisitions centered around software and services like cloud computing and big data.

As a company started with Internet hardware equipment, in order to promote its core competitiveness in the digital transformation market, Cisco pays more attention to the acquisition of enterprises in the field of software and services. Effectively connecting standardized hardware through software will enable Cisco to continuously upgrade its overall solutions and endow hardware with soul. In the newly promoted M&A cases, Cisco still adheres to its existing principles and policies, namely, whether it conforms to the general direction of Cisco's transformation, whether the acquisition risk is controllable, and whether the acquisition contributes to the long-term development of the enterprise.

Acquisition of IoT companies. Cisco's acquisition of an IoT startup, Jasper Technologies, for $1.4 billion in cash and stock in 2016 was notable. It is not only a big deal for Cisco in recent years, but also regarded by many in the industry as one of the biggest mergers in the Internet of things. Jasper will not only provide Cisco with a platform for the Internet of things, but also expand Cisco's security, advanced analytics and other IoT services. In addition, Cisco has acquired CliQr ($260 m), a hybrid cloud service provider whose core technology is to help customers select the most suitable cloud service providers. Synata, a cloud search start-up, was acquired to support end-to-end encryption for Cisco Spark, a cloud-based collaboration service owned by Cisco. In addition, the acquisition of chip maker Leaba, cloud search start-up Synata, and cloud security company CloudLock are mainly used to enhance Cisco's security technology in the cloud, aiming to enhance the depth, differentiation and integrity of Cisco's overall layout in cloud computing applications.

Acquisition of data visualization companies. In 2017, Cisco completed its $3.7 billion acquisition of App Dynamics, a cloud application and business monitoring provider, making it a company capable of providing visual data services to end users of network infrastructure. The company helps enterprises transform application data into business insights and provides end-to-end insight into their technology stack. The acquisition will enable it to develop visual services across networks, data centers, security and applications, drive the company's digital transformation, improve the customer experience, and help customers monitor the impact of each line of code on business results. A month before Cisco's acquisition, applied performance management filed for an IPO, and Cisco had been in contact with the company before its IPO filing and abandoned the talks at the end of 2016. The news was a turnaround, with Qatalyst, the investment bank, arranging the paperwork in 48 h. Founded in 2008 and headquartered in San Francisco, application performance management offers a range of services for managing and monitoring application capacity, scalability, troubleshooting, and user experience, as well as mobile monitoring and business analytics. The company had raised $314 million in six rounds of financing, and Cisco's offer of $3.7 billion was a good price and may set a positive precedent for future related acquisitions and financing. The combination with Cisco will improve its visualization, intelligence and security from network to application end to end and will help Cisco take its network data analysis and visualization business to new heights.

Strengthening intention-based networks. Network based on intent refers to the built-in machine learning mechanism through the network, the data in the automatic interpretation of the situation, and providing the user with a visual analysis. This can lead the network through machine learning, artificial intelligence, smart analysis, digital network architecture (DNA) centers, and network automation and learning engine set up. Centralized management dashboards enable network administrators to customize and put intention into action, across the design, configuration, strategy and guarantee for entire IT department provides the visibility and situation of the network. To build a network based on ideographs, people must trust the network, so network security and privacy protection become more important. For this reason, the network can also identify threats in encrypted traffic without decrypting them and compromising data privacy. A software-defined Access (SD-Access) through automation strategy is used to simplify network access by automating routine tasks (such as configuration, troubleshooting). The new data platform and assurance serves as an analysis platform that categorizes and correlates all data running on the network, translating machine learning into predictive analytics, business intelligence and operability through the DNA centrality assurance service. Encrypted traffic analysis security software uses Cisco's Talos network intelligence and machine learning to analyze metadata traffic patterns, enabling IT departments to detect threats in encrypted traffic with up to 99% accuracy.

Cooperate with telecom enterprises to lay out 5G technology. As companies increasingly move to full digitization, mobile operators are demanding the high speed, low latency and dynamic set-up capabilities offered by 5G networks to meet growing user demand and meet new service trends. By working closely with Verizon, the US telecom company, Cisco has seized the perfect moment to build the world's largest 5G field trial network. Cisco has provided the key components of a 5G-ready mobile architecture for the pilot operation of Verizon's 5G commercial pilot project, including: (1) simplifying the registration and operation process of VNF through Cisco services platform, accelerating the service speed and realizing real-time delivery of applications to customers; n the area of network transmission, rolling out the mobile return infrastructure to fully realize the faster gigabit bandwidth that 5G can provide; (2) virtual management services, rapid deployment of security and network services through virtualization, automation, data analysis and cloud computing; (3) jointly study the connection and performance of 5G network and how to make full use of this technology in vertical industries. New business applications, such as augmented reality or virtual reality, demand the low latency, high quality service and large capacity advantages that 5G offers across the network. This will enable the enterprise to bring unprecedented interaction and immersive experiences for users.

Cisco's layout in the construction of the Internet of Things. In 2014 Cisco reckoned that only 1% of the world's devices were connected; in 2016, 92% of the 64 million machines worldwide were not yet connected to the Internet, meaning companies now have the opportunity to make their production environments smarter and more efficient. Cisco's research team predicts that by 2020, there will be 50 billion connected devices. About 45% of such loT devices are limited by battery power and require a long-distance Internet of things connection. As a result, Cisco is offering a solution for LoRaWAN™ that combines low-power wide area networks with WiFi and cellular technologies to connect billions of such battery-powered Iot sensors at low data rates and over long distances economically and efficiently.

According to Cisco's techno-optimism, there is a huge scope for the Internet of things. Cisco offers a complete suite of solutions for networked machines that enable customers to transform machine data into valuable real-time insights while continuing to grow their daily business by working with machine manufacturers to securely connect devices. By implementing networked machine solutions, Cisco's manufacturing customers will be able to benefit from the expertise of machine manufacturers to drive continuous machine process improvement through real-time corrective action and continuous predictive maintenance. In IoT applications, Cisco offers services such as: (1) pluggable micro services that can reliably integrate IoT sensors with cloud applications in a very secure manner while processing data closest to the machine; (2) connection flow analysis, using fog applications to support secure connection machines for small deployments on IE4000, extract machine data reliably, and provide real-time insight. The success story is the iSMART factory built for the world-renowned Japanese machinc tool manufacturer MAZAK. Cisco combines lox-enabled fog applications with connection flow analysis via IE4000 switches and Cisco networked machine solutions via SmartBox. This application facilitates the free flow and sharing of data in process control and operational monitoring by enabling advanced manufacturing units and systems and comprehensive digital integration technologies. Under this concept, by connecting to the industrial Internet of things (IloT), manufacturers have increased levels of efficiency and productivity to unprecedented levels.

Build-up networked factories. Based on complete technical architecture and system, Cisco networking factory provides customers with a complete industrial park solution. It simplifies network management and expands the scope of the Internet of things, supports customers' securely connected machines and sensors, and quickly gets from Internet of data real-time insight information. It can find hidden dangers and problems in production and can greatly shorten the production cycle, improve equipment availability and efficiency and reduce risk. Some customers are realizing their value through the overall networked factory architecture. One of the more successful examples is the total solution of the connected factory offered by Lordan, a Cisco Israel heating and cooling systems manufacturer. Lordan has a worldwide reputation for providing high quality custom design and flexibility in provisioning. In order to promote its Internet strategy and improve the overall efficiency of the workshop after installing Cisco technical equipment, the company's chief operating officer, said: "In two weeks, we can make the overall equipment effectiveness (OEE) report, and to make decisions based on the real data rather than the subjective evaluation, a month, we will produce the workshop production efficiency is improved by more than 10%."

Cisco's networked factories include the following technologies: first, factory automation networks, including industrial Ethernet, wireless control, and Internet of things connectivity. Second, fog calculation. In the process of factory production, a large amount of data will be generated, and there are two kinds of requirements for data processing: first, timely control of machine tools and equipment, which requires fast processing of this information on the edge; second, if you do not conduct edge processing directly into the wan or cloud computing center, it will bring pressure on the network bandwidth and computing resources, therefore.

Third, machine learning and automatic configuration. No matter the network infrastructure or the data center, it will change from the original manual semi-automatic configuration to an automatic configuration. The network infrastructure will predict the resource demand in the future according to the current network or computing resource model and conduct automatic scheduling. Machine learning method will be used to help enterprises adjust automatically. That is to say, in the future, network or computing resources can be adjusted and serviced by themselves through independent learning and independent management, without requiring too many IT personnel to carry out daily maintenance. You simply present your policy and requirements settings at the beginning, and the machine will run and implement automatically.

Fourth, equipment interconnection and equipment service. Internet of things technology will install industrial control equipment and network connections on CNC machine tools, which are of great value to small and medium-sized enterprises. Because the cost of CNC machine tools or high-end machine tools is relatively high, it also needs to be constantly updated. Small and medium-sized enterprises can use these CNC machine tools or high-end machine tools through lease rather than purchase. Enterprises providing equipment and services can ship CNC machine tools to SMEs for an hourly fee, enabling SMEs to obtain machine tool services at a lower cost. In addition, they can also be integrated with numerical control machine tools and robots, forecast and plan in advance of the whole system production lines, equipment uptime, equipment state, when you need to customize upgrading, maintenance, effective supervision of manufacturing equipment health status, monitoring each time to detect problems, and timely adjust when problems occur. At the same time, it can also carry out rapid business optimization according to business logic requirements, so the entire production or machine operation efficiency is continually improved, along with the overall level of intelligent manufacturing, management, decision-making and operation and maintenance of manufacturing enterprises.

To build a cloud-based office communication platform for SMEs. Cisco has teamed up with TCL to develop the Ketian cloud to help small and medium-sized enterprises solve office automation problems. Generally, large enterprises have their own conference video systems, but the input–output ratio of building this system is not cost-effective for small and medium-sized enterprises. How can companies meet the cross-enterprise and cross-regional office communication and collaboration needs of small and medium-sized enterprises? Through the development of the virtual cloud model, Cisco helps enterprises build cross-enterprise, cross-regional video conferencing system; small and medium-sized enterprises are assisted through dedicated hardware terminals (such as mobile phones, pads, etc.), through the cloud conference connection, at relatively low cost to rent services, such as weekly or daily production coordination meetings, video conferences with upstream and downstream suppliers; through the integration of video and monitoring technology, customers can also see the state of the production line remotely.

Development of fog computing applications. Since fog computing was formally proposed in 2011, Cisco's fog computing has been applied in North America and Europe, but this is the first time for the Chinese market. Compared with the mature development cycle of cloud computing, fog computing is still in its infancy, but its technical principle is suitable for industrial Internet of things application scenarios, as it can solve network delay, terminal security and other technical problems. What is fog computing? Fog computing refers to the arrangement of computing, communication, control and resource storage on the device or node closest to the user or data source for calculation and control. Cloud computing virtualizes resources and concentrates them within the core network at the top of the network, thus realizing the resource sharing within the whole network. While fog computing pulls the cloud from the core layer to the edge, the terminal data does not need to be sent back to the data center, and it is directly calculated and processed at the edge of the network. The equipment used to carry the fog computing may be an edge router, a mobile phone, or even a light pole. Fog calculation of a typical scenario, such as in many large manufacturing companies are fitted in the workshop of "robot", the precision of each arm movement will directly affect the line qualification rate of products, when the "robotic arm" is running a few years into the development period of fault, the factory can deploy video capture camera real-time acquisition "robotic arm" row data, WiFi, bluetooth and other network to pass data to the nearest one implementation of the data mining on a router and calculation. The resulting feedback on the quality monitoring platform allows the maintainer to keep track of each robotic arm. The above scenario can also be extended to the application of large industries such as city, transportation and electric power. For example, in the field of smart transportation, in the future, not only will there be cameras on both sides of the streets, but every vehicle will be equipped with sensor devices to present road conditions more accurately and identify and avoid traffic jams. However, if all the sensor data are sent back to the background, the massive data generated will cause great pressure to the transmission network, and more importantly, lead to network delay. In 2015, Cisco, ARM, dell, Intel, Microsoft and Princeton University's edge computing lab announced the Open Fog alliance. France telecom and Inria, the French national institute for computer and automation, established Discovery, a research project on fog computing and large-scale distributed clouds. In addition, the theoretical model of fog computing can be seen in relevant projects of core manufacturers. In 2017, fog computing was officially introduced to China.

Build-up a shared cloud supply chain platform. Cisco has an intelligent manufacturing cloud project in Panyu, Guangdong province. This is a cloud infrastructure platform for the Internet of things. On this platform, an ecosystem will be formed. This platform has two values: one is to help customers achieve remote equipment use, equipment management, real-time monitoring of the production line, improve production and operation efficiency; the second is private clouds that help smart companies do smart manufacturing. These companies do not need to build their own cloud platforms but obtain cloud services by leasing. On this basis, Cisco helps enterprises establish intelligent supply chain management systems. Cisco is able to provide these services because the model has already been implemented within Cisco itself. Cisco has 187 manufacturing plants in China to help the production of various kinds of Cisco products. Cisco produces the cloud model at its 187 factories and its upstream and downstream supply chain collaboration. In order to satisfy the demands of its orders based on networking and change, enterprise production functions occur daily and include monitoring production meetings to assist companies in upgrading their systems. Network-based production is one of Cisco's core competitive advantages and is an important basis for Cisco to transform its capabilities into exported products and services.

Build-up a global digital business platform. On the basis of integrating the original technology system with the acquisition technology, Cisco quickly built the all-digital business platform, including the all-digital network architecture with comprehensive functions, the all-digital solution driven by results, and the development environment supported by the global partner ecosystem. Among them, Cisco's all digital network architecture (DNA) is a software driven architecture for all digital business, which can organically combine data, connectivity, security, automation and analysis. New hardware platforms and virtual network services have been launched in 2017, extending virtualization to branch offices. On the basis of building and upgrading technological capabilities, Cisco's digital transformation strategy continues to advance in various industries. In 2016, Cisco launched the network data analysis of the Tetration Analytics TM platform, the platform in the industry that took the lead in implementation of the existing large-scale data center and Yun Ping on real-time acquisition, storage, and analysis of network traffic. This helped Cisco users in the cloud era to realize the automatic network operations to upgrade and provides a new perspective and a variety of possibilities.

Cisco supports the digital transformation in retailing. In 2015, Cisco conducted a comprehensive research and evaluation of the digital value of different industries, reviewing the digital potential value of 16 industries through customer research and analyzed the digital cases of 350 enterprises. Cisco's research found the realization of digital potential value is mainly seen in two ways: first, through digital investment and innovation to bring a new source of value; second is the transfer of value from "losers" to "winners" through the use of digital technology capabilities in different enterprises and industries. The survey found that six sectors, including manufacturing, financial services, retail, operators, healthcare and oil and natural gas, will capture 71% of the potential value of digitization between 2015 and 2024. Despite a promising future, none of the six sectors delivered more than 29% of digital potential in 2015, with retail delivering only 15%. To help retailers close the gap, Cisco released a report titled "Digital value roadmap for the retail industry." The report identifies the top 10 sources of digital value for the retail industry and provides a roadmap for retailers to begin leveraging digital strengths and achieve long-term success. According to its research, a retailer with $20 billion in revenue could save $33 million of potential annual IT costs and generate $823 million of annual pretax profit, if the retailer adopted a comprehensive digital strategies and procedures. The capacity construction of digital transformation of retail enterprises mainly includes three stages: first, the construction of enabling digital capacity; second, realizing brand differentiation through digital capability; third is defining new business models through digital disruption. To that end, Cisco is offering in-depth seminars in Europe, South America and North America to nearly 200 retail executives from brick-and-mortar retailers, e-commerce, apparel manufacturers, food services and other retail sectors. In the digital transformation process, the strategy of self-financing is very important, which will help enterprises generate new revenue sources while achieving significant operational/IT savings. These gains and savings can then be reinvested in new digital solutions to drive continued innovation.

The digitalized technical service system of retail industry mainly includes four aspects: (1) full-field WiFi, indoor and outdoor WiFi coverage, automatic authentication and broadband control; (2) indoor positioning, including real-time positioning and positioning accuracy management; (3) passenger flow detection, including real-time monitoring, historical data statistics, visiting connections and flow control; (4) indoor navigation, including navigation accuracy management, three-dimensional navigation and reverse vehicle search.

Starbucks, for example, has taken a step forward by linking its own mobile payment app to its customer loyalty program, a pioneer on its own. Starbucks then decided to address new customer concerns, known as "line trouble." Starbucks built on the success of its mobile payment application by creating a mobile order and pay (MOP) application. The app allows customers to order drinks and pay for them without having to wait in line to pick them up at the store of their choice. Starbucks says purchases on mobile apps now account for more than 21% of total purchases, with nearly two-thirds of payments made through MOP. The success of this application has created new opportunities for online (digital) advertising. Because MOP is tied to the stock management system at each store, it can provide a channel to improve cross-selling opportunities to spur buying behavior, for example, would you like a muffin with your latte?

How Cisco is helping the digital transformation of finance. In Cisco's point of view, digital is deepening and expanding existing organizations' informatization, connection and reconstruction. Digital practice is mainly embodied in five aspects: providing a fully digital customer experience, which improves customer satisfaction, experience and loyalty, increases the profit of enterprise income, providing customers with exemplary customer service, consulting and communication, promotes customer analysis based on 360° upward and cross-selling, and personalizes loyalty management. The second is to optimize the business process and business model to provide a fully digital collaborative office environment and conditions, increase the response speed to customer needs to make the internal operation more efficient. The third is a fully digital business operation: fast service delivery to shorten the innovation cycle, reduce the investment cost of infrastructure and application development through the automation operation of cross-cloud service providers and data centers; reduce operational risks based on visualized operational data; business insight based on real-time analysis of production data. Fourth, risk and information security: meet regulatory and internal control compliance requirements, ensure the reputation of the institution, avoid losses, and use strong information security capability as an endorsement of the credibility of the institution. In order to achieve these goals, Cisco's existing network technology hardware and software services will play a supporting role. These services include Cisco's many offerings such as visual experience, remote expert, intelligent interaction center, mobile experience technology, position analysis, physical security video systems, platforms as a service, a hybrid cloud, the cloud management, service exchange platforms, the Internet, network monitoring and trace, data visualization, and information security event monitoring. Fifth, empower employees, improve their work efficiency and innovation ability, and attract and retain excellent talents. According to Gartner's survey of 396 CEOs of 30 enterprises, 50% of the CEOs believe that the change and transformation of their companies in the coming years will be driven by the wave of digitalization, thus putting forward higher requirements for employees' thinking, quality and skills.

In Cisco's view, technology alone is not enough to go digital. It also requires the company to rethink the way its entire business operates and delivers to provide new value to customers and partners through rapid innovation and greater operational efficiency. To succeed, companies cannot simply equate digitization with basic automation. Instead, they need to revolutionize systems and tools to establish an ongoing cycle of innovation for the company's product portfolio and business model.

The potential value created by all digital innovations in the financial world is huge, with retail banking alone generating a potential value of $405 bn between 2015 and 2017. In 2015, however, financial services as a whole captured less than 30% of these opportunities. Tight, complex regulation and cyber security vulnerabilities are the shackles that slow growth and stifle innovation. Combined with competitive pressure from nimble Fintech disrupters, four of the world's top 10 retail Banks will be knocked off the list within three years. Realizing full digital transformation is the only way for the financial industry to maintain its competitive edge and win market share. Cisco's solutions for the full digital transformation of the financial industry include a comprehensive integrated system architecture to ensure smooth transformation of financial customers and enhance the interactive experience of financial institutions, agents and customers. Based on the infrastructure, Cisco cooperated with the SDN based strategy management and automation architecture, built the PaaS platform, conducted the application life cycle and multi-cloud service provider management, provided IT service ordering, and guaranteed the security of the cloud and data center with the excellent security and analysis capability of Cisco Tetration Analytics.

How Cisco is helping build digital cities. In Cisco's point of view, digital city construction has occurred mainly in the following areas: network assets (asset management and asset tracking), logistics, supply chain management, goods to trace), wisdom city (intelligent parking lot, streetlamps, waste management, etc.), intelligent buildings, utilities (water, gas metering), agriculture (soil, irrigation management). The Hamburg port authority (HPA), a long-time Cisco customer, has fully realized the value of LoRa® technology. As part of its digital transformation strategy, the HPA deployed Cisco LoRaWAN™ solutions and installed sensors along the Kattwyk bridge at the entrance to the port. The bridge was one of the first facilities to deploy LoRa® technology, which can be lifted to allow cargo ships to pass. Sensors allow technical maintenance departments to accurately plan maintenance and repairs in advance, thus reducing maintenance costs and downtime. Operations are now significantly improved using LoRa® technology and the sensors in the life bridges on Elbe River. Managers no longer have to wait for problems to arise, but to proactively address them before they do. This will be one of the important results of sensor research, and the port will deploy additional technologies, including the LoRa® gateway currently in use at the port authority center, to facilitate smarter transportation, maintenance and logistics.

How Cisco is helping digital health. Internet of things technology has set a new definition for medical devices, which can transmit the basic data of the body to doctors without requiring patients to go to the hospital in person, thus addressing the geographical limitations of traditional medical services and the traditional diagnosis mode. The advent of wearable medical technology and analytical tools enables real-time monitoring of users' health, including calorie consumption, food intake and sleep quality. The data collected from the device can be used to monitor the user's own health, and the data generated from the device can also be used for medical research and reference.

In 2015, Health care provider Cyrcadia Health designed a bra with sensors for Internet of things technology called the smart bra (iTBra). The invention can detect early signs of breast cancer by detecting small temperature changes in breast tissue, allowing patients to be treated early and reducing the potential risk, more effectively than conventional X-ray technology. The invention of this product is a landmark event in the medical field and has a far-reaching impact.

In the United States, there is a movement called VITAS, which aims to provide distance observation and care for the dying so they can live out their final years meaningfully. Only 20% of the 11,000 medical professionals in the scheme are in hospital or hospice care, with the rest staying at home. Cisco plans to build robust data centers and mobile devices that will allow medical professionals to monitor patients remotely, integrate and analyze data, and connect patients and medical professionals through technology.

9 The Role of Leaders in Strategic Transformation

Leaders in charge of corporate transformation tend to have strong convictions. The belief of Cisco's leaders plays a crucial role in its transformation. Among them, 10 key ideas play an important role in the transformation and ultimately contribute to the realization of Cisco's transformation.

Look at the future in terms of the future. It means looking to the future, not the past or the present. Usually, it's easy to think about what is not going to happen in the future, not what is going to happen in the future. In this process, Cisco tries to realize the transformation of the way of thinking. They pay great attention to the thoughts and behaviors of young people, and often invite them to attend high-level meetings and express their opinions to obtain their views on the future through their comments and input.

Face reality. Although it can be challenging to face stark realities, it is important to be realistic. It is essential for companies to put facts and figures on the table for open discussion. Individuals may have different definitions and understandings of current circumstances, however, only by facing reality and looking at the problem from different perspectives can the problem be truly addressed. If people see only the reality they want to see, rather than an accurate view of the true situation, it is difficult for enterprises to achieve sustainable development.

Create a Shared vision of what people want. Cisco focuses on building a common vision that everyone is willing to accept, at least by the 80/20 rule, which means that this vision can be supported by a majority of people. The key here is to have a Shared vision that draws people around it, because experience tells us that when an individual's vision and a company's vision become one, the company is able to succeed.

Communicate, communicate, communicate. You have to communicate, communicate, communicate. A lot of research shows that a person needs to receive a message repeatedly before they can truly comprehend and accept it. So, companies need to repeat messages to make sure recipients eventually internalize them.

Build team cohesiveness. If the new CEO or other senior leader stays on top, they don't fit in well with everyone else. In this case, employees are not willing to accept and implement many of the ideas and practices of leaders. So, leaders must build their own teams and make sure that all the members are consistent with their own vision. Especially in the case of change and transformation, there are always some people who will not agree with change. Employees will look at the performance of leaders and, thus, leaders must find ways to ensure that everyone on the team supports them.

Train star employees. Get in touch with your employees to see which ones you can trust and rely upon, which ones are the most important, and which ones you need to focus on. Leaders must take care of the people who are important to their success, not by taking care of them in a different way, but by giving them the power and responsibility to convey the vision and confidence of the leader.

We need to be both principled and flexible. Principle is very important, and cannot be shaken. This refers to the good character of a leader who on the issue of principle cannot compromise. But at the same time, leaders need to be flexible in some aspects. They need to measure situations and adjust in time. They need to also be flexible in adapting to changes in the environment.

Passion drives execution. Once there is a strong team, members must work and strive to achieve the goal, without giving up, with efficient means to implement the plan. The lesson at Cisco is that if you have a team, a plan, and a vision, you may execute it quickly.

Keep doing the right thing. It is very important to keep doing the right thing. It can be very lonely to be a leader in a period of transition, when the leader may be the most unpopular person, and it may take a lone Wolf to drive that transformation and change. Then, leaders need to ask themselves questions to make sure they are doing the right thing, and, with that belief, they need to persevere.

Overcoming inertia in organizational transformation. In the stage of rapid change, leaders need to judge the future direction of the industry, understand how to achieve differentiation in the fierce industrial competition environment, and understand the differences between the strategic visions of the company and competitors. On this basis, leaders can see the focus of developing competitive advantage, opportunities and challenges, and lead the team to act quickly. As previously described, Cisco describes employees who resist the state of change as the different animals in the "resistance zoo": ostriches, cochlear cows, dogs, moles and tigers. Only by understanding the inner needs of animals and the real reasons for their resistance to change, and taking corresponding measures, can zoos be more harmonious and more receptive to change. But if the source of resistance is not found, the animals will certainly continue to cause trouble. Therefore, senior leaders should pay more attention to and analyze the reasons why employees resist change and try to overcome this resistance. The specific process is as follows: (2) draw an achievable vision so that employees understand where the value of change lies; (3) identify the core steps that can be taken; (4) reduce the psychological cost, reduce the economic cost and cost of participants and collaborators, and manage the pains of change.

In terms of specific change processes, Cisco according to their own practice to summarize it into five stages: think about why there is a need for change (change consciousness), how to participate in change (change participation), know how to change (change process and knowledge), the implementation of new skills, new action (change), and to preserve change situation (secure the achievements of change). In this process, if the work at any stage is not done well, the change will fail, and these failures are mainly attributed to the failure of the leadership.

As a leader of Cisco, the following questions need to be seriously considered in the process of change and transformation: from an incremental perspective or a transformational perspective? Where are the opportunities for corporate transformation? Are you fast enough? This is a dynamic world, a Shared market, where competitive advantage depends on how quickly the leader ACTS, so act quickly. The tough style of transformational leaders can sometimes be frightening and stressful, where leaders need to really think in terms of quality, in terms of people. Because what you do may not be popular, leaders need to have the courage and faith to do the right thing, even if it can be very lonely. Sometimes leaders need to take a step back so they can focus on what it takes, what the rewards are, and what the goal is, and then focus on moving toward that goal. In general, a transformational leader is someone who has the courage to focus on doing the right thing.

10 Summary

Enterprises can survive in the fierce competition; what is most important is the ability to carry out continuous transformation and change.

Sustained transformation depends first and foremost on the long-term perspective and unique understanding of the future of the industry of the core leaders of the enterprise, which is usually conveyed through the vision of the enterprise. A leader's perception of the company's long-term position in the industry determines whether it chooses a sustainable industry, which is usually reflected in the company's vision. For example, Cisco's vision that the Internet will change people's lives, work and study reflects the long-term and far-reaching position and value of the Internet. This vision is stable and has not been out of date in the 34-year development history of Cisco. It provides a long-term direction and sustained impetus for the development of the enterprise. Therefore, it is very important for the enterprise to choose an industry with long-term development prospects for its survival and development.

Secondly, an enterprise in fierce competition to continually seek and find the fast growth of markets and technology found that customer demand changes constantly, especially focus on the developmental trends of disruptive technology, timely adjustments to their own system of technology and products, market strategy, and quick application of new technology to new markets lead the enterprise into regular new growth cycles. This transformation process should be the normal state of the enterprise, as it cannot be stopped. Once a fresh idea emerges, it is easy to be eliminated in the new market and technology transformation period. This is the process of enterprises' self-transcendence and self-transformation. Only through ongoing transformation can enterprises survive. It is difficult for many enterprises to engage in this as they focus more on their competitors and blindly imitate them, which makes it difficult to become market leaders and creators. However, Cisco attaches great importance to customer research and regards customer demand as a weathervane leading the enterprise transformation. The broad development space brought by customer demand brings inexhaustible internal and external power to the sustainable development of the enterprise. For a mature, successful enterprise, its reliance on an existing pattern and path as the focus of internal and external enterprise changes is problematic. When the new technology, especially following the appearance of disruptive technology, still clings to old technology, ignoring the value of new technology, it loses market opportunities in technology transformation influence and leadership. Cisco facilitates its own transformations by constantly discovering emerging markets and new industry applications. When the growth rate of the enterprise slows down, shareholders will press for change. The enterprise can only reduce costs and increase profits by reengineering or slimming down.

Finally, the internal transformation in the process of enterprise transformation should overcome all kinds of difficulties caused by organizational inertia and human inertia. Organizational inertia comes from the inertia formed after the internal structure and the overall processes are stable. When an enterprise pursues efficiency, it needs stability, but stability will restrict the flexibility to cope with changes. How to balance the stability and flexibility of an organization is a concrete manifestation of the dynamic capability of an organization and a challenge of change management. People's inertia comes from people's thinking. People at different levels have different motivations for change due to their varied perceptions of challenges and crises in the external market. Therefore, it is the important responsibility of leaders to reach consensus on the issue of change through adequate communication. Cisco has made transformation and change a part of its corporate culture, a normal part of its business operation, and a counterbalance to inertia. For high-tech enterprises, the life cycle of technology and products is decreasing, and the market competition is becoming fiercer. If an industry leader cannot change quickly enough, it is likely to be surpassed by the latecomers.

Chapter 4
Innovation System

1 Introduction

Innovation systems emphasize the flow of technology and information between people, businesses and institutions, which is the key to the innovation process. In the process of innovation, good ideas are turned into processes, products, and services that can be accepted by the market and customers. Technological innovation system is a dynamic network for the generation, diffusion and utilization of technology by all demographics of people under specific institutional environment and infrastructure conditions. Silicon Valley's unique innovation environment is mainly manifested in: the innovation culture centered on Stanford University and the cultivation of innovative and entrepreneurial talents and the willingness of a large number of young people who master certain new technologies and not fear failure (many of whom are new immigrants with the "American Dream") willing to explore innovation and entrepreneurship. There is a wealth of venture capital willingness to support young people's entrepreneurial ideas. Thus, a large number of people from different professional backgrounds gathered in the region and interacted with each other, and there is a positive and interactive relationship between large and small businesses, i.e. through acquisitions the dynamism of large enterprises is stimulated, and small business entrepreneurs are funded and new small businesses are hatched.

Innovation activities are particularly active in the transition period of technology, and innovation with technological transitions as the core shows the process of combining new technology with social application, which is a process of social change. In this process, changes occur in user practices, rules and policies, as well as changes in industrial networks (supply chains, value chains and ecosystems), infrastructure and culture. Therefore, the process of technology transformation and innovation is a process of reconfiguration of social-technology systems, in which the dominant enterprise plays an active role in applying new technology to transforming society. This process requires seven elements.

X. Dong et al., *Cisco*,
https://doi.org/10.1007/978-981-19-7870-8_4

Innovation Center: Silicon Valley in USA

(1) Entrepreneurship and activities, whose main role is to transform new knowledge into business opportunities.
(2) Knowledge development. Enterprises should continue to research emerging technologies, but also to learn and understand customers, markets and industries. In this process, enterprises have a lot of search-based learning and side-learning activities; the former is reflected in the independent research and development, mergers and acquisitions and partners continue to integrate new technologies into the market; the latter refers to enterprises in order to integrate the technology system into the social system constantly looking for the best entry point and path.
(3) The interaction and diffusion of knowledge. A very important mechanism in an innovation system is that people from different backgrounds participate in a lot of interactive opportunities, learn from each other in the process of interaction, and generate new ideas and experiences through the interaction between technology developers and users, technology developers and sellers, etc.
(4) Search guide. This part of the activity refers to the community's relevant stakeholders on the needs and expectations of new technologies, especially the government, customers, partners and competitors. The results of the search can be optimistic or pessimistic, and companies need to make trade-offs based on limited resources to decide whether to adopt a focus ingress or portfolio strategy. The balance between the two is important, too much focus may put the treasure in the wrong direction, too much combination may also lose focus and lead to waste of resources.

(5) Shaping the market. Emerging technologies are often difficult to compete with existing technologies, so they must create a market segment that penetrates and spreads.
(6) The liquidity of resources. This mainly refers to the flow of funds, talent, information is very convenient with few obstacles, while resources can always find its greatest value of the place.
(7) Advocacy Alliance. The concept of advocacy alliance comes from the field of political science, which refers to the emerging political groups by competing with interest groups representing different ideas and gradually changing the cognitive and interest patterns within the political system. The emergence of new technologies will often encounter the tenacious resistance of existing mature technology systems, and emerging technology enterprises usually do not necessarily choose to confront them directly, but instead form new ecosystems with soft and circuitous ways to market and form a new ecological system, while gradually replacing the existing technical system.

2 The Main Obstacles of Innovation in Large Enterprises

After establishing an industry leadership position, large enterprises often have five barriers to driving innovation and energizing the business:

First, excessive security. Large enterprises often occupy the leading market position in the industrial environment. With a large market share and rich resources, highly complex organizational structure and technical systems, in general, small enterprises may find it difficult to challenge the competitive position of large enterprises in a short period of time, resulting in the lack of innovation momentum of large enterprises.

Second, there is enough cash flow, there is no problem with production, and there is no incentive to innovate without the pressure to survive. Stability is the most important issue for a company that doesn't struggle with the death line, and innovation is often the second priority. For many start-ups, they are often supported only by very limited venture capital funds, so they must desperately explore and develop to solve the problem of survival.

Third, a great deal of time is not spent on innovation. After years of technical accumulation, management optimization and market development, large enterprises have gradually accumulated a set of internal and external operation management system. Past successes have enabled it to operate with complex resources and systems, to become less sensitive to new technologies and to turn a blind eye to the risks posed by external competition or alternative technologies. As a result, big business is like a giant dinosaur, often running in the last of the competition to get into the market first. In practice, enterprises that can emerge from the blue are often enterprises with fast innovation, especially for technology companies. For the innovation of large enterprises, how to avoid taking too long to complete innovation is the key. There are many reasons for the loss of time for innovation: slow management decisions, delays in each department, and difficulty reaching consensus. For Cisco, 18 months to complete the entire process from creativity to product sales requires changes in the innovation process, internal organization coordination, decision support mechanisms, and cultural construction.

Fourth, there are redundant employees. Big business has to endure too many meetings when deciding on innovative projects, too many leaders agree, and in the process, there are many people who express their opinions and who want to step in to manage, but there are not necessarily enough technicians who really do the work. To increase innovation efficiency, Cisco attempts to develop, produce, and sell the entire process with short, compact business units, focused on a new technology with no more than 50 people per business unit. Cisco innovation teams average 50 people during product development. If the scale of product sales expands, then new members are added.

Fifth, paying too much attention. Good potential innovation projects in the enterprise are interesting, and therefore, everyone wants to participate in them. The project team leader may be constantly called out to introduce the situation and make comments. Cisco, however, takes a nearly closed approach, not calling, emailing, and even announcing new projects in office locations, thereby remaining relatively independent and confidential to ensure that the innovation team can focus on research and development projects and minimize unnecessary attention and distraction.

Cisco also extends its life as a growth business as much as possible, delaying its entry as a mature business. Silicon Valley has a lot of start-ups and strong companies, especially information technology companies that attract a lot of young people, along with many small businesses that attract innovative talent. In order to attract talented people, Cisco has also explored ways to recruit new graduates from prestigious universities, not only for high salaries, but also to allow doctoral students to practice in their third year. Cisco also works at attracting talented young people with salary, stock options, and remote work. At the same time, Cisco holds seminars on future leadership issues, often attended by scientists from within and outside the company. These experts have in-depth discussions about difficult issues facing the industry and technology development to attract promising young people.

Both companies founded by Tuqiang Cao, a Chinese scientist, were acquired by Cisco, and after the first self-employed company was acquired by Cisco, he wanted to leave for a few years because he believed that big business's innovation environment was less than that of small businesses. But a few years later, he was supported by Chambers' in-house innovation fund and started a second venture, sharing Cisco infrastructure and resources while enjoying the freedom, dynamism and independence of small businesses. Tuqiang Cao's second venture was successful and was reacquired by Cisco, where he has now been for 12 years. Referring to Cisco's entrepreneurial and innovative environment, he said that while Cisco is a large company, he still notes the relaxed environment and similar freedom of small business start-ups. This allows for regular communication with senior management to discuss innovative concepts at any time. Yet the company remains concerned about the product at the lowest level of development and technology at the forefront of the trend. Cisco tries to avoid bureaucracy, red tape, a mountain of paper work and a sea of meetings, which have often been regarded as large enterprise diseases.

In Tuqiang Cao's view, a successful enterprise not only to live in danger but also in peace and security. Kodak and Xerox failures serve as examples that the success of enterprises is determined by the market. Failures are often eliminated by the market and consumers, therefore, a leading enterprise will always have to operate and manage as a start-up company and pay attention to what customers care about. In order to achieve this goal, enterprises should set up a keen intelligence radar system to monitor the environment dynamically and find new trends in the market timely. Cao also spoke specifically about an important way for Cisco's innovation success to continue to turn new innovations into standards, occupy the high end of intellectual property value, and, in the process of innovation, combine seemingly contradictory things in order to integrate different concepts, technologies, and resources so mature companies remain high-growth.

3 Three Pillars of Cisco's Innovation System

Cisco's innovation strategy consists of three pillars: one is self-development, the other is strategic alliances and partners, and the third is mergers and acquisitions.

3.1 Independent Research and Development

Of these three pillars, independent research and development is the core of innovation. In 2011, Cisco's investment in research and development accounted for 13% of total revenue with total corporate sales of $5.8 billion. More than 20,000 engineers worldwide are involved in innovation, and the results of independent research and development will determine the core technologies that companies will have in the next 3–5 years. This is due to the benchmarking of other high-tech companies (Intel is 17% and Apple is 15%). The R&D investment of high-tech enterprises in Silicon Valley generally accounts for 13–14% of the sales revenue. The R&D investment of some small high-tech enterprises is overall larger, while that of large enterprises is relatively small. Over the past four years, Cisco has invested $25 billion in research and development. Thirty technology labs have been engaged in new technology development, filed 700 patents each year, increased return on investment from $28 billion to $36 billion, and increased return on investment by 25%. Cisco's research and development focuses on scaling and strengthening the core technologies and markets that have established leadership in areas such as routers, switching voice and wireless technologies, emerging collaboration, video, data centers, and virtualization and energy applications.

3.2 Strategic Alliances and Partners

Cisco's Strategic Alliances and Partners are an important strategy for forming an industrial ecosystem with external resources, and in the process of developing and maintaining strategic alliances and partnerships, Cisco gains a competitive advantage by leveraging its leading position in the industrial chain to form a community of interests and a strong market force (see Chap. 6 for details).

3.3 Mergers and Acquisitions

The third pillar of the innovation system is merger and acquisitions. The core of the merger and acquisitions strategy is to increase the differentiation of the technology system and form the richness of the technological ecology. Cisco's acquisition is a strategic initiative that does not blindly focus on big business as a core goal but looks for disruptive technologies that complement Cisco's overall market and technology ecosystem to maintain a continuous technology leadership and differentiation of technology systems; this can spread the risks of large enterprises in R&D directions. Cisco acquires companies that are complementary to their technology systems through mergers and acquisitions. On Cisco's big platform, the product positioning and direction of the acquired company will not change significantly, but the sales market and channels are greatly broadened, and its products are sold not only to small businesses, but also to large enterprises through Cisco's partners and channels. After the merger and acquisition of technology will gradually form a market size according to market changes, emerging technologies will take 3–4 years (such as telepresence, high-quality video has not yet been formed), while some will take 10 years to form a market size. Cisco will also make mistakes in the merger process, but it will reflect on and analyze the reasons for the failure of the merger and avoid a repeat in the future. Cisco, when screening the acquired company, pays special attention to the cultural compatibility, considering whether the vision sits well, whether the top is like-minded, whether technology complements each other, whether they know each other, and whether the culture is compatible. Cisco does not acquire competitors for cultural compatibility reasons.

In the past five years alone, Cisco has invested more than $9 billion in more than 30 companies, generating one-third of revenue in new markets and more than 7,000 new employees, which is invaluable in IT. The secret to its success is not only to see mergers and acquisitions as opportunities, but also to see them as risk management and control. Even if a merger fails, Cisco will study it well, learn its lessons and avoid reoffending. Cisco acquisitions often target companies that are aligned with the company's strategic objectives, second, help the company seize market transformation opportunities, third, help the company achieve one-two leadership positions in the market segment, fourth, establish a shared culture with the company to successfully integrate into Cisco, and fifth, further promote the company's relationship with the market segment customer. How to measure performance during the merger process? Market share, market size, revenue or profit growth, ROI, profit contribution, and retention of talent are all important metrics. Cisco's primary goal in acquiring high-end technology is to enter strategic markets such as unified communications and video technology, often to companies with a small market size but a very large market space for the technology. An example of this might be Cisco's acquisition of Tandberg Video Technologies, which cost $3 billion. The goal is to enhance the differentiation of core technologies and to acquire disruptive technologies and talent through acquisitions. Cisco also creates new technical capabilities by acquiring disruptive technologies early through the acquisition of external technologies or small and medium-sized enterprises, integrating acquired technologies with existing technology and product systems through Cisco's brand, capital, and channel advantages.

Sometimes, some companies develop disruptive technologies, and Cisco chooses to invest in these companies to operate as independent entities. Cisco's requirements for target companies are that pioneering technology meets Cisco's technical standards, that products meet Cisco's business model, and that innovation meets the needs of specific customers. Cisco will decide whether to acquire based on business relevance and priority. This acquisition is the best of both worlds, both to maintain the vitality, passion and creativity of a start-up, while taking full advantage of Cisco's size, management capabilities, market development and financial strengths as a large company to bring together talent and intelligence. Cisco has a precedent for this acquisition in areas such as fiber, computing, and data centers.

Cisco effectively addresses the intense competition and challenges of the market through a combination of three pillars to enable the exploration, development, and sale of new technologies (Chap. 5 also discusses). The combination is mainly reflected in the following three aspects:

A combination of progressive and disruptive innovation. Cisco's research and development innovation system is progressive and disruptive, with 80% of the technology portfolio. Progressive innovation focuses on the technology ecosystem that the enterprise has matured to ensure the continuity, reach, depth, and combination of ongoing technologies through complementary technology combinations and operationally superior business models. Continuous technology and products are an important guarantee for enterprises to form large-scale market sales and market share.

Disruptive innovation softens on early new technologies, which often influence the direction of technology development, replace existing technologies, or change the field of technology applications and the direction in which markets are adopted. Cisco's technology innovation system has always followed a strategy that ensures a balance between incremental and disruptive innovation, ensuring that both exist. Progressive innovation ensures maximum market value through a superior operating system, typically 80% of Cisco's technology portfolio. But if mature technology companies focus solely on sustainable technologies and ignore and reject disruptive technologies, they risk being marginalized in the new wave of technological transformation. Small businesses with the right disruptive technology will grow into mainstream companies after being accepted by the market. As a result, Cisco also attaches great importance to disruptive innovations. In the independent research and development system, the department that develops disruptive technology is called the emerging technology team. Emerging technology teams look at researching disruptive technologies that will impact the future and seek innovative technology spaces through in-house incubation. These teams start with a few people, looking for profitable business models and market space for businesses through ideas, and they have the ability to create billions of dollars in market space. Cisco allows the team to evolve in an unconventional way, allowing the research and development team to enjoy a unique space for innovation beyond the company's culture, performance, and operating systems. It's not easy for Cisco to turn ideas into market opportunities, however, it is not about the lack of good ideas, but rather about creating too many, and screening out ideas that are of business value. To this end, Cisco has developed an evaluation system and a replicable process from creativity to large-scale market sales that filters, selects, values, and incubates processes design and optimization to truly turn ideas into business value. Over the past few years, Cisco's annual proportion of new products has remained around 28%, which is closely correlated to its innovation system.

Allocation of research and development funds. In the company's overall sales of 16% of the research and development funds, the allocation of funds also reflects the combination of technology product innovation, of which 3% was pledged to invest in new technology, especially high-end technology. Only a small number of professionals were required to participate in the project, and the total number of projects was approximately 15. Seventy-five percent invest in technologies with a broad market in the future, especially 20 emerging technologies with significant market potential in the next 1–2 years. Twenty-two percent is used to strengthen today's technology architecture and improve existing product technologies, primarily Cisco's traditional products, routers, and switches. In terms of investment, Cisco's technology portfolio of research and development investments includes enterprise collaboration, video, virtualization technology, and energy.

Dynamic balance between progressive and disruptive innovation. The coordination of progressive innovation teams with disruptive innovation teams is a very important element. There is a leadership mechanism within Cisco that coordinates the two teams. Coordination of the two teams falls to management under Chambers who is in charge of operations. Cisco's coordination is divided into two parts: one is strategic coordination. Before you budget each year, the budget allocation is weighed between the two teams. Second, business coordination. Both types of business units often integrate business or product. For example, there is an integration between the conference system and the high-end telepresence system and, in accordance with user requirements, it is now possible to start the conference system of Netcom and The Telepresence system of Tengbo. The two business units often communicate regarding the product. By properly planning the two business teams, Cisco builds a sustainable structure that contributes greatly to the sustainability of innovation.

At Cisco, progressive innovation teams generate relatively high margins, while disruptive innovation teams start out with low profits and high costs. As a result, employees of the progressive innovation team may feel dissatisfied, even while they are generating a lot of money, but that the budget spent is not as good as that of a disruptive innovation team. On this issue, it is important to ensure that the two teams are able to coordinate with each other and not be affected by negative emotions. The 1,000-person team led by Yuan Zheng, Cisco's vice president of research and development in China, includes people who do regular web conferencing products and people who develop new products. He leads both research and development teams and tries to keep the two integrated rather than merged. When a disruptive and innovative business matures, it is incorporated into the conventional business. The reason why the two innovation teams cannot merge is that for incremental innovation, users are already using the products they offer and do not need to have disruptive innovations, otherwise users will feel uncomfortable. For example, Cisco now produces routers that are provisioned with commands, and users will not be comfortable if they suddenly develop a router controlled by an iPad. Therefore, incremental innovation requires incremental advances to ensure consistency in the user experience. Instead, exploratory businesses need disruptive innovation because they do not have their products tested by users.

4 How to Match Innovation with Business Model

The innovation strategy of enterprises should match the market positioning and business model of enterprises. There are two types of business models: the centralized large customer model and the large-scale small customer model. The centralized large customer model focuses on large customers and provides comprehensive, systematic, comprehensive, complete solutions and one-stop services for the problems faced by large customers, which are generally owned by governments, large enterprises or super-large groups or organizations. This model is characterized by a small number of customers, complex problems, organizational systems and demand differences. Companies that serve such customers can provide customized and specialized solutions tailored to the needs of a wide range of customers only if they have comprehensive, systematic and integrated methodologies, talent teams, solutions and experience. For technology enterprises, it is necessary to have a complementary, serialized, compatible technology system, technical capabilities and product lines to help customers solve complex problems. In other words, companies that focus on the large customer model as their primary business model have the core competency of having a more complete technology, product, talent, knowledge, methodology, and management of operations to address the complex needs and problems of customers (such as IBM, SAP, and Cisco). The more resources and capabilities an enterprise has, the stronger the ability to differentiate, and the stronger the competitive advantage and the ability to obtain a premium.

The market positioning of the large-scale small customer model is aimed at the needs of a large number of individual customers in the market, through large-scale, standardized production and operation systems and brand building, the production of standardized products and services for domestic or global customers (e.g., Haier, Procter and Gamble, Apple, etc.). Such enterprises focus on the specific needs of our customers (such as home appliances, daily necessities and electronic products), to produce systematic, constantly updated products, through high-quality products, services and brand building to form a market influence, to attract customers to continue to buy the enterprise's products, The core competitiveness of such enterprises is reflected in the innovation of technological innovation, functional development and product design, through the innovation of the management operation system, to bring products to market with lower cost and higher efficiency, and to show their uniqueness and competitive advantage in the combination of price, quality, performance, psychological experience and other value elements. The innovation of the large-scale small customer model mainly focuses on three areas: First, the innovation of the operating system, through the supply chain process management, end-to-end value chain management system, enterprise-wide process information construction to achieve operational excellence and high efficiency. Second, product innovation, enterprises through the development of new technologies, with the new technology constantly embedded in the product system, so that the function of the product is unique and differentiated. Third, customer intimacy innovation, enterprises need to constantly understand customer needs, through durable marketing and brand building, strengthen customer awareness and recognition of corporate brands and product brands, while constantly breaking down customer demand to find market segments to enrich their product lines.

The core competency of the centralized large customer model lies in the ability of enterprises to discover and resolve complex problems, which come from the following four sources:

(1) **Long-term professional knowledge and industry experience accumulation**. Through independent research and development, mergers and acquisitions, and strategic alliances, the more complementary product lines and system-solving capabilities are formed, the wider the complementary product lines that can be dynamically combined, and the stronger the ability to solve complex problems.
(2) **The comprehensiveness and uniqueness of the talent pool, methodology and technology system**.
(3) **In the large number of customers of awareness and reputation, enterprises continue to produce innovative ideas, insights and forward-looking ability**.
(4) **The ability to integrate internal and external resources**. To ensure the sustainability of these capabilities, the innovation focus of such enterprises is focused on three areas:

1. **The emergence of new ideas**. Through the social network, consulting methodology and communication system with large customers as the core, we can realize a comprehensive understanding of our customers' complex needs and provide them with effective solutions through the discovery of

lighthouse customers,[1] to produce demonstration effects in the market and industry.

2. **Technological innovation**. On the basis of understanding the complex needs of customers, we constantly improve the methodology, technical capabilities, product systems and service systems to solve complex problems.
3. **Management and service innovation**. Through the innovation of the organizational structure and the innovation of the internal communication mechanism, the process and information collaboration platform are continuously optimized to realize the cross-functional rapid response mechanism with the customer as the core.

For Cisco, it strategically expands its innovation space at two levels: an understanding of customer changes and complex needs, an ongoing search for technology and market transformation opportunities for changing customer needs, and a direction and timing for large-scale sales of new products. Second, according to market transformation opportunities, through independent research and development, mergers and acquisitions and strategic alliance partners three ways to enhance, deepen, expand or update the enterprise's technology system, product system and market service system to efficiently meet market demand. That's why Cisco is so focused on communicating with big customers, understanding their realities and potential needs, and one of the reasons Chambers calls at least 200 CEOs in the World's Top 500 companies twice a year. Based on a more comprehensive understanding of the potential or emerging needs of customers, Cisco can clearly position its technology gaps and future directions. At the same time, in the organizational system design, Cisco's inspiration to us is the need to enhance cross-functional and cross-product line collaboration and collaboration capabilities, according to the needs of major customers, with rapid integration of internal and external resources to achieve the strategic objectives of the market.

5 Judging the Value of Innovative Projects

Cisco believes that innovation is valuable only when it provides an economic reward for the business, and that innovation differentiates Cisco from its competitors enough and makes customers willing to buy Cisco products or services and pay extra.

In the selection of innovative projects, Cisco focuses on two types of technology: first, the core technology, which is the core technology of the enterprise with independent intellectual property rights, is to bring continuous competitiveness, differentiated technical capabilities, but also the key technology and product system that the enterprise is different from the competitors. It is usually the technology or product that the customer is willing to pay for. Second, peripheral technology, where usually the enterprise has the peripheral technology and competitors of the difference is not

[1] The so-called lighthouse customers, refers to customer demand and enterprises can provide technical solutions to match, while other customers have a certain role in demonstration.

vast, but it cannot bring the core competitive advantage of the enterprise, rather the core competitive advantage has a supporting and supporting role.

The choice of innovative projects is a very difficult and complex issue, if the early project selection misjudgment, will not only bring the loss of resource spending, but also will cause enterprises to lose the valuable time to enter the market quickly. Steve Steinhilber, Vice President of Emerging Solutions Ecosystems at Cisco, points out five questions for companies to identify themselves when judging the value of innovative projects: First, is the potential market for innovation projects large enough? If the short-term look is not big enough, 5–7 years later will there be a large market? If so, is it also of investment value? Second, is the timing of the selection of new technologies and projects appropriate? Many companies choose a good technology project, but the timing of choosing to develop or market it is not appropriate. How can you tell if the timing of the technology project is appropriate? It may be too early if no one on the market has done this project; The ideal state is that there is still room and opportunity in the market, but only small companies or regional companies do. When technology is more decentralized, not yet systematized, industry integration is very low, it is a good time for large enterprises to enter this kind of technology.

Third, is the new technology chosen highly relevant to the company's current core business? The more relevant, the more integrated the technology is, the greater the differentiation of the technology system, the greater the likelihood of sharing the supply chain and sharing customers, and the greater the value of innovative projects.

Fourth, where are the opportunities to impact the market with new technologies? What are your technical differences compared to the products your competitors already have? An important strategy Cisco uses to impact the market is to select the customer, rather than the customer choosing Cisco. Cisco typically chooses to use the product and believes that the product has addressed the real-world pressing problems of the customer, rather than the customer whose demand level exceeds the product's capabilities, the lighthouse customer, so that Cisco can upgrade its product and service capabilities to solve more complex problems on the basis of addressing the primary issue. This rolling sales strategy is known at Cisco as a bowling strategy: hit easy-to-hit targets first, then gradually hit hard-hitting targets. In the market, those most willing to accept technology solutions are often faced with challenges. If enterprises help solve urgent needs, customers may be willing to accept new technology or new products and satisfaction may be relatively high. Only if the market has accumulated enough early adopters of new technologies to further promote the product and the new product has been continuously optimized to improve and upgrade, then enterprises have the opportunity to enter the next sales cycle and form a larger market size. In developing its sales strategy, Cisco is not targeting high-end customers who are looking forward to version 2.0 or 3.0, because if they are only offered version 1.0, they will be very disappointed with higher expectations and market sales will tumble, making it difficult to bridge the market divide.

Fifth, can new technologies achieve lasting differentiation? This is the most important question. What if a company develops good technology and products and all the competitors begin imitating you? How can you achieve lasting differentiation?

Global companies often have two competitive strategies: one is to create more and more differentiation to separate their products from others, and the other is to continuously integrate and integrate existing technology products, to be systematically and modular, to increase the complexity of technology, and to prevent competitors from imitating and overtaking.

In the strategic choice, is it the road of differentiation first, or the road to improve the integration of technology system? Cisco's approach is to place great emphasis on understanding the broader context of market, customer, and technology development. Second, in the process of integration and evolution of technology systems, Cisco's innovation path is to do differentiation technology, create a market, and then, according to the needs of customers and the market, constantly develop, add and combine related technologies through additional comprehensive solutions, to achieve technology and product system differentiation. On the Internet, Cisco continues to integrate highly relevant technologies and products to expand market space. For example, Cisco starts with data-based, adding networks, voice, video, wireless, and collaboration technologies, and adding the Internet of Things, sensors, computing, energy applications, and as a result more as technology applications expand. Guided by this concept, Cisco developed and acquired integrated technologies, further enhancing the differentiation of the company's technology system. For example, when Cisco makes telepresence, it first looks for a single high-quality product, and when the product first enters the market, there are many imitators, in which case Cisco gradually integrates mobile phones, web conferencing, and recording technology to enhance its overall strength. In other words, it is an important way and method for Cisco to innovate by having core technologies and creating a market for them, and then building complex technology applications around them. To achieve this, it is necessary to have a long-term and open view of the development trend of the whole industry, and to identify outstanding problems in the industry.

Cisco has created an analytical framework to assess the market potential and business value of new technologies and products, inspire as many ideas as possible early on, and develop a holistic view of the innovation world. However, after continuous evaluation, 98% of the ideas are eliminated, leaving behind the idea of real development value, through employee creation, into a truly marketable product with the full commercial value of the product solidified within 2–3 years.

6 How to Speed up Innovation

The speed of innovation is important to Cisco, and how to achieve speed advantage in the organization has always been a central issue of Cisco's organizational transformation. Cisco's overall organizational structure is functional, not matrix. To enhance cross-sectoral collaboration, Cisco has attempted to accelerate decision-making by establishing business councils and committees to achieve cross-sectoral collaboration. The Business Council is responsible for $1 billion in project decisions and is responsible for achieving $10 billion in project decisions over the next three to five years, and innovative young talent plays an important role in the council and the committee. After the council and the committee have mandated decisions, they aim to take 45 days to turn ideas into action without compromising the quality of their products. The effect sits on this approach has yet to be tested further, but Chambers believes it should be patiently waiting for it to come into play.

The speed of innovation requires effective internal collaboration. The high dispersion of the organizational system, the simultaneous progress of many bulls and many directions will reduce the efficiency of innovation. The slow response to the market has become the biggest obstacle to the development of enterprise, and improvement of the efficiency of innovation has become an urgent task. As mature customers demand more demanding products, and emerging markets demand a large number of localized products, Cisco is constantly looking for a way to rapidly develop new products and technologies. While reasonably controlling research and development costs globally, Cisco enables some good ideas to be quickly identified and produced to maximize returns on the global value chain by accelerating in-house research and development. But how can the management costs of global research and development be effectively controlled? The biggest challenge to solving this problem is establishing collaboration on a global scale.

Establish a global research and development platform. To address the global distributed research and development problem, Cisco uses a product lifecycle management system (PTC) developed by Parameter Technologies to enable simultaneous product development around the world. Managing global innovation processes requires consistency to support rapid retrieval of innovation results and effective management of research and development data. In this regard, Cisco uses distributed research and development with the primary purpose and benefit of managing and improving the visualization of new product development globally through a reliable and efficient product lifecycle management system, efficiently enabling engineers in global design centers and remote research and development centers through rapid data transfer of comprehensive security and protection of critical data design, applications, and infrastructure by applying and optimizing data center infrastructure and WAN bandwidth.

Use rich media to facilitate innovation team communication. In a connected business environment, the innovation team includes people with the right skills and experience who work together to find the best solutions, solve problems, and make decisions. Effective collaboration and mutual support through the use of rich media in such an innovative team.[2] Rich media is used as an application tool to enable human interaction with advanced technology. Rich media can be used to inspire people to innovate. Teams can work together within 24 h and execute goals quickly and effectively, across all borders, regardless of geography or time. An important benefit of a rich media environment is that people can communicate at a much faster

[2] Rich media, refers to embedded in the internet site or web page, can be downloaded and played offline files, these files usually contain animation and video, such as multimedia in 2D and 3D animation, images and sound, technology including HTML, JavaScript, Interstitial window gap, Microsoft Netshow, RealVideo and RealAudio, Flash, and others, the list is likely to grow further as technology advances.

pace and share ideas. Experts and decision makers can connect more easily and the cycle of acquiring prototypes is shortened, and collaborative relationships are formed between teams for project implementation and delivery. Rapid innovation allows businesses to rapidly develop and test new concepts and make ideas viable as quickly as possible. While innovation inevitably implies the possibility of failure, rapid and innovative approaches allow companies to identify errors and make adjustments and modifications early on.

7 Establish an Efficient Innovation Process

Emerging technology exploration. Cisco has always attached great importance to research and development and, in recent years, the focus of research and development with the strategic transformation of enterprises to the consumer market, emerging technology business models, cultural atmosphere and team composition is different, and the need for enterprises to have star talent leadership has increased. In particular, Cisco has created a unique atmosphere and incentives for emerging technology teams, giving them more space to explore and experiment. In this process, Cisco's research and development team not only continues to learn, but also build brands, increase the market display, and make technology more intelligent.

The composition of the new technology innovation team. In order to improve innovation efficiency, there is a need to configure the right team. Some people are highly suitable for research and development, some people are good at marketing, and some people are experienced in improving efficiency. Leadership should address the needs of the innovation process to configure different characteristics of talent, just like in a relay race, the baton is handed from one person to another, and everyone has to play their own role. Successful innovators need a good market sense, and sometimes many knowledgeable Ph.D. students find it difficult to play a central role in new technological innovations because much of their knowledge comes from the past, they don't perceive new problems facing humanity, as they are using intelligence to meet the challenges of innovation, but the results of research and development are often not what the market needs. Innovators need sensitive intuition and perception of the real world in order to focus on the problems that the market needs to address.

Often people value their skills and intellectual background when choosing innovative team members, but often ignore the enthusiasm, energy, and passion of employees, who are important to the success of innovation. In the process of selecting talent, the background of knowledge is often overemphasized, while passion and motivation are ignored. In the eyes of the leaders of the Cisco research and development team, skills and knowledge can be developed and taught, but passion is not taught, so Cisco seeks out passionate people who can find their way, maintain a positive and optimistic spirit in difficult times, and choose to be persistent when others want to give up. It is this passion that drives innovation projects forward.

Creative choice. The choice of new technology depends on the general trend of technology and market development, and the process of selection is quite difficult.

Typically, 15 of 1,000 ideas can be considered, but perhaps only two are deemed real business values to be generated. In the process of selecting new technologies, an important reference system is the larger environment and mainstream trends in technology applications, although this trend is often like deep-sea subcurrents and is not recognized by the general population. People often predict the future based on the inertia of thought, but technological innovation and change have not evolved linearly, but are growing exponentially in a subversive or alternative way, and those who cannot foresee the big trends of the future often miss out on the opportunities presented by new technologies, which is a challenge for all high-tech companies.

Reject old projects before a new project starts. Before starting new projects and product developments, Cisco first looks at what is in existing products and which ones can be culled. In this way, resources can be freed up for new products. IBM has done an exceptionally good job of this. When IBM switched to services, its PC business was out of competitiveness, so it chose to sell the PC business and make a big profit. At the same time, management needs to pay attention to the product life cycle, timely put forward some business or eliminate some products. Once a business or product is eliminated, the company has the resources to innovate other products or services, which goes back to the "exploration stage" and innovation continues.

Develop ways to quickly filter ideas. Once Cisco has acquired the idea both internally and externally, it needs to filter it as quickly as possible in order to find a valuable project. To this end, Cisco proposes the concept of opportunity and the concept of an internal venture capital function diagram. The concept diagram of opportunity refers to the semantic network of the company's technology and products in a visual way, the inherent correlation of the technology product system through concept, connection, and the potential relationship between the new idea and the original technology system. The opportunity concept map includes collaboration, video, data centers, virtualization, and energy, which are market opportunities that Cisco currently considers to be important. Building on the core areas, Cisco created an in-house venture function diagram that helps Cisco focus resources on a few potential projects.

Adopt ideas globally. To expand the source of ideas, Cisco has created ideas among young people through thousands of competitions around the world, offering awards of up to $250,000 to creative winners. Based on thousands of ideas, Cisco invites 60 leaders in the enterprise to evaluate them from different perspectives and to collectively screen them. After selecting ideas that have development and application value, Cisco forms an action learning group to turn ideas into products and propose targeted customer solutions. On that basis, Cisco's sales team is trying to bridge the market divide and turn creative products into products with hundreds of millions of dollars in market value.

At Cisco, multiple leaders determine the choice of innovative projects. If innovation fails, leaders need to take greater responsibility. Leaders need to analyze the information available to determine whether innovative projects are feasible. The main reasons for innovation failure are in the project selection and judgment stage, and fewer cases lead to innovation failure due to errors in the execution process. Therefore, collaboration is important in the early decision-making phases.

Innovation projects that are "isolated". At Cisco, the president has $10 billion to $20 billion in innovation funding, and employees are looking for academicians or engineers to plan together to negotiate the benefits of new ideas for the company's future. If the project is approved by experts and engineers, employees can independently form a team to develop, at which point the project team operates like an investment company. Sometimes, creative teams leave Cisco to share Cisco resources and infrastructure while enjoying more independence and freedom, free from Cisco culture, incentives, and even work hours, and maintaining time and space isolation from Cisco. This time and space isolation allows these innovative teams to enjoy more freedom and atmosphere for start-up small businesses, free from the constant thinking and operating patterns of large enterprises. Once the product has been developed to enter the market, the company buys the project back, and the purchase price of some projects is predictable. If the creative team hatches within Cisco and enters the mass manufacturing phase, the company-designed process will be incorporated into and become part of the mature product production system. Cisco's technology and products are incubating, growing, integrating, and recycling, constantly enhancing the depth and breadth of the product system and enhancing the difference severity of the entire product and solution. Technology and product innovation are accompanied by innovation and optimization of management and operational processes, innovation in sales patterns and business models. This combination of innovation greatly improves the efficiency of innovation and overall competitiveness.

Think of failure as the twin brother of innovation. The key to reducing failure is to spot failure in a timely manner and make a decision. If the market and time prove that a project in development is not a key project for Cisco, stop the bleeding on the right end and transfer talent and money to the next innovation project. It's a circular process, but when new technology development has accumulated to a certain extent, it's very difficult to eliminate the high-tech being developed, and Cisco sometimes does not do well in that regard. The process is very painful and means that some people must leave, but even so, it is still especially important for the enterprise to engage in the process of new creation. For Cisco, failure is part of innovation, an inevitable experience and process in the innovation process, not shortcomings and errors. A lot of growth can come from failure; thus the key is to be able to grow in spite failure and not let the same failure be repeated.

Reconsider the idea of the first phase of sieve. Cisco often reconsiders market size, timing, relationships with core products, destructiveness, impact, and so on, and the ideas that are sieved are not thrown away, but are shelved. Cisco may not be ready to develop these products at the moment, but if things change, they will reconsider them. These ideas can be filtered based on the above criteria.

Project execution and management. According to Chinese engineers working at Cisco, there are differences between East and West cultures during the project development phase, and Cisco emphasizes collaboration, which is important during the decision-making phase, but when decisions are made at the top, they need to be executed efficiently and collaboration is less important. U.S. employees often present their views during the project implementation phase, challenging high-level decisions and influencing the progress and efficiency of project execution. At Cisco

China's research and development center in Hangzhou, the project team's execution is very strong, team members work hard and are very efficient. In addition, after the successful product development and launch of the market, the need to pay attention to the user's attitude towards the product and the cost-effectiveness of the product, once found that the product is not liked by users, its benefits decline, we should consider the product cancellation, elimination. Some teams can make products, but don't know how to sell their products. The cycle of innovative products is very short, and if a product cannot be quickly delivered to the hands of customers and put into use, the product will soon lose its vitality; thus, the marketing process of innovative products must be rapid.

8 How to Match Innovative Projects with Market Maturity

The time it takes to put innovative products and technologies on the market is very important, and the return on investment of innovation is closely related to the maturity of the market. Cisco divides the market into three types of maturity: growth, mature, and declining markets, with different innovation strategies for different maturity markets.

8.1 Innovative Strategies in the Growth Market

The main characteristics of the growth market are: disruptive technology has the opportunity to rise, new technology is in the early stage of acceptance, the potential demand of the market is huge, sustained high growth trends will maintain in a longer period of time a, and new technology as the core of products and services have a lot of open and combined space. Therefore, innovators need to use the leading edge to quickly establish their core position and expand market influence. Through research and development, mergers and acquisitions, and partners, we continue to enrich our product and service portfolio around new technologies, enhance differentiation, complexity and concentration of technology systems and product lines, and build barriers to competition to prevent competitors from catching up quickly.

Cisco has three main innovation strategies for growth markets:

One is disruptive innovation. Disruptive innovation refers to the use of different paths from the past technology systems and business models to subvert or replace the past technology and products. Most of this process involves gradual movement into the market, with new technologies and new business models gaining consumer acceptance in an unobtrusive way to share in the market share of companies that have established leadership positions in the industry. In the early days, disruptive technology products were often questioned or despised by most people, unlike familiar product concepts, consumer behaviors, standards and value chains, but it was these technologies that triggered a new wave of economic growth. Disruptive innovation requires reshaping the entire value chain and supply chain, and it requires constant trial and error in the market to find opportunities for success, so it is risky, costly, and the exploration process is long, and thus few companies are truly successful in the market.

Second, application innovation. It is in the existing product system by combining new elements or changing the relationships and structures between technology and product elements and tapping into new uses of existing products to open up new markets. Applied innovation is the realization of innovation through local optimization in existing technologies and product systems, so it can operate on established value chains, and innovation is less difficult than disruptive innovation, but the market space is limited.

Third, platform innovation. It creates a simplified and superior product layer to integrate its inherently complex, diverse and vast resource and product systems, and to form a community of interests through internal technology structures, governance mechanisms and mutually beneficial mechanisms, thus forming an integrated technology or market ecosystem. There are two types of platform innovation: the first is to treat a market space as a platform, constantly overlay ingress with combination products, extending and expanding market penetration on the platform. Cisco, for example, sees the Internet or grid as a platform that develops new technologies and product systems by constantly recognizing the platform's application space and customer needs, and ensures a competitive advantage on the platform through a portfolio of products. The second is to create a platform that can be either open (e.g. Android) or closed (e.g. Apple), and platform creators need to master the most core and scarce strategic resources (such as prestige, brand, technical standards, and architecture) throughout the technology ecosystem, and then build multiple applications, integrate various internal or external resources to form a community of interests. The platform creator innovates primarily in the business model, and the business ecosystem it creates is hard to beat by competitors in a short period of time.

For growth markets, Cisco pursues five innovative ideas and practices:

(1) **From the product to the system.** This is the conclusion Cisco has reached in the innovation of its security products. Security is the number one problem for the internet, and the market is full of Internet security devices. "Most firms prefer to develop security products on a case-by-case basis and address performance requirements on a case-by-case basis, which may be feasible for a business that is not well-grounded, but for mature companies, the evolution from product to system is the key to a sustainable competitive advantage." Cisco is positioned to provide integrated system products, build a complete product architecture, and comprehensively address security issues.

(2) **Do not be superstitious towards technology, pay attention to the direction of market transformation.** At the height of the Internet, the market's focus began to shift from routers to switches. Cisco is a leader in the router market and had no involvement in the switch market. However, Cisco chose to follow the trend and immediately acquired four switch makers.

(3) **Customer demand is the source of enterprise innovation**. At Cisco, customer-driven has a new meaning: let the market take you where it wants you to go. If you enter the market with the idea of serving the market, you can find a trusted customer, and once the customer asks, listens and follows the direction it points in, you can find something innovative. Cisco has held several customer advisory committee meetings to support the work of the business committees, assign senior management to meetings and communicate with each client committee member, list action, and announce actions taken in response to the results of the previous meeting at the next meeting. In this way, Cisco gives "customer-driven" a deeper meaning.

(4) **Rapid access to the market through acquisition and cooperation strategies**. For Cisco, the need is to quickly build market capabilities through cooperation with strategic peripheral enterprises.

(5) **Realize incremental innovation from product and system integration to solutions**. In practice, Cisco has found that once a user accesses the Internet, customer businesses may lose control of Internet services, such as failing to prevent customers from using network resources endlessly or charging reasonable fees. Therefore, to address this issue, Cisco has added a service transaction layer to the network architecture, in particular for service providers. By providing solutions to telecommunications service providers, Cisco helps them validate users, allows them to develop policies, implement them, and ensure network reliability. In the process, Cisco has also transformed itself from selling products and systems integration to providing solutions to providers.

8.2 *Innovative Strategies in Mature Markets*

In mature markets, modern technologies have dominated, and the products and services surrounding them have become saturated. In mature markets, the growth momentum of categories gradually flattened, the combination of technology and combination of products gradually reduced space. Cisco has four main innovation strategies for mature markets:

First, product extension line innovation. According to customer demand and market research, for the existing product system to combine a unique sub-category and application to meet the needs of the new segmented customer baseor through the upgrading and replacement of old products, the market sales cycle of products must extend, further deepen and expand mature markets.

Second, enhanced innovation. Focus on products with market extension possibilities, discover their market trajectory, and optimize the product portfolio through innovation. The greater the change to the intrinsic core infrastructure of the product, the deeper the degree of innovation, the greater the impact, and the smaller the change to the product's core infrastructure, the closer to product appearance improvement, the less it is innovative.

Third, marketing innovation. The purpose of marketing innovation is to continuously enhance customer awareness of the product. In this process, companies are very concerned about the differentiation needs of customers (especially valuable customers) in the process of purchasing products or in the process of interaction. This innovation is reflected in the interaction with customers, not in the design and production of products, with the aim of selling more products than competitors.

Fourth, experiential innovation. To give customers an understanding of enterprise products, Cisco adopts a strategy that is close to the customer: first let the customer experience the enterprise's philosophy and products, make a good impression on them and then become an enterprise user. The purpose of experiential innovation is not the differentiation of product functionality, but the experience of a product or service.

8.3 Innovative Strategies for Declining Markets

In the declining market, the market competition is hot, the enterprises that adopt imitation and follow-up strategy will usually enter the market with low-cost advantages, first from the low end to gain market share, and then upgrade the existing technology system and product quality, gradually entering the middle and high-end market. In homogenized product supply, the market demand is gradually saturated, product categories have been completely developed, existing technology and product remaining development space is very limited, product systems may be completely closed, and it is more difficult to find opportunities for innovation. When a new wave of disruptive technology emerges, the original technology system will be abandoned and replaced, and the life cycle of technology will come to an end. In this environment, enterprises still have to find a living space to maximize the market value of their products and technologies. In addition to the research and development of enterprises that are constantly looking for new growth market, the declining market cannot be given up lightly. Cisco adopts two innovative strategies:

First, value engineering innovation. The main purpose of value engineering innovation is to reduce costs. By reducing material and manufacturing costs for existing products, companies replace early, high cost, manually integrated custom component designs with low-cost, standardized components and integrate with existing sub-systems without changing external attributes. "Enterprises can compete with new market entrants and imitators by meeting the needs of market segments at a lower cost at a large scale."

Second, integration innovation. Integrated innovation reduces the maintenance costs of customers operating complex products by integrating dispersed components into a single centralized management system. The improvement in the management system of integrated innovation is reflected in process innovation, which is designed to reduce waste in the production process and eliminate valueless steps in the production process.

Cisco's innovation experience in mature markets is that innovation must be done at the integration level of the system architecture to ensure backward software compatibility. Cisco's integrated innovation focuses on the network operating system (IOS), which contains 24 million code, and Cisco's product features are monitored and managed by the software. As the complexity of the system increases and the technology scale increases, no matter how much effort the enterprise has done in documentation of the system, there are always omissions, forgetting to document the system features those some maintenance personnel must know about, which leads to the lack of expansion of the expertise contained there. In addition, as key employees retire or leave, their expertise is lost. To counter the pressure of the dynamic changes in these things, organizations often have their teams rewrite the entire system. But this violates the market's inviolable value proposition that the new version of the system must be compatible with the previous system version, or the company will suffer irreparable loss of benefits. Cisco made the same mistake in the 1990s, but it turned back time, redesigning the mainstream version of IOS into a subsystem module with clear boundaries and strict intermodulation rules. If vulnerabilities occur, the architecture embraces them and systematically tracks them. If the enterprise needs to modify a particular function, the ability to remove the appropriate modules for reconstruction, completely independent of the rest of the system, are the benefits of integration innovation. As we enter new markets, subsystems are first imitated and modified to operate in new environments. This refactoring process can be carried out at a given speed without affecting the operation of the original system, so the core technology of the system has a high degree of elasticity, which brings new hope for Cisco's integration innovation. All integration processes greatly bridge the gap between Cisco's products or services and direct competitors. While these competitors are able to outperform Cisco in the performance of a single product, they cannot deliver Cisco's value proposition and provide an integrated network structure.

"The innovation strategy of an enterprise typically combines a growth market, a mature market, and a declining market to meet the new technology challenges of new growth markets and to maximize the business value in mature and declining markets through operational excellence and management innovation." There is also a dynamic switching mechanism for innovation and operational excellence that empowers new technologies to continue to be transformed into markets.

Cisco's innovation for growth markets is primarily disruptive, with a focus on breaking the rules and concepts of existing technologies and product systems, designing and developing products from a new mindset, and disrupting and replacing existing technologies and products. Once accepted by the market, a new space for market growth will be created. Focusing on demands that are not currently being noticed in the industry often presents opportunities for disruptive change in the market. Focusing on new markets and new technology applications, disruptive innovation with engineers as the core explores unknown areas, so has the characteristics of uncertainty, high risk, high investment, high return, high return, and high profit, representing the growth and increment of the enterprise. Innovation for mature and declining markets is incremental innovation, optimized and improved in a progressive, routine, low risk, established core business, maximizing market returns through operational excellence.

9 Summary

Cisco's innovation is a complete system engineering. It looks from a large social background, first to find the future market business opportunities and fast-growing industries where, where customer needs are located. After determining the direction through the rapid use of a variety of external and internal channels, innovative activities are carried out and new technologies and products are combined with previous technology to develop a differentiated product system and reuse strategic alliances and partner channels. In order to realize the efficient operation from strategic insight to marketing, Cisco will make the process from leader's strategic insight to marketing as fast as possible by creating a highly collaborative organization and highly adaptive culture, in order to grasp market opportunity and ensure high revenue. As a result, Cisco's innovation system does not focus solely on research and development and new product development, but integrates strategic transformation, innovation and marketization processes to ensure the market value and business success of innovation through continuous operational management optimization, enabling innovation systems to seamlessly interface through information-based and efficient collaboration organizations. Multi-system consolidation is an important competitive advantage for Cisco.

Cisco uses a range of innovative approaches to activate endogenous power, avoid big business disease and organizational inertia, and enable large enterprises to maximize the flexibility and creativity of small businesses while maximizing their resource advantages. These means include constant self-reflection and awareness of the causes and pitfalls of the failure of big business, constantly reminding themselves of self-awareness. As Chambers says, all successful companies need a strong sense of crisis and fear, which is the only way to keep pushing forward. At the same time, by constantly making emerging markets a core force for activating businesses, companies do not stop, as Cisco's leadership puts it, "The core of our focus is on customers and markets, not just competitors." Encouraged by future market opportunities, Cisco will integrate companies with strong correlations with its culture, technology and products into its own system through mergers and acquisitions, external adoption of innovation, and inward-spin acquisitions, especially by incorporating these Talents for Small and Medium Enterprises into Cisco to stimulate itself with the vitality of small and medium-sized enterprises. Break any pattern and inertia that might make it rigid.

One of the key stakes in the success of Cisco's innovation system is the high degree of alignment between the research and development system and the management operating system to maximize corporate earnings by combining to meet the needs of growth markets while also meeting the needs of mature and declining markets.

Among them, the innovation side focuses on radical technology and emerging technologies to meet the needs of the future and potentially fast-growing market and the operating party through the operation and sales advantages. This allows for the largest scale of sales of existing technology products and may bring substantial profits to the enterprise. Once emerging technologies are used quickly, Cisco combines new technologies with existing technologies to bring a new round of scale sales. In this sense, Cisco's success is not just about the leadership of the technology itself, but also on the success of the technology-driven market and the success of the customer. Driven by this kind of thinking, the focus of enterprise innovation must be the market; in relying on their own technology and knowledge to pursue the success of the market, the enterprise must have the resources, ability and motivation of sustainable development.

Chapter 5
M&A Strategy and Management

1 Introduction

In order to enhance the competitiveness of enterprises and maintain sustainable development capabilities, enterprises need new technologies. In the era of higher demands for rapid innovation and increasing complexity, enterprises should obtain competitive advantage through internal research and development and through mergers and acquisitions and strategic alliances. In the process of mergers and acquisitions, the main driving force is access to valuable resources, such as human resources, technical resources, market resources and physical resources. Many mergers and acquisitions fail to meet expectations due to problems in the implementation process. First, it is associated with strategic misalignment. The enterprise's own needs and integration ability are not clearly understood and the complementarity of the two sides of the merger and acquisition is unclear, resulting in failure of the expected assumption. Second, people use it improperly. In the process of merger and acquisition, means of appointing the senior executives and core personnel of the acquired enterprise is important. In the process, establishing a full trusting relationship between both organizations, designing incentive mechanisms, and full application of talent and professional value are crucial to the success of the merger and acquisition. Third, merger and acquisition integration. If the merger is a large enterprise or a good performance of the enterprise, the integration of the information system, ability system, management system and culture is a very difficult endeavor. The integration of information systems, data consistency, and consistency of management processes may conflict, and the management system and culture integration is more difficult. Fourth, the transfer of technology and ability is the most difficult activity in merger and acquisition management, especially in the process of a rapid merger and acquisition. If there is no trust in the new relationship, much hidden knowledge and valuable talent will be lost. Thus, it is important to retain the hidden knowledge of the acquired enterprises following a merger and acquisition.

X. Dong et al., *Cisco*,
https://doi.org/10.1007/978-981-19-7870-8_5

2 Evolution of Cisco's Merger and Acquisition Strategy

Cisco's mergers and acquisitions are part of the innovation system, and its acquisition strategy is developing and evolving. Cisco began the merger process in 1999. In the 1990s, Cisco primarily marketed new technologies through sales channels, and when Cisco focused on the Internet as a strategic investment and began to serialize and differentiate technologies and products with routing switching technology at its core, mergers and acquisitions became an important strategy for entering adjacent technologies. Between 2000 and 2008, Cisco developed advanced technologies, expanded its networking business, and entered new markets in an attempt to diversify Cisco products to improve their overall competitiveness in terms of market, technology, and business models. Since 2008, Cisco has focused on high-tech, expanding the strategic relevance of its network, driving major market changes, and developing a range of new businesses with markets valued at more than $10 billion. At the same time, Cisco continues to drive innovation in its core areas, increasing the value of key advanced technologies to more than $10 billion and delivering superior operational performance. Cisco has also been innovating in the associated market segment, achieving sustainable business development through a comprehensive innovation system of research and development, mergers and acquisitions, and cooperation. In terms of mergers and acquisitions, there is a focus on technology companies and how emerging technology companies can integrate into Cisco's existing technology and product systems to enhance Cisco's ability to differentiate. For the past five years, Cisco mergers and acquisitions have focused not only on technology-innovative companies, but also on companies with strong business models, not only on business models that are appropriate for advanced economies, but also on promising business models in high-growth emerging markets.

By 2013, Cisco had completed 160 acquisitions. Cisco made 14 acquisitions in 2013, with an average of one every six weeks. In the merger case, there were only a few small companies, but also a larger company, the largest of which was the acquisition of Atlanta Technology, involving 7,000 employees, with a value of $1.2 billion. Cisco often has $30 billion in cash reserves dedicated to mergers and acquisitions. In Cisco's view, the best acquisition size is a small company with 50–100 people with a certain size, performance and customers. However, 100 people is optimal, as these people can be placed in different departments. If you acquire companies with more than 150 people, consolidation is more difficult. As of 2015, 25% of Cisco's employees were from acquired companies, and more than 15% of the directors' leadership was from the acquired company with a retention rate of 80%.

3 Strategic Objectives and Value of Mergers and Acquisitions

Cisco regards mergers and acquisitions as one of the three pillars of the innovation system and an important way to achieve its corporate strategy. As a high-tech company, Cisco believes that mergers and acquisitions can achieve three main objectives: first, to enter into new technology application markets through mergers and acquisitions, second, to better integrate and utilize technology, to deepen and expand existing products and technology systems, and to enhance the ability to achieve sustainable differentiation, and third, to build a business ecosystem through strategic investment alliances to ensure its leading position in the market and to gain a large market share.

Specifically, the objectives and value of mergers and acquisitions are mainly reflected in the following four areas:

First, through mergers and acquisitions to enhance the core capabilities of enterprises, reduce the risk of technological innovation, to ensure that enterprises continue to lead the position. In the low-speed development period of the industry, most product development and technological innovation come from within the enterprise, enterprises have enough time to carry out new technology and new product research and development. But when the market accelerates, it is difficult for companies to keep up with the needs of customers and markets simply by relying on internal forces, and it is thus difficult for them to gain market leadership status if competitors launch new products at a faster rate. In this case, companies need to quickly acquire the latest technology from the outside through mergers and acquisitions and convert them into market value with the company's original sales system. In this process, the choice and judgment of the object of merger and acquisition, the ability to integrate the object of merger and acquisition, and the ability to market the acquisition technology and products play an important role in ensuring the effect of the merger and acquisition.

Another value of mergers and acquisitions is the diversification of the risk in the direction of research and development, through external resources, to obtain complementary value to the Cisco technology system of enterprises. Cisco believes that there is a certain risk in the internal research and development of enterprises (investing in previous research projects, conducting in-house research) in two main ways: First, the previously mature technology system may become an obstacle to the acceptance of new technologies, and enterprises in technology research and development may develop blind spots. This has been replaced by disruptive technologies from start-ups. Second, early developed technologies often cannot be converted into market-accepted technologies or products for various reasons. When enterprises fail to detect the trap of research and development at an early stage prior to a high investment of money, the result of the program was found to be unrealistic. Conversely, small start-ups tend to have the ability to discover emerging technologies and market segments, often focusing on demands ignored by large enterprises, being sensitive to new technologies and responsive to the market. Having small businesses verify that a new technology meets market needs reduces the risk of large businesses choosing new technologies. In the process of market validation, businesses must set up a series of test stations, closely track to observe whether the products designed by small enterprises meet customer demand and are accepted by the market, effectively help large enterprises judge the value of these small business mergers and acquisitions, and eliminate some of the risks in the choice of new technology. When the market proves the commercial value of new technologies, Cisco's inclusion of them can reduce risk and increase returns, while small businesses can develop rapid market-oriented capabilities with the help of large companies' brands, capital, and sales channels.

In the strategic vision of the Cisco mergers and acquisitions team, try to avoid acquiring advanced technology developers with limited market value, and instead pay close attention to companies with disruptive technology development results, while taking full advantage of their in-house technology to create the best incremental technology products on the market. Once the technology or product is in place, Cisco acquires the start-up and integrates its products and employees into Cisco's operating systems.

Second, through mergers and acquisitions to integrate resources and services to ensure the sustainable development of enterprises. Cisco is adept at taking advantage of market turmoil: on the one hand, to further consolidate existing market positions in mature areas, and on the other hand, to consolidate existing resources through mergers and acquisitions, strengthening the ability of companies to differentiate in technology and product systems. In mergers and acquisitions aimed at integrating resources and services, the consistency of the acquired company's business with Cisco's strategic business is an important indicator. For example, for Cisco's traditional hardware and equipment industry, the degree of change in the post-merger business model is a key indicator of the target of mergers and acquisitions. Because if the target company is culturally and strategically far apart from Cisco, and the two companies are quite different, then the challenge of convergence is more difficult. Therefore, success depends on whether the acquired enterprise is consistent with Cisco's development direction and objectives, whether the strategic direction is consistent, whether the business model is complementary, whether senior leaders have commitment and other indicators, and whether the success of the merger is important. In addition to these elements, Cisco also takes market trends into account when making merger and acquisition decisions, as it is also important to capture the best point of access for technology and market development.

Cisco rarely acquires companies of homogenization, and the ability to quickly enter new market segments is an important consideration when choosing an acquired company. For example, Cisco already had relevant products and partners when it entered the smart grid market, but in order to enter the smart grid market more quickly, Cisco chose to acquire Arch Rock, which significantly accelerated the pace of entry into the field.

Third, through mergers and acquisitions to enter new markets or achieve rapid transformation of enterprises. Cisco's acquisition strategy is not just to acquire more new technologies or produce more new products, but more importantly to find a way to radically increase their market size and make more money. Guided by this strategy, Cisco is constantly looking for opportunities to enter new markets through mergers and acquisitions, with the aim of rapidly moving the capabilities already in place to new markets, expanding the boundaries of the enterprise, and expanding the company's territory to areas that were previously less involved. From 2004 to 2011, Cisco opened up a number of markets, including consumer, video, software, collaboration, content security, virtual computing collaboration, through mergers and acquisitions, and achieved significant growth in size like the underlying market. In FY2003, Cisco successfully entered the consumer market through the Linksys merger, and in FY2010, Cisco entered the wireless services market through the acquisition of Starent, and successfully entered the video and telepresence markets through the acquisition of Tandberg. Cisco continues to build new product portfolios to transform the industry.

Cisco's acquisitions in different parts of the world have also helped it quickly shorten its learning curve and quickly integrate into emerging markets. Cisco has made a growing proportion of acquisitions overseas in recent years. To maintain a strategic balance, Cisco will combine mergers and portfolios in mature and emerging markets, currently investing $2 billion a year in different emerging technologies and markets.

Fourth, use mergers and acquisitions to obtain talent. Cisco's acquisitions sometimes focus on the core backbone and employees of the business, or the intellectual property that the company has, not simply the products and infrastructure of the moment. Cisco is more focused on the future value of its employees and acquiring second- or third-generation products that employees will develop in the future.

4 Search for Radical Technology and Inward-Style Mergers and Acquisitions

Cisco is concerned with missing out on new technology opportunities, and it has focused on small start-ups in search of disruptive technologies. Although Cisco carefully examines its leadership team, cultural compatibility, technological uniqueness, and potential business value when it researches and examines acquired companies, it has adopted an inward-led approach to mergers and acquisitions to reduce risks and uncertainties in the course of acquisitions. Inward-linked mergers and acquisitions are those in which Cisco, when evaluating candidates, looks for disruptive technologies that match its technical standards, as well as products that fit its business model and meet the specific needs of its customers. The difference between spin mergers and acquisitions is that Cisco invests in the business early and buys the company when the invested company's sales reach a preset number of customers and milestones. In this process, to ensure return on investment and reduce investment risk, Cisco oversees corporate management when necessary and sends key employees to candidate companies to provide guidance in order to ensure the successful operation of the invested enterprise.

The advantage of spin mergers and acquisitions is that Cisco can share technology, experience, and product roadmaps closely with acquired companies to collaborate in the development of well-integrated products that can be part of Cisco's technology architecture in less time. With in-spin mergers and acquisitions, Cisco can link the acquisition price to product revenue and related profits. This results-oriented approach to mergers and acquisitions avoids the uncertainty that usually exists when evaluating the value of the business. Cisco has acquired new technologies through this approach, enhancing the requirements of the enterprise for market transformation, further enhancing the differentiation of existing technologies, driving Cisco's creativity through small businesses, and enhancing the vitality of the enterprise, while Cisco's established enterprise size, brand, management system, market channels and financial strength provide a higher visibility for small businesses and new technologies.

Inward-turned mergers and acquisitions also have drawbacks: Cisco's employees may face career-risk as they constantly re-position their businesses, thus Cisco must motivate them. In addition, the cycle of completion of internal spin mergers and acquisitions is longer than the traditional merger cycle. If Cisco's goal is to acquire disruptive technologies in the peripheral markets, and time-to-market is not a primary consideration, then spin-on mergers and acquisitions are very effective. But if the time to go public is imminent and the business model is new, Cisco typically chooses a traditional approach to mergers and acquisitions.

5 Six Principles of Mergers and Acquisitions

Principle 1: Consistency and integration of the vision objectives of both sides.

This principle implies the idea that the employee who is invested in the acquisition is part of the overall merger and acquisition transaction, and that the conflict between the core backbone and the vision objectives will ultimately undermine the expected value of the transaction. For Cisco, the most important value is acquisition of intellectual assets, and Cisco can only make a correct assessment if it fully understands the vision objectives of the acquired company. This principle requires that the target company have clear industry and product prospects to integrate with Cisco's vision. In Cisco's view, the ability to be accommodating is considered a necessary condition for a merger.

Principle 2: Do not make competitive mergers and acquisitions.

Cisco is not involved in competitive mergers and acquisitions, and there is an exclusive agreement in potential merger negotiations that the target company will only negotiate with Cisco, not with other companies simultaneously. Sometimes, bankers or intermediaries take the initiative to bring projects to Cisco to inquire about merger and acquisition intentions, but Cisco is less involved and communicates directly to the target company. The reason for this is that Cisco wants to control the entire acquisition process to get to the target market as quickly as possible. When Cisco anticipates market trends, it also makes acquisition decisions quickly and moves expeditiously after a target is identified. During one Cisco merger, talks between the target company and Cisco occurred over a period of nine months, however, it took just 10 days for Cisco to make the final decision. This exclusive acquisition gives Cisco more control over the entire process.

Principle 3: The culture of the target enterprise is integrated with Cisco.

Culture and values are one of the key criteria for Cisco's assessment of potential acquiring targets, and in the reconciliation of culture, Cisco focuses on values, beliefs, and behaviors. At the heart of values are honesty and trustworthiness as well as a customer-centric mentality; at the belief level, specifically, values include a consistent vision, goals, and views of the market, and behavior directly influenced by values and beliefs that require employees to be consistent with their work behavior. When examining the target of an acquisition, the culture of the target company is investigated to determine whether it is compatible with the Cisco culture. While the culture of the two enterprises does not have to be exactly the same, the key requirement is that the big goals are consistent. Cisco does not ask the acquirer to address this in detail, but it pursues compatibility and inclusion from a cultural and macro perspective, and cultural integration is central to the process.

Principle 4: Mergers and acquisitions should value long-term profitability.

Cisco carefully weighs each acquisition and evaluates the long-term strategic impact of the merger on relevant stakeholders, such as new employees, customers, shareholders, and so on. If Cisco believes that a merger is not in the interests of either party in the interest group, it will choose to abandon the acquisition despite its short-term profit prospects. This principle is mainly embodied in practice in two aspects: first, whether to retain employees. Cisco believes that the primary purpose of the merger is to obtain the most valuable employees, and that the purpose of the acquisition is not only to purchase existing product series, but also to support the products that those employees are developing or are about to develop. Incentives are for employees to offer stock options, the means of restriction is to sign a competition prohibition agreement, employees are required to sign a two-year non-competition agreement, that is, for two years following employment with Cisco, employees cannot be employed in other enterprises in the same industry. Second, whether to get closer to the customer. The advantage of being close to customers is that you can quickly understand customer needs and changes and respond quickly, improving the ability to customize them according to different customer needs, and at the same time helping to improve service levels and reduce logistics costs.

Principle 5: The acquired company is geographically close to an important market or supply chain.

Cisco Systems' geo-proximity standards come from the goal of fully integrating the target enterprise. The proximity of geographical location will have a great impact on the integration of the target enterprises.

Principle 6: Peer-to-peer mergers are not accepted.

In Cisco's view, the ideal acquisition target is a private enterprise with fewer than 100 employees and a product that can be marketed. The size of mergers and acquisitions will affect mergers and acquisitions in three ways: one is to increase the risk of mergers and acquisitions, the other is to increase the merger and acquisition process, and the third is to reduce the speed of integration. Cisco typically acquires small businesses with good technology and products that lack global sales channels and platforms. They also seek out small businesses that already have a good product line, but lack the financial support to continue to grow. The assets of these companies are complementary to Cisco, and through mergers and acquisitions, they can achieve win–win goals. Cisco believes that the merger of companies of the same size complicates the integration of employees, and that the integration of the two corporate cultures may be long and difficult.

In 2013, Cisco's mergers and acquisitions teams had a very clear strategy, with the direction of the merger remaining close to the company's core architecture. Within the architecture, there are three core business elements and corresponding service systems: infrastructure (technical services and advanced services), platforms (platform services and managed services) and applications (consulting services, IoE exchange). Of these three elements, a unified platform is expanded within four areas at the infrastructure level: unified data center, core network, network access (wired and mobile) and network security (access control, context aware, content awareness, and threat awareness). The application level is also divided into four areas: third-party and content open-source systems, business processes, enterprise applications, IoT solutions and industry applications, video and collaboration. All Cisco mergers and acquisitions are conducted under the guidance of this business architecture, with clear objectives and controlled results.

6 Acquisition Process and Methods

The timing of the merger. Cisco has established two key points based on the dynamic growth curve of the enterprise (see Fig. 1), one is the timing of the investment (e.g., the internal spin merger) and the other is the opportunity for the merger and acquisition of the firm. During the launch of innovation and early adoption, there is an opportunity to invest, to promote the maturity and development of new technologies at this stage, and to accelerate the maturity and development of the market during early adoption and late adoption.

The process of mergers and acquisitions. The process for each Cisco merger is not exactly the same, and this is related to the governance structure. Merger and acquisition decisions are made by three main entities: the board of directors, the CEO, and the CFO. The usual process is for the business unit to form a team responsible for investment, with expected collaboration between the investment team and the business unit who will work together to identify prospects for an investment or

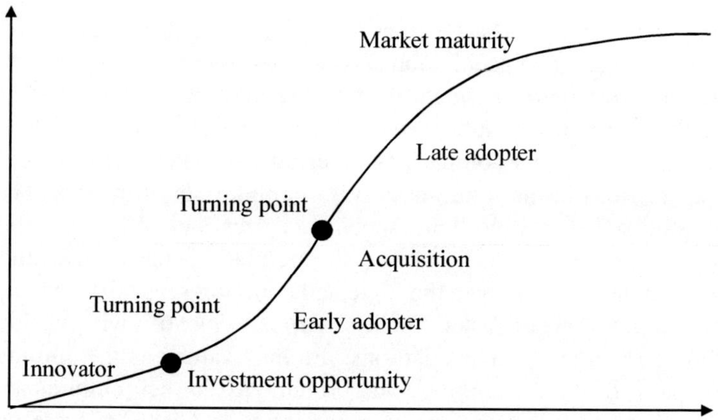

Fig. 1 Dynamic growth curve of enterprises

merger. Following this, the investment team optimizes the idea and reports back to the CEO. The discussion is focused on ensuring that the merger proposals were aligned with the company's overall strategy and objectives.

Next, the CFO and COO (CEO) are involved in reviewing the financial data supported in the decision-making process. In discussions with the CFO, there is a large team involved, and participants ensure that financial results are forecasted, at which time the commitment and responsibilities of each department person are clear. The merger proposal is then submitted to the board, where a committee responsible for investment has a committee dedicated to the merger to discuss and make decisions about the merger plan and to ask the investment team tough questions and examine any potential blind spots in the decision. The merger is finally approved by Chambers. If the merger exceeds $6 billion, it needs to be unanimously approved by all members of the board of directors, and if the merger is to measure 40 performance metrics, it is rare to initiate a shareholder meeting process for approval.

To improve the efficiency of acquisitions, Cisco institutionalizes the processes required to ensure that key elements and resources in the acquisition are integrated into every step of the execution process. The goal of process institutionalization and continuous optimization is to clarify what to do before solving the problem, rather than spending a lot of time communicating, discussing, and negotiating during the merger process to significantly reduce repetitive work. Several key elements of the merger and acquisition process are the team responsible for the merger, the financial evaluation of the subject of the merger, the pre-merger tasks, the pre-task evaluation and the merger integration process.

The team responsible for the merger. Cisco has approximately 15 teams that work on integrating acquired companies, with more than 60 dedicated teams working across the company once acquired, and 400–600 employees associated with the merger and acquisition process. Cisco typically targets 100 companies at a time and conducts careful research and negotiations in groups of 10, later resulting in the acquisition of a company. The 1% rate shows that Cisco has room for improvement in the area of mergers and acquisitions.

Financial assessment of the subject of the merger. Mergers and acquisitions must take the return on investment into account, and Cisco's financial performance measurement of the target company to determine whether it meets the company's growth expectations in the future has a very complex set of metrics. These criteria are also optimized over time, with specific metrics including investment income statements, income statements, balance sheets, market shares, and other financial objectives to financially analyze the logic and common sense of their acquisitions.

Carry out pre-merger tasks. The first step is to identify what problems can be solved through mergers and acquisitions: are they valued as the employees of the target company, or their technology and products? Can their cultures and products be integrated and will they be easily integrated with Cisco? Cisco's investigative projects include an audit of the financial, legal asset value of the target company, and an in-depth investigation of ethics, integrity, teamwork, professional specificity, customer commitment, and more.

Evaluation of pre-task. The pre-task evaluation is an evaluation of the completion of the task by a Cisco Systems' project team, whose team leader is usually the head of the business development department and is composed of representatives from marketing, engineering, and product manufacturing. Representatives of each department are responsible for evaluating and judging matters related to their departments.

Merger task process. Cisco's complete consolidation process consists of four main phases. Phase 1: Trading forecasting. The main task of this phase is to scan and identify business opportunities and mergers and acquisitions in the market and to evaluate those opportunities and businesses. On this basis, the business development team and the business unit responsible for the merger and acquisition report to a higher level of the core team, which is the next step of technical review. At this stage, the early integration team is involved in research and developing integration strategies and program recommendations to support the next step in implementation.

Phase 2: Business case studies and pre-approvals. This phase is the key link of the merger and involves further evaluation and analysis by the acquisition team to issue pre-approval and develop of terms and conditions. At this stage, the specific workflow includes writing a business case, clarifying the value of the case, and analyzing the results of the merger and the return on investment. At the same time, it is necessary to carry out predictive research, focusing on the early business situation. After this early intelligence research and documentation work is completed, a draft of the integration intention program is put forth. Following this, the M&A project enters a substantial implementation phase, with the support of management, business units and functional departments. The joint team holds a pre-final decision approval meeting, and if the merger is approved, the merger negotiations begin, drawing up a terms sheet and engaging in substantive negotiations. The goal of this phase is to conduct pre-transaction surveys of the acquired companies, assess their capabilities, determine the overall integration strategy, clarify the vision of mergers and acquisitions, and establish a value-driven model for the success of the mergers and acquisitions.

Phase 3: Transaction execution. This phase is a substantive operational phase of the merger, starting with due diligence (including due diligence at the technical, financial, legal, operational, key employee levels), negotiating the merger agreement, identifying and negotiating with key employees, and addressing the specifics of due diligence and negotiations. Create a FAQ for follow-up. On this basis, the merger enters the final approval and signature phase, when Cisco has drafted the merger agreement and public statements, but internally, there is a series of approval process work in progress, especially to obtain approval from the CEO and the board of directors. After the project is finally approved, there will be relevant legal documents and confirmation of the financial closing conditions and documents, and Cisco will begin to make an official statement to domestic and external partners after an agreement has been reached with the acquired company. At this stage, the operating conditions of the acquired company are still subject to a detailed investigation to eliminate unnecessary risks. The core objective of this phase is to develop an integration and business transformation plan based on a detailed investigation and analysis of the acquired company, and to put the plan into practice.

Phase 4: Communication, integration and evaluation. At this stage, the merger has actually entered the consolidation phase, and Cisco will ensure a smooth and secure integration process within 100 days, such as new employee orientation, to make the employees of the acquired company feel a sense of belonging. At the same time, Cisco integrates efficiently in information systems and related infrastructure and functions, and the non-core business units of the acquired company are integrated into Cisco's unified systems. The integration of acquired companies into Cisco also brings new changes to Cisco itself, so at this stage, Cisco will evaluate the new knowledge and experience those new businesses bring and effectively manage the changes that will be brought about by the merger. After 100 days of the merger, the consolidation optimization phase includes consolidation optimization of products and platforms, the release of merger and acquisition reports, quarterly audits, payment processing and monitoring, and, if the metrics meet Cisco's expectations, the consolidation is declared complete.

7 Cultural Integration and Business Integration After Mergers and Acquisitions

After the merger is completed, the integration of the two companies begins. At Cisco, consolidation is very powerful, with integration experts in every function, including financial or human resources experts. On the tax side, there are more than 100 people in charge of consolidation, which also extends to the technical field to ensure full acceptance of mergers and acquisitions. For example, a Cisco merger two years ago involved more than 100 people in the integration effort, although they were not in charge of integration full-time. In the integration process, Cisco has a strong framework, managed centrally by headquarters, and in the process, centralized management and strategic structure and methodology are critical.

Departmental integration. The first step in Cisco's acquisition is departmental consolidation, which typically integrates human resources, manufacturing, sales channels, customer service, and finance into Cisco's organizational structure, while engineering, marketing, and sales departments are typically integrated into Cisco's mergers and acquisitions departments. After each merger, Cisco's authorities have a business unit that is connected to the acquired company so that it is not lost in the process of being integrated by Cisco.

Cultural integration. Cultural integration is not an easy task in the process of mergers and acquisitions. First, Cisco's core values and culture will not change significantly, no matter how many companies are acquired. Cisco uses a variety of ways to understand and digest its cultural characteristics, cultural background and connotations in the corporate culture of the acquired company, without forcing the other party to accept it. In Cisco's view, the Chinese convergence of the merger process depends on how they adapt to each other to meet the needs of the market.

Of course, it may take a long time to achieve cultural docking with Cisco through the use of face-to-face "companionship". Bringing employees from both parties together and holding regular briefings by pairing members of the target enterprise with members of the Cisco team on equal footing. In this way, employees of the target company can get timely answers to the concerns from those who were acquired early.

One core aspect of Cisco's culture as a global enterprise is a commitment to the convergence of a global culture, both the core values and codes of conduct of the parent company, and the due focus on local cultural characteristics of each region, such as Cisco China, Cisco Norway office features and work in a different way than Cisco headquarters in San Jose. Communication is different, but that doesn't mean they're independent of Cisco culture.

In the early stages of consolidation, Cisco manages communication between employees in the target enterprise and establishes an integrated work team to select key internal agency employees from 10 to 15 functions to form the team. This team acts as an intermediary for Cisco's communication with target employees and controls the content of the communication. In the integration process, there are several other issues that are critical:

(1) **Dealing with stock options**. Keep employees focused on long-term returns, extend the option exercise period from 4 to 5 years, and allocate options annually.
(2) **Clear placement of the acquired employees**. Cisco strives to place key positions for the key members of the acquired company to motivate management to stay and continue working but is not eager to retain managers who do not want to stay on after the merger. At the employee meeting of the acquired company, the employee and the position of the acquired company will be identified. In order to enable the acquired company's employees to quickly integrate into Cisco, Cisco welcomes the addition of the acquired employee in a variety of ways. When the merger is announced, the acquired employee receives a Cisco

cup that says, "Welcome to the team." At the initial employee announcement meeting, they will bc provided with information about Cisco and future work.

(3) **Exclude uncertainty**. As part of the merger, Cisco will clarify which employees it wants to keep and which it does not want to keep. This allows employees to know whether their work is protected and eliminates the uncertainty of the future. For example, in the merger of Cerent, there was an agreement that Cisco could not fire the company's employees without the CEO's consent, nor could it make significant adjustments to their work.

(4) **Quick action**. Cisco Systems typically begins to enter the acquired company within hours of the announcement of the merger and acquisition announcement and begins the assimilation absorption process with the aim of integrating the acquired employees as quickly as possible. For small business acquisitions, Cisco will take about 90 days to consolidate, and for large enterprise consolidation, Cisco will take 12 months to complete.

(5) **Integration through information systems**. Cisco focuses on communicating using network technology to facilitate the smooth integration of its mergers and acquisitions. Cisco employees can access links to employee information under the Cisco Systems Corporation website, which can be found in most of the internal operations of Cisco that need to be known. The Management Information System (MIS) provides the manager with real-time sales information, such as orders, bill lists, etc. Executives of acquired companies are assigned to conduct operational training on the Cisco Information Platform. Cisco Systems' information systems department adapts the information infrastructure of the target enterprise and Cisco to accommodate each other and provides training for acquired employees to overcome barriers to information system conversion. Cisco also familiarizes new employees with using telepresence as a face-to-face communication tool, enabling the company to quickly connect with acquired companies and enhance cultural consensus. Telepresence meetings and Web Office can greatly improve meeting collaboration and communication, making it easy to integrate team data sharing.

Product integration. The product integration solution is the process of converting all the products of the merger into Cisco products, and Cisco has adopted an integrated approach to transform the acquired products into Cisco's standardized manufacturing systems, making them part of the Cisco product system, including:

(1) **Ciscoization of product numbers**. All products acquired receive a Cisco-based Manufacturing Resource Planning (MRP) database product number and require this to be done within a 90-day schedule. The significance of this change is that first, salespeople and customers can use product numbers to order products from the target company; second, to make communication steps simple because the numbers reflect information about the product in the MRP system, and finally, from the customer's point of view, they are doing business directly with Cisco. The goal of cisco providing customers with a unified terminal-to-terminal solution is achieved.

(2) **Product transfer**. Within 30 days of the acquisition, the Cisco Manufacturing Integration team will initially determine which products will be fully transferred to Cisco for manufacturing and which products will be manufactured by the acquired employee. In making this decision, Cisco considers whether the product is easily obsolete, whether Cisco is in urgent need of acquiring the technology, the complexity of the product's manufacturing, and whether the technology is easily transferred.
(3) **Ciscoization of the suppliers**. Cisco has a dedicated team that works with current or potential vendors and evaluates them. The group will also assess all vendors of the acquired companies. The seller of any acquired company is evaluated in accordance with the same set of acceptance criteria.
(4) **Ciscoization the products acquired**. Cisco Systems determines an outsourcing process for the acquired product within 90 days of the acquisition target, which is an important part of the manufacturing portfolio process.
(5) **Ciscoization of the product tests**. Cisco has developed its own automated test system for manufacturing products, which is not only a standardized system control system for Cisco management, but also a means of managing virtual plants when manufacturing outsourcing products that meet quality standards and meet the specific needs of customers.
(6) **Ciscoization of quality monitoring**. Cisco Systems uses its own various process-based quality monitoring procedures, which are based on the automatic detection system test results, after the acquisition, the original process quality monitoring program of the acquired company to be modified to adapt to the Cisco Systems Company's methods.
(7) **Make predictions in a Cisco way**. The acquired company is asked to provide a forecast of the acquired product to the Cisco Enterprise Level Marketing Group, which is affiliated with it. Cisco's marketing team provides feedback to new employees and ultimately arrives at agreed forecasts. The final forecast figures will be adopted by The Cisco Manufacturing Resource Plan, which will then determine the production requirements. Cisco's forecasting method is adopted by the acquirer within 30 days of the merger.

8 Keys to the Success of Mergers and Acquisitions

Clear strategic objectives. The Cisco mergers and acquisitions team spends a majority of their time making sure the strategy is clear: Why buy the company? What are the expected goals? How can we get to the market more efficiently? How can Cisco's strategic advantage be enhanced after the merger? How can we capitalize on the complementary advantages of the two sides? These are the issues that need to be analyzed before a merger.

Efficient integration process. Cisco's merger and acquisition integration process is divided into eight major steps: opportunity assessment, business case, evaluation and analysis, pre-approval and terms, due diligence, final approval, contract execution, announcement of acquisition closure, consolidation stabilization, and integration optimization. The eight major steps are followed by a breakdown of specific tasks and activities (see Fig. 2). Cisco has processed the merger process based on past acquisition experience and has actually developed a set of efficient merger methodologies. Under the guidance of this method theory, the problems and risks that may be encountered in the process of merger and acquisition are avoided as much as possible, and the employees involved can understand the workflow as soon as possible, thus greatly improving the efficiency of the merger.

Focus on the consistency of both businesses. The consistency and strategic consistency of the acquired company's existing business with Cisco are important to the success of the merger, but sometimes it is difficult for the business to achieve complete agreement and the other is unique in its business model. In this context, the commitment of the two leaderships and the adjustment and complementarity of business models are very important. For example, Cisco has traditionally been a hardware and outsourcing company, selling primarily through channels rather than directly to customers; in the merger and acquisition process, if the other side sells directly to the end customer, the interface between each is difficult. Methods for finding ways and means to integrate the new model must be made without further financial commitments. It would be challenging for Cisco to manage a merger in which a company sells directly to customers. In addition to differences in business models, differences in organizational structures can also make integration difficult. For example, Cisco expects to integrate the relevant functions directly, but in the process of consolidation, different levels in the division of labor and duplication of business require incremental adjustments by Cisco. The key principle here is to capture each other's core values. These core values are mainly reflected in three aspects: first, the financial situation, second, strategic considerations, and third, to attract talent and morale, so that people feel that mergers and acquisitions are a positive experience. Sometimes the number of people who remain after integration can even indicate the success of the merger. Under the traction of the core value, the difference severity of the merger process can be properly resolved.

Due diligence. Cisco will conduct in-depth due diligence before a merger is announced, with the investigation focused on the strategic level. A second due diligence will be conducted after the announcement of the merger. The second due diligence will focus on the tactical and execution dimension, with Cisco trying to identify specific questions that the acquired executives have not previously answered, such as how the business operates, how the team is formed, what the business model is, and how the business with integrate with the Cisco team.

Blueprint planning. Blueprint planning is presented in the form of a process that reflects what the two companies look like when they are integrated. During the blueprint planning phase, Cisco will engage in a very detailed discussion with the target enterprise, which involves a very large number of details, such as whether a product is included in Cisco's pricing system, how the pricing structure is created, how to incorporate the target enterprise's product into the Cisco product family, and so on. The planning phase is a very detailed process. The blueprint not only shows

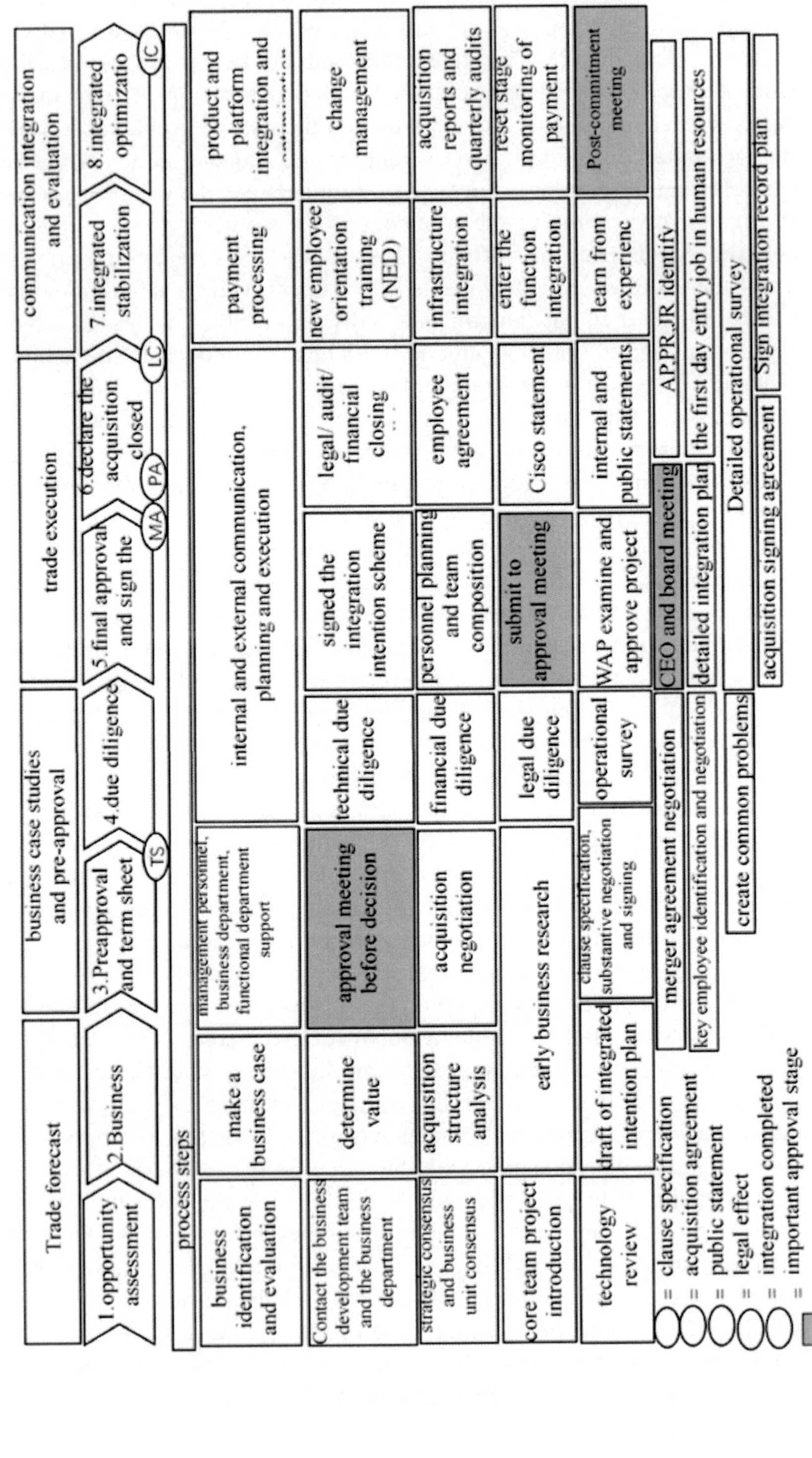

Fig. 2 Cisco's merger and acquisition integration process

the expected results, timetable and specific implementation plan of the merger, but also has important guiding significance for the acquisition operation. In developing a blueprint, the investment leader spends approximately 80% of his time communicating with the business unit to ensure that they understand all strategic details and that both parties are satisfied in the integration process to ensure the success of the merger and acquisition project.

Integration as part of the merger. Cisco's merger integration process is a complex process of 62 steps, with the merger beginning with an opportunity assessment, so subsequent consolidation issues are already being considered at the time of the opportunity assessment. Cisco's success rate of 70% in mergers and acquisitions demonstrates that the acquisition team knows exactly how to make the business successful from the start, so the goal is clear before the merger process is started. Cisco also places great emphasis on integration and treating integration and mergers and acquisitions as a whole, with close collaboration and a high degree of collaboration across the integration process. Cultural integration is the most difficult process of integration, and Cisco can achieve the same culture and core values regardless of how many companies are acquired. When observing an acquired company, Cisco understands and examines the culture of each and their characteristics at multiple levels. Leadership tries to digest and understand the cultural background and connotation of the other party in the pre-merger preparation process. If there are differences in culture between the two sides, the integration may be fostered through discussion and consultation, if necessary, but also compromise, and both may adapt to each other in order to achieve common goals. If leadership finds that the other party's culture does not really integrate successfully with Cisco culture, they may consider abandoning the merger. It is not Cisco's strategy for some multinationals to adopt a shark-like merger or acquisition model, regardless of whether the other side wants to do so. In doing overseas mergers and acquisitions, given the importance of globalization strategies, Cisco will think carefully about how to draw on the characteristics of the corporate culture of the acquisition and establish a common cultural benchmark to unite both and find success together.

Work effectively with external consulting firms. Cisco is very strict in selecting external consulting firms, and it is less likely to consider hiring an outside company unless it is particularly short of staff, typically involving contractors because of their low cost and efficiency. Even an outside consulting firm must adopt Cisco methodologies and processes if hired. Cisco often uses Deloitte's consulting services. In terms of fees, Deloitte is in the middle compared to competitors. Cisco's choice of Deloitte is not its own lack of acquiring-related capabilities, but rather is mainly based on the need to rely on each other's human resources. Cisco sets performance goals for consulting firms that match the company's bids, and when introducing consulting firms, its culture and code of conduct follow Cisco's system and follow Cisco's culture and values.

International mergers and acquisitions should pay more attention to attracting high-end talent. In overseas mergers and acquisitions, Cisco is very focused on maintaining and attracting the original team of the acquired company, especially the senior executives who are away from the U.S. headquarters. Although communication with the other party sometimes requires translation, Cisco's mergers and acquisitions team ensures that there is an opportunity to communicate with middle managers in the other business unit to understand their feelings about and expectations of the merger. Cisco believes the company will only be able to function properly after acquisition if the original group remains. At the same time, Cisco will embed its talent in the leadership team of the acquired company so that it can bring Cisco's culture into it. In the process, instead of sending airborne troops in to put them above each other, Cisco's managers are integrated into the other side's management team so that the team can better integrate into the Cisco headquarters network. The hardest part of mergers and acquisitions is methods for integrating the networks of large companies. After the merger is completed, Cisco will redecorate its office, placing all of Cisco's logos, banners, and image brands in the new office, so that the acquired company feels physically and psychologically integrated into Cisco. In such an environment, they develop a sense of identity, not a sense of alienation and being marginalized.

In summary, the key elements of Cisco's consolidation success are:

(1) Integration team, including specialized and experienced integration experts, professionals in areas highly relevant to the integration object, and backup external resources for the integration object.
(2) Early preparation, clear expectations, according to the results of planning.
(3) Paying attention to the feelings of customers, partners and employees to promote value transactions.
(4) Using information technology to facilitate the integration of transaction processes.
(5) Integrating the best employees and doing a good job in change management.

9 The M&A Cases in Cisco

Case I: Starent Company

Starent was founded in 2000 and went public in 2007. Headquartered in Tuxbury, Massachusetts, the company employs approximately 1,000 people worldwide. As of December 31, 2008, the company reported revenue of $254.1 million, an increase of 74% over the previous year.

Cisco's integration process consists of four phases: transaction outlook analysis, business case and pre-approval, transaction execution and communication, integration and evaluation, in eight phases, as follows:

Opportunity analysis. This is the first step in a merger to evaluate the companies that may be acquired and to determine whether the company meets the conditions of the Cisco merger based on the above-mentioned merger principles and development plans. For example, whether the company's outlook goals are consistent with Cisco's, whether the acquisition of the company will bring short- and long-term profitability, whether the target company's top executives are aligned with job adjustments, and so on. If one of these conditions is not met, Cisco may not make the acquisition. With Cisco's announcement of the acquisition of Starent, consolidation enters its second phase.

Business case, value assessment and analysis. Work to be done at this stage includes business case research and development, value assessment determination, merger and acquisition architecture analysis, early operational discovery, and integration planning. In this merger case, Cisco concludes that two things should be focused on early management meetings for consolidation: identifying common values and matching adjustments to product, market entry, and business prospects.

Pre-assessment and schedule. At this stage, Cisco held its first pre-approval meeting for a merger and acquisition project, and the merger integration process reached its first approval milestone. In addition, merger negotiations will be undertaken at this stage, a list of terms and an exclusive agreement (no-shop) will be completed, and a draft consolidation plan will be drawn up following the previous phase.

In the Starent case, the Cisco Integration team concluded that during the due diligence phase, the subject of due diligence needed to be analyzed against the core transaction strategy and value-driven elements of the acquisition, as well as a preliminary assessment of the integration impact factors in the investigation, as reflected in the financial model.

Due diligence. The issues to be undertaken at this stage include technical due diligence, financial and legal due diligence, business due diligence, negotiation of merger and acquisition agreements, identification and negotiation of key employees, such as the CEO of the former company, and, finally, the production of answers to frequently asked questions.

In the Starent case, Cisco concludes that early decisions should be made on the employment contracts of the acquired employees, assess ingenuities that may be encountered in future implementation, and seek solutions. As work agreements are reached step by step, obstacles will gradually decrease.

Final approval and signing. This phase is a critical decision-making phase in which Cisco will finalize the details of the merger intent and merger consolidation through the first four phases. During this phase, a final approval meeting is held to finalize an intention to consolidate the plan, a VAP approval is initiated, and a briefing is made to the CEO and board of directors to refine the integration plan and operational system, leading to an agreement.

Key points from Cisco's summary are the harmonization of regulatory communication tools to cope with the next corporate shutdown, the consolidation of grants to allow merger and acquisition consolidation to take place quickly, and the use of an integrated approach to buy into the company by Starent's leadership.

Announce the merger to close. From this stage onwards, the acquisition of Starent has officially entered the phase of integration. This phase requires company employees to sign an agreement with Cisco and issue a notice to Starent within the company and the public to announce that the company is in the closing phase, and to conduct a detailed functional evaluation to end the consolidation logging program.

In the Starent case, Cisco concludes that at this stage it is important to build relationships with people in the integration team and to focus on stabilizing those employees affected by the merger, including Cisco and Target. At the beginning of this phase, go to the target company to make field trips and ensure the unification of internal and external messages.

Integration stabilization phase (1–100 days). On the first day of consolidation, the target company completes a legal shutdown. Cisco needs to change the way it manages and communicates, prepares sales and channels, and starts enabling employees. In the Starent project, Cisco attached great importance to activities and communication on the first day of integration, and changes in management were significant.

During the 1–100 days of consolidation, Cisco completes the payment process for acquisitions, trains new employees, integrates organizational structures, and integrates into the market. In the Starent project, Cisco uses public events to build momentum, such as the mobile phone world. Use cross-company sales to mobilize the corporate atmosphere in the integration process. At this stage, Cisco begins to translate the operations of the target company into Cisco's operational model and expected behavior and redefines the positioning framework for new employees based on business expectations. Cisco uses a management framework to overcome difficulties in the integration process.

Integration optimization phase (after 100 days). This phase is the optimization phase of integration, in which the primary task is to optimize the integration platform, and complete merger and acquisition reports and quarterly reviews. In Starent acquisitions, Cisco focused on maintaining the power of consolidation and adjusting its plans as needed, but always focusing on long-term goals. Cisco places a strong focus on the situation of its employees, ensuring that all employees are 100% active after the merger and acquisition. At the same time, Cisco focuses on quarterly reviews of consolidation. Eventually, in the final stage, the target company is introduced into the company's mainstream business.

Case 2: Tandberg

The Tandberg merger is a good example of how Cisco is using mergers and acquisitions as a corporate strategy. When Cisco looked at the collaborative market, it found that it had a lot of potential: it was worth $34 billion and was growing rapidly. Cisco has entered this market with telepresence technology before, but it cannot complete the entire product delivery process on its own. Cisco realized that the portfolio could be built faster through mergers and acquisitions, enabling the delivery of collaboration products independently.

At the time, Tandberg was the world's second largest manufacturer of video conferencing equipment. Cisco has a strong brand, strong customer relationships and smooth sales channels, and an authoritative Internet solution. Tandberg mastered advanced video conferencing live broadcast technology, so the two technologies have the possibility of convergence, and in the product portfolio can play a complementary role. In addition, Cisco believes that the channels and consumers that Tandberg bring can effectively drive Cisco's growth in the video market. At the same time, both Cisco and Tandberg share a "people-oriented" vision and similar core cultural values. All these have laid a good foundation for successful integration. Cisco finally chose Tandberg.

In October 2009, Cisco announced a $3.4 billion acquisition of Tambo. Cisco at this point had built long and strong track record in mergers and acquisitions. As of August 2010, Cisco has completed more than 140 acquisitions. Of these, Tandberg was Cisco's biggest cross-border acquisition as far as the time. Given the complexity of the acquisition and the size of Cisco and Tandberg's global presence, the Tambo merger has faced the following challenges: first, to manage negotiations, second, to develop a consolidation plan, and to consolidate and manage it.

To overcome the difficulties in the merger, Cisco and Tandberg's top executives held numerous video conferences to negotiate deals and terms of employment, kept in touch with the bank at all times to clarify their financial contracts, and launched an integration program to ensure that every Tandberg employee has a new job because the merger is not about creating a property crisis for anyone. It's about making progress for both companies.

The success of a merger also depends on the integration, and the success of the integration depends on the attitude of the management team. Cisco formally completed its acquisition of Tandberg in April 2010 because of the smooth integration strategy. In the 30 days of the deal, Cisco hosted more than 40 "ice-breaking" events, connecting more than 1,000 Cisco and Tandberg employees.

With the integration of Tandberg into Cisco, Cisco has provided a full range of support, especially in the common technology development, and soon after Cisco launched the consumer version of The Cisco "TelePresence" video conferencing system, creating the world-renowned audio video conferencing webcast solution This high-end brand is worth $34 billion and is growing rapidly.

Other facts also prove that Cisco's acquisition of Tandberg has been a success: more than 97% of its employees remained in office, market share continues to grow as a result of the business merger, more than 1,200 partners have been invited to join the new Telepresence video licensing technology provider program, and the sales team remains highly aggressive during such a dramatic change. Orders rose more than 30% in the first quarter, and momentum continued unabated in the second quarter.

Experience the Telepresence conference

The acquisition benefits Cisco in three areas: first, creating market opportunities to increase the company's wealth; Although Cisco's acquisition of Tandberg cost about $3.4 billion, the acquisition of Tandberg has resulted in even greater profits for Cisco from a long-term development perspective as Cisco has captured changes in the Internet and video markets in a timely manner. Now, Cisco believes that it is this merger that makes the company the leading provider of video and collaboration products.

10 Summary

Mergers and acquisitions reflect the ability of enterprises to integrate external resources quickly and effectively, and how to integrate the resources into the original system of the enterprise to create new value together is part of the dynamic evolution ability of enterprises. Cisco's mergers and acquisitions are an important part of its dynamic evolution, strategic transformation, innovation and technology system differentiation. Merger is the process of internalizing external knowledge, managing external talents, technology, knowledge and ability and enterprises facilitates an effective integration of the system, and co-creates the new value realized by each other, determining whether the merger is successful or not. The key to Cisco's choice of mergers and acquisitions as part of its innovation system is that in a highly competitive and fast-growing environment, leading companies may overlook new technologies and markets with future potential value, especially those that could lead to aggressive innovation. At the same time, the speed, flexibility and acumen of research and development among leading companies is likely to be less than those of small businesses, thereby depriving them of opportunities for technology and market transformation. However, the sales channels, brands and capital that large enterprises have to cover the global market are precisely the resources that small businesses need to translate research and development into market value. In this context, the advantages of large enterprises and small enterprises complement each other and resources, so that the two sides in the fierce market competition complement each other.

Mergers and acquisitions are part of the enterprise strategy and innovation system. For fast-growing high-tech enterprises, successful mergers and acquisitions are an important starting point for the success of enterprise evolution and transformation. Cisco's success is primarily due to the expertise it trains in the field of mergers and acquisitions, a complete set of processes and methodologies, and the knowledge built up through continuous learning and refinement of lessons learned. Effective analysis and management of the various potential risks and issues encountered in the merger process, from project scanning and due diligence, to process control and management of mergers and acquisitions, every detail and step is to ensure that the acquired company's talent, technology, systems can achieve rapid and effective docking and integration with Cisco. Cisco's basic principles in choosing an acquired company help it filter and focus on the businesses that will really be with them in the future. At the same time, Cisco's emphasis on acquired talent and technology reflects its greater emphasis on the future value and development of the acquired company.

The core goal of mergers and acquisitions is to enhance the differentiation of product systems. Some enterprises may become large scale in a short period of time through mergers and acquisitions, but more in depth research around how to do this well. Cisco, in selecting the acquired enterprise, takes its existing technology and product system as its core, and selects those enterprises that can establish deep connections with existing technology and product systems, enhance the differentiation of its own technology and product system, and have rich technology and product ecology. The differentiation of this technology and product system has brought unique competitive advantages and premium capabilities to Cisco's future development, while also raising barriers to technological catch-up and meeting the market's need for a new product portfolio, especially providing the basis for a comprehensive solution and transformation from a product-led enterprise to a service-led enterprise. In other words, Cisco is able to deliver more integrated solutions through continuous acquisitions, rapid acquisition of new technical capabilities, transition slots into new markets, and expand and combine more comprehensive technology systems. In this process of evolution, mergers and acquisitions serve to achieve the optimization and reorganization of talent, technology, products and market capabilities. They may also eliminate the industry-leading enterprise thinking solidification, technology system aging, organizational rigidity and development of stagnant large enterprise disease, through the injection of the vitality of small and medium-sized enterprises to bring enterprises to new development space.

Chapter 6
Strategic Alliance and Partnership Management

1 Introduction

Strategic alliance refers to the relationship between one or more organizations through the integration of resources, in which the participants can continue to create high value. Between enterprises that form strategic alliances, the first is due to the product and technology life cycles that may be getting shorter. The market gives companies an opportunity window that is limited, and thus requires the enterprise to occupy the global market quickly, when the enterprise may lack internal resources but can get external resources through strategic alliances to achieve success. Next, enterprise expectations in cities seek to obtain a larger share and stronger economies of scale to participate in the competition and achieve good investment returns. However, it may be difficult to obtain the necessary resources and capabilities in the whole value chain to acquire an enterprise, therefore, in order to expand the industry value chain in the ecological status and influence, other resources and the ability of enterprises to form alliances is important. Finally, customers have higher expectations and higher degrees of personalization. Both enterprise customers and consumers want more integrated comprehensive solutions and one-stop services to meet their needs. This pressure also urges enterprises to provide competitive products and services through strategic alliances.

The parties to a strategic alliance should share assets, technologies and resources and focus on developing a strategic long-term and stable relationship. Typically, there are five types of strategic alliances: joint ventures, investment alliances, sales alliances, regional alliances, and solution alliances.

Strategic alliances usually have four characteristics: first, significant business influence and sustainable value among the participants. Significant means that strategic alliances have strategic value for all stakeholders; sustainability means that everyone can achieve a satisfactory profit margin over a period of several years. Second, strong organizational commitment from all participants is critical. This commitment must be passed down from the CEO, with senior management team members having a clear sense of ownership and responsibility in the strategic alliance.

X. Dong et al., *Cisco*,
https://doi.org/10.1007/978-981-19-7870-8_6

Third, each party of the strategic alliance has the input of talents, capital or intellectual property. Fourth, consistency and coordination of strategy must occur. The participants share the same goals and, although their cultures may differ, mutual trust and dialogue mechanisms must be established.

A partnership is a relationship with a supplier or distributor that includes operational (short term), tactical (medium term), and strategic (long term) partnerships. Two or more partner entities can create a collaborative solution for joint selling, resales based on accurate competitive intelligence sharing, value chain integrated marketing, etc. Both parties reduce common costs and utilize new approaches to enhance competitive advantage.

The difference between a strategic alliance and a partnership is that a strategic alliance is a long-term and stable strategic relationship based on mutual recognition of each other's value, while a partnership is a special project or sales system based on mutual benefit formed according to market and customer needs.

2 Value Orientation of Strategic Alliance

Strategic alliances are an important part of Cisco's strategy. Through the establishment of alliance relationship, Cisco has built the industry platform and industry standard with Cisco as the core. The relationship between Cisco and its strategic alliance is like a marriage. Cisco makes high commitments, and it also guarantees that it will meet with its allies every three or four months, hoping that the relationship will be closer than just financial communication.

Cisco sought strategic alliances in the first place because early leaders considered that Cisco needed allies as it had far less influence in the industry than Microsoft or Intel. Second, Cisco is unlikely to acquire all ancillary and potential replacement technologies, and executives are reluctant to acquire technologies that deviate too far from the company's core technologies. Finally, the strategic alliance will directly benefit the marketing of Cisco, which will help Cisco establish smooth sales channels worldwide and bring greater market opportunities.

Under the following four circumstances, Cisco will choose strategic alliances and partners. First, from the perspective of providing solutions, Cisco can provide better solutions and corresponding supporting services to customers by cooperating with its partners. Cisco creates a strong business process and business plan, and partners provide complementary hardware and software so that both parties can identify more business opportunities, add new revenue streams, and expand the size of the deal. This value chain is accomplished by Cisco and its partners, who provide Cisco with complementary technologies and expertise to make up for its own shortcomings. Cisco combines its technical capabilities with the marketing capabilities of its partners to form a Shared value chain. Cisco alone cannot do all work required to move up the value chain.

Take Cisco in the mechanical field: Cisco has no prior experience in this field, and its partners have significant advantages in mechanical manufacturing, such as robotic arms. However, the partners used to use the dedicated network platform, through collaboration with Cisco, thus making its products more common, and Cisco therefore entered new markets, opening up new business opportunities.

Second, from the perspective of innovation, Cisco has three modes of innovation: independent research and development, external acquisition and cooperative development. For a large enterprise like Cisco, it is very difficult to carry out internal innovation, so Cisco will adopt merger and acquisition strategy when new technologies emerge. For example, Cisco has acquired many enterprises in cloud computing. In some cases, Cisco does not own the core technology, but if the target enterprise is large, Cisco may not be able to complete the merger or the merger cost may be too high, in which case Cisco may use the cooperative development approach to innovation. Cisco, for example, has been working on a unified computing platform since 2007, in which it collaborates with external companies (such as Intel, VMware, oracle and Microsoft) on everything from hardware and products to software and hardware packaging.

Third, from a market perspective, through partners, Cisco can bypass mergers and quickly enter markets with high barriers. It is expensive for companies to enter a new market, but Cisco thinks it can do so by seeking partners in nearby markets. For example, the market of Apple, REIM, HTC, Samsung and other mobile phone manufacturers is not the market that Cisco will enter, but these voice access devices are related to networks, and Ip-based networks are Cisco's strength; thus, Cisco cooperates with them to enter the network market of voice access devices.

At the same time, such a partnership can also stimulate the demand for the current and future products of both sides, because different companies think from different perspectives. Such close partnerships can enable both sides to think from a multi-dimensional perspective, create sparks and come up with new ideas to expand the market together.

Fourth, from a financial and distribution channel perspective, this partnership can increase Cisco's revenue. Cisco's partners create and increase demand for existing and to-be-produced products, through which Cisco gets 80% of its profits; meanwhile, 14% of Cisco's products are sold directly by the company, and the remaining 86% are ordered by partners. The value created by strategic alliances and partners for Cisco is reflected in expanded sales and service channels, hardware and software support, the convergence of new technologies through technical mutual support, seizing new markets quickly, and industrial transformation and evolution through partners.

Cisco tries to maintain long-term, strategic relationships with its partners, but sometimes companies may decide not to work with Cisco because of conflicts of interest. However, for Cisco, it is still necessary to maintain a good relationship with its partners, because each is of great strategic significance to Cisco. With the development of the market, the two sides may have more cooperative opportunities in the future. Of course, in order to avoid the loss caused by the unilateral withdrawal of partners, Cisco will list six to eight independent action plans before the action to ensure the final success.

3 Evolution of Cisco's Strategic Alliance

Partnerships based on expanded marketing. In the 1990s, Cisco sought marketing and service relationships with partners to form alliances with manufacturers of complementary products. Such companies including Japan's electronics industry, mainly in the field of Internet and wireless communications enterprises (such as NEC, Hitachi, Fujitsu and Softbank, etc.) and IBM (Cisco, one of the major partners; began selling Cisco equipment in 1992, at the same time combined Cisco products with their own products; eventually IBM gave up their own network manufacturing equipment to become the most Cisco equipment sales intermediaries).

Product-based partnerships. The goal of Cisco's alliance with hub makers, most importantly Hewlett-Packard, is to combine their products with routers made by Cisco. HP has been an important partner for Cisco, first in hubs and later in ATM and LAN products.

Partnerships based on technology promotion. Looking for partners in the exchange technology market, Cisco's strategy is to make IOS software widely available to users at the lowest cost to promote it as an industry standard. In the early days, Cisco licensed IOS software to Cascade and 20 other companies to help them implement routing on phone switches. Then Cisco teamed up with MCI to develop wireless services and manufacturing. Cooperate with NEC to develop ATM switch technology; Alliance with Nortel, into Ethernet LAN switching technology area.

In the late 1990s, Microsoft, Intel and Cisco formed a network of multimedia links. Chambers had been reluctant to join the alliance of potential competitors, but as Microsoft and Intel began to use their hardware and software to enter the lower end of the networking market, Cisco inevitably had to work with competitors as it grew. However, as Mr. Chambers expected, conflicts soon arose: some of the core software of the three companies is functionally redundant, and Cisco competes directly with Intel in hardware networking products. Although Cisco and Microsoft worked together on areas such as multimedia security and network directory services, the alliance eventually collapsed after Intel pulled out a year after it was launched.

Partnerships based on customers' overall solutions. Cisco has teamed up with consulting firms such as Cambridge technologies partners, Ernst & Young and KPMG (which helped Cisco build its internal Internet systems) to advise clients on how to build internet-based information systems and set up the Internet business solutions group. For example, an alliance was formed with AT&T to add value to network solutions; Cisco allied with PeopleSoft for large enterprise web-based applications.

As you can see in this process, Cisco has moved from manufacturing individual products to integrating technologies and providing business solutions. In this process of evolution, Cisco has become more and more demanding and dependent on its partners, who provide increasing added value. In the process, partners can continue to increase profitability (and Cisco will make sure of that), so Cisco's market path will widen.

In fiscal 2008, more than 80% of Cisco's revenue came from partners, which means partners generated nearly $32 billion in revenue for Cisco. Cisco employs more than 15,000 salespeople worldwide, a number that would rise to 282,000 if the sales force of its 55,000 channel partners were included, almost 20 times as many as Cisco's own.

4 Main Types of Partners

Cisco has five types of partners: supplement manufacturers, service providers (e.g., AT&T, BT, Orange), systems and technology companies (e.g., Apple, IBM, etc.), consulting firms (e.g., Capgemini, ACS, CSC, etc.), and strategic consulting firms (e.g., McKinsey & Company, etc.). The peripheral part of the company, for the non-core part of Cisco's business, realizes the rapid response to market changes by outsourcing to partners.

Cisco's sales partners are very important. 80% of the revenue from product sales is sold online and through channels in more than 100 countries. Cisco's sales channels include direct sales (14%), service provider channels (17%), resellers and secondary resellers (15%), value added resellers, and system integrators (54%). Overall, 86% of Cisco's orders go to partners. Enterprises in different stages of development have different partners, and in the mature stage, more partners.

- Direct sales channel: mainly refers to the branches located in different places, selling new products to large enterprise users.
- Tier 1 partner: a system integrator who has a direct contractual relationship with Cisco to sell its mature products.
- Tier-2 partners: dealers and resellers. Resellers buy Cisco products from resellers and sell them to customers, mature products aimed at small and medium enterprise users.

Cisco's sales channels have changed significantly with the development of the enterprise. Cisco began working with tier 1 partners in the early 1990s to expand distribution channels; with the increasingly fierce competition in the network equipment industry, Cisco began to add two-tier partners from 1996, and expanded the product sales target from the top 1000 companies to the top 4000 companies in the world, and extended the product sales antenna to small and medium-sized enterprise users.

In terms of product distribution channel selection, Cisco's original approach was to use direct sales for new products, with large routers sold by tier 1 partners and more mature and less expensive products sold by tier 2 partners. The problem with this approach is that different products sold at different times, if there is a price difference in different sales channels, will have an impact on the high-priced channels. In order to avoid channel conflict, Cisco no longer adopts the method of product differentiation in channel separation, but takes customer scale as the dividing standard, and at the same time adopts a different discount structure and certification system to distinguish between dealers.

Cisco will consider looking for partners before entering a large new market, because partners can make it much cheaper for Cisco to enter the city. When choosing partners in new markets, Cisco gives priority to the market share and regional advantages of potential partners but does not choose partners based entirely on the market share it already has. For example, at the beginning of the cooperation between Cisco and apple in the field of mobile phones, apple's dominant share in the mobile phone market was zero, but Cisco saw the unique features of its products, so finally decided to cooperate with Apple.

5 Evolution of the Evaluation Mechanism of Sales Partners

For larger sales partners to provide a greater discount in Cisco retail and distribution in the process of the old tradition, this way to make some of the biggest partners use quantity discount they buy a lot of Cisco equipment, at the time of Cisco 55,000 partners, one of the biggest 10 partners accounted for more than 10% of the total business Cisco. But as a result of this approach, Cisco's partners tend to sell equipment quickly by volume, regardless of pre-sales and post-sales needs. This practice is in conflict with Cisco's values of giving its customers the greatest attention, so Cisco must step in from time to time to ensure that customers are getting the value they need.

By 2001, Cisco came to rethink certain policies to ensure it was meeting its own standards. Cisco's ideal partners should be able to provide real value for customers, which means a partner is required to provide to the customer the biggest technical problem-solving skills, have unique insights, the vertical segment of customer focus, and even hire a certain number of certified, specially trained staff. While such a shift could mean a fundamental game-changer for Cisco's big old Allies by accepting different terms of engagement, Cisco decided it had to. Only by creating a competitive arena that encourages the right values can Cisco's partners shift the focus from competing for profits to delivering benefits to customers.

As a result, Cisco needs to redefine how it rewards its "best partners", not by volume discounts but by performance. Cisco plans to reward companies that design complete "end-to-end" solutions for customers, as well as those that help Cisco win big customers or gain a foothold in new vertical markets. By redefining the way partners are evaluated and incentivized, Cisco enables partners to stand united and serve to maximize customer value.

6 Treatment of Partners' Interests

Cisco's strategy is to take the value chain as the core, through the common value innovation to take advantage of each. In this process, Cisco attaches great importance to the relationship of trust between each other and maintains the partnership through a common governance framework, a common vision, a constructive dialogue mechanism and a code of conduct. As a strategic cooperation, Cisco commits to maintaining the partnership with each other for at least 3–5 years. The partnership will end as soon as one party damages the other.

Cisco may encounter a situation where the interest demands are quite different from those of its partners. At this time, Cisco and its partners will make a list of requirements before the cooperation, indicating what Cisco wants to achieve through cooperation and what the partners want to achieve to ensure that both parties can achieve their goals.

As for the distribution of partners' profits, Cisco first made clear what profits could be given up before negotiating with partners and reached an internal consensus. At the same time, the goal is to make the pie bigger through teamwork, and as long as the new market share continues to grow, Cisco can make more concessions in profits. During negotiations, both sides should keep communicating with each other on this issue. If the other thinks that the profit distribution is not equal, the cooperative relationship may be easily destroyed.

Sometimes, partners are concerned that Cisco's entry into the market will affect their own position in the market. Cisco's solution to this problem is to make a list of what the other party wants before cooperating, and clearly state how Cisco intends to accomplish it and what value Cisco can provide to its partners. For example, Cisco has very strong sales channels. Cisco has a very large share of the switch and router market. Many other companies do not have the technology or foundation to allow their products to enter this market. But Cisco still works with these companies in this area and benefits from it. The reason for this is that Cisco hopes to use its technology and market advantages to bring more value to each other.

In summary, the key elements of Cisco's successful partnership development are:

The change of cooperation mode should be consistent with the change of market and enterprise strategy. In the process of personalized product generation, technical specialization, integration technology, business solutions and other aspects, the development of partners should be consistent with the development of Cisco. Cisco is looking for partners that fit its business model. When Cisco wants to integrate into different industries, it can achieve industrial transformation and evolution through partners.

The partners should take the value chain as the core and give play to their unique advantages. Cisco's partnership with its partners is centered around the value chain. When it comes to core new businesses, Cisco will buy if it cannot do it itself. For the parts that are not Cisco's core business, if Cisco is not skilled in the area, it will adopt alliance strategy. By then, Cisco had completed 160 mergers and acquisitions and had 30,000 business partners. Cisco will adjust the merger and alliance strategy according to the industry situation. A merger represents total control. If strong control is not required, Cisco will become a partner with the other party.

Build a comprehensive relationship of trust. Cisco has built a bond of trust with its partners, and the main factor in achieving this is how they work together to create value. It needs to be clear what the goals of each company are and turn them into a code of conduct. If one party steals the other's technology, the relationship quickly ends. In addition, Cisco and its partners conduct staff training together, share their visions, and truly open up; Then establish a good personal relationship, so that there is a deep relationship of trust between individuals. This may lead to a common governance framework and constructive dialogue.

Build alliances for competitive advantage. Cisco sees strategic alliances as strategies that promise a partnership to last at least three to five years (if the partnership is too short, it's just a strategic alliance, profitable but ultimately difficult to build trust).

Distribution of profits between partners. The distribution of profits between partners is also a major concern for Cisco. Before negotiating with its partners, Cisco identified what profits it could forego and reached a consensus within the company. At this point, the CEO's opinion is very important. Cisco and its partners will work together to expand the market share pie. Cisco believes that as long as the new market share can continue to grow, it can make more concessions in terms of profits. In the process of negotiation, it is necessary to communicate constantly, because once the other side thinks that the profit distribution is not equal, the relationship is easily destroyed.

Success factors and evaluation of strategic alliances. According to Cisco, there are five key factors for the success of strategic alliances: agreement, understanding of industry positioning, distribution of reasonable profits, a clear management model, and quantification of performance. At the same time, the following indicators are used to evaluate the success of cooperation: trust, business model, industry evaluation, local needs of the value chain, core and peripheral capacity building, optimization of scalable and repeatable business model, effectiveness of personnel training, etc.

It can be seen from the above that in the cooperation between Cisco and its partners, "win–win new business path" is the constant theme. In today's continuously developing society and changing user needs, it is only by seeking flexibility based on the win–win principle that Cisco can finally pave the way for common successful development of its partners, end users and Cisco.

7 Construction of Partner Ecosystem

Cisco's approach to the market will create an architecture that includes all of its partners. This framework will also provide a roadmap through which Cisco can assign roles to its partners.

Cisco's approach to adding partners comes in stages. Many partners are not necessarily the best partners in this segment, but Cisco will gradually add partners in this phased way.

The cooperation between Cisco and its partners will obtain the commitment of each partner, so that Cisco will provide differentiated products to the market and create a certain market height, so that people will be willing to use Cisco's products.

The collaboration between Cisco and its partners is unprecedented, bringing together CEOs from different companies to create a billion-dollar application. Cisco has taken its partners to the next level, collaborating with them to create a competitive advantage, drive products, and create solutions that customers are looking for.

Cisco does not have a service product, but it has generated a demand of $1 billion, which makes Cisco and its partners enthusiastic about developing this product. Cisco has also devised a joint venture structure to ensure that partners are highly aligned with Cisco. A joint venture structure can announce Cisco's commitment to other partners in the ecosystem, while also limiting product overlap between service participants, making better commitments to customers, and developing a sustainable approach to integrated development.

At the same time, Cisco will create a new business model that will make products available to its customers in a way that has never been done before. In managed services, for example, Cisco has partnerships with large companies that provide global services with which Cisco products can be packaged and sold.

8 Impact of Partners on Cisco's Value Chain

The partners influence Cisco's value chain in three ways: first, they expand Cisco's sales and service channels (geographic areas, integrated solutions, vertical experience); Second, Cisco and its partners support each other in software and hardware. Third, Cisco and its partners support each other in technology provision. Hundreds of Cisco technology partners contribute expertise that enables Cisco and its partners to bring together new technologies that complement Cisco technologies. In addition, in some cases, mergers are too expensive, and through partners Cisco can bypass them and quickly enter markets with high barriers. At the same time, Cisco's partners have created and increased demand for existing and to-be produced products (14% of Cisco's products are sold directly by the company, the remaining 86% are booked by partners: 54% through primary resellers, 15% through secondary resellers for smes, and 17% through service providers).

Partners are so important to Cisco that Cisco takes a set of steps to ensure that the partnership is successful. Cisco identifies five areas with its partners: first, revenue metrics. Whether it's Cisco's own sales or those of its partners, sometimes the goal is to increase market share, rather than making profit a core measurement. Second, the partnership is not focused on one project, but a series of projects with partners, gradually, so as to ensure success. Third, the customer approves the project. Fourth, how different business models align. Fifth, executives on both sides of the partnership establish standards that are scored at each review. Cisco has summed up these five points to be confirmed in continuous practice. If these five points are achieved, cooperation will often have a high success rate. And these details will be confirmed in the cooperation contract between the two sides, so as to provide a solid backing for the partnership.

9 Summary

In a highly dynamic market environment, the industrial structure and pattern often change, and it is difficult for an enterprise to compete with powerful rivals when it is fighting alone. From internal ability, every enterprise has its own unique competitive advantage, but, if it is difficult to leading the industry in all aspects of competitive advantage, needs through strategic alliances with partners to build industry ecosystem, seeking common development space, the enterprise, through the resources complementary form relatively stable and safe environment of survival and development, at the same time, brings to the competitors to enter the barriers and obstacles.

The relationship management between strategic alliance and cooperative partner is an important part of enterprises' ability to obtain resources. Cisco is known for its technical and engineering capabilities. However, the market capability of technology enterprises is also important. The technology development is so fast that if the technology products cannot be quickly marketed, the market opportunities may be lost in a short period of time. As a result, Cisco outsources 80% of its market capacity. Through partners, Cisco can bypass mergers and acquisitions, quickly enter markets with high barriers, or through partners, reach customers it cannot reach, or reduce the cost and risk of entering a new market.

Seeking win–win results is the basis for ensuring long-term partnership. Cisco is closely interdependent with its partners, forming a set of methods for selecting, managing and evaluating partners to ensure the stability and reliability of the relationship. In this process, Cisco takes the value chain as the analytical framework. The partners have their own uniqueness in the value chain. They are complementary and dependent on each other. At the same time, a common governance framework, Shared vision, communication and dialogue mechanisms, and common codes of conduct are also important for building trust between partners. In order to maintain a stable and reliable relationship, reasonable distribution of benefits is also crucial as an important part of the core interests. Cisco aims to make the pie as big as possible by clarifying which profits are negotiable and ensuring that the partnership has value for all parties.

Chapter 7
Build Highly Adaptable Corporate Culture

1 Introduction

Culture is made up of common values, understandings, assumptions and goals. Culture is strongly inherited, passed down from the previous generation, influenced by the current generation and passed on to the future generation. Social and cultural differences exist between countries or regions, and organizational culture differences exist between different organizations, companies, institutions or groups. Organizational culture reflects the expectations, codes of conduct and common goals of members of an organization. Organizational culture is influenced and changed by national cultural values, as well as by social culture. Culture has a strong influence on management. Some people believe that the influence of culture is more significant at the individual level than at the organizational level, which is the result of assimilation. Assimilation refers to an individual's management style moving closer to that of other individuals. When we try to impose our system of values on other societies, the impact of culture on the way we are managed will be significant. The way many people in the world understand and communicate with others is always based on their own cultural background. This tendency is called the self-acceptance criterion. The research team of Global Leadership and Organizational Behavior Effectiveness (GLOBE) summarized the research on cultural dimensions in recent years and defined nine cultural dimensions. These nine cultural dimensions can effectively distinguish different social and cultural characteristics and have important management significance. They are confidence, future orientation, performance orientation, humanity orientation, gender difference, avoidance of uncertainty, power scope, collectivism and individualism, and groupism. Professor Hofstede's famous research puts forward four value dimensions to measure cultural characteristics: Power scope, uncertainty avoidance, individualism tendency and "resolute" values. The scope of power refers to the acceptable degree of unequal distribution of power in a society. Uncertainty avoidance refers to the degree of environmental uncertainty that people can accept. The tendency of individualism refers to the degree to which people consider the interests of individuals, small groups and society. The

X. Dong et al., *Cisco*,
https://doi.org/10.1007/978-981-19-7870-8_7

value view of "fortitude" is a kind of value form based on the traditional view, which is dominated by self-confidence, materialism and lack of concern for others.

In the view of Cisco, corporate culture is the code of conduct for leaders when they are not present. The formation of culture is formed by the life experience of leaders. It is the projection of the personal behaviors of the top leaders and reflects the behaviors and values of leaders. Differences in leaders' values and codes of conduct contribute to differences in corporate culture. For example, Oracle's corporate culture is shark culture, while Cisco's focuses on and emphasizes team spirit.

2 Core Values in the Cultural System

Cisco's corporate culture has 12 core values: Customer success, high quality team, empowerment, outreach, market transformation, teamwork, open communication, no technology worship, accountability, fairness, integrity, culture, fun, frugality. Chambers has repeatedly stressed in his reports that leaders need to build trust with their employees, treat others with respect, and find opportunities for self-criticism when they make mistakes. Cisco's egalitarian culture is reflected in the company's daily routines, such as leaders having the same size offices and parking Spaces as employees. As for the reimbursement of travel expenses, the company only pays the coach expenses, while the first-class expenses need to be paid by itself. One of Cisco's Asia–pacific chief executives once mentioned that his office is the same size as Chambers' when he chose Cisco over the good conditions of his former company, which also shows the influence of Cisco's egalitarian culture.

Interactive Conversions with Chambers

Customer success. "Cisco doesn't have a technology cult," Chambers says. "Listening to customers is the most important thing. He attaches great importance to customers' Suggestions and complaints and spends 55% of his time dealing with them. He stays connected with 15 key customers by phone every day, and deals with problems as soon as he finds them. In his first 10 years, he contacted 10,000 clients and attended more than 200 mass meetings.[1] in fact, Cisco's leaders have always placed the needs and interests of their customers in the highest strategic position and regarded them as the most important mission and primary value in Cisco's corporate culture. Cisco believes that only by helping customers succeed can an enterprise succeed. Cisco, which has grown from $18 billion to $53 billion, has been looking for growth in line with the needs of its customers. In 1993, Boeing, which used Cisco's routers, told Cisco they would order converters from Crescendo and stop buying Cisco's routers because Cisco did not have them. To meet this demand, Cisco acquired Crescendo, which became one of Cisco's most successful businesses. Another example is when Cisco provided technology products to insurance companies, customers complained about the complexity of software installation and wanted Cisco as a consultant. Driven by customer demand, Cisco bought related software companies. In 2001, Cisco was impacted by customer complaints about the quality of its server products. Mr. Chambers says the company needs to change its culture and improve the quality of its products for its customers. Cisco's culture is to gradually integrate customer needs and products into the system by listening to customers.

To build a sense of importance to customers across the company, Cisco linked customer satisfaction directly to employee bonuses. If the score is low, the company would ruthlessly deduct a large part of the employee bonus. Cisco takes two steps to improve customer satisfaction: Open forums and case banks. The function of open forums is to help customers solve complex technical problems. The forum answers customer questions in the following steps: Analyze the question, after the key words in the "customer online service questions and answers" search for the answer; at the end of the search, the system will provide a series of solutions based on previous experience, and provides the answer to the customer according to the matching degree of the keyword. If after the search the system fails to return the relevant answer or the answer fails to meet the customer's requirements, the customer can rephrase the question in a different way, or send the question to a Cisco professional by clicking the "Send to Forum" button. If they cannot come up with an answer that satisfies the customer, the system creates a new case named after the customer in the case library of Cisco's technical services center, which is then answered by a senior customer service specialist. These experts are knowledgeable and experienced, and they can answer questions on the spot or after conducting appropriate tests or asking other departments for assistance. When customers submit their questions to an open forum, the company sends them an email prompting them to read the answers. After the customer accepts the answer, the question and the answer are added to the database

[1] Guang Yang, Xin Yang. Why Cisco Surpassed Microsoft's Network Culture [J]. Chinese and Foreign Management, 2000, (7).

of the customer's online service system. In the future, similar problems of other customers can be solved by searching the database.[2]

The customer-centric culture is also reflected in the incentive mechanism for dealers. The traditional incentive mechanism is based on the number of sales of dealers, rather than on the value they create for customers to decide which offer they will seek, but cannot encourage dealers to provide more value-added services and create more new knowledge for customers. To address this, Cisco has reduced the use of "volume" to determine commissions, encouraging dealers to help customers succeed by improving service quality and adding value.

High quality team. "A strong, high-quality workforce will help Cisco remain the industry leader and make Cisco the best place to work in the world," Chambers said. The fundamental factor of an enterprise's success lies in the joint efforts and contributions of high-quality employees. In order to build a high-quality team, new employees must be strictly vetted, and all employees must be required to adhere to the principle of organizational interests over personal interests. Leadership should not be limited to only a few people. Organizations should try their best to cultivate future leaders. This personal leadership gives employees room to grow and enables the organization to attract high-quality candidates. Once the right opportunities are identified, the company will focus on training and employing high potential employees and develop them into leaders who can adapt to future changes. Of course, companies will not always hesitate to fire the wrong people, and, no matter how talented, some staff will be asked to leave.

Authorization. In many enterprises, the most decision-making power is usually held at the top level. In Cisco, managers of different business units have certain entrepreneurial consciousness and enjoy certain decision-making power. Chambers not only puts a lot of responsibility on other executives, but also gives Cisco employees a chance to feel that they are really doing something unique. By being empowered, valued and given the opportunity to use their talents, great people are motivated to be creative, dedicated and enterprising. In such a system, the senior management of each department is tightly integrated to form a cohesive whole and work together to achieve the strategic goals of the company.

Stretch your goals. Extension goals are about encouraging employees to do what others think is impossible and to push themselves beyond their limits. Chambers expects employees to find solutions to achieve their goals as much as possible, to expand and exceed their capabilities, which can effectively motivate employees to adopt distinctive new methods to achieve their goals, and to stimulate the work team to make continuous progress to achieve higher professional standards. But Chambers does not require all employees meet that goal, but rather to do their best; even if the extension goal is not reached, the enthusiasm of employees is mobilized, and their efforts are significantly improved, thus promoting the continuous improvement of the company's performance.

---

[2] Zhinong Chen. A network of affection for customers-the connotation of Cisco's service culture [J]. Chinese and foreign corporate culture, 2005, (6).

Market transformation. The Internet is one of the rapidly changing industries, and the speed at which products and services are updated is changing. Cisco recognizes that the Internet economy is an unprecedented new industry and environment, with no precedents or similar models to follow. Therefore, the company must continue to meet the challenges, embrace change, and promote transformation. Since Chambers took over, Cisco has undergone seven major transformations that have been based on sharp market observation and effective decision-making. Cisco's long-term goal is to become the most powerful and influential company in history, so the company is able to seize the opportunities of market transformation and grasp the trends of market development by facing the challenges brought by various changes in the process of moving toward the goal. The key to Cisco's successful transformation over the past 34 years, Chambers said, has been "listening to our customers and having a healthy paranoia, which has been a key driver of our growth."

Teamwork. Cisco executives recognize that the power of one person is limited, and in today's society, only teamwork and collaboration can lead to success. In the face of the increasingly detailed division of labor, technology and management of what is increasingly complex, the individual's strength and wisdom appear to be negligible, and even a genius may need the assistance of others. However, such cooperation must be based on the benefit to all concerned. Teamwork is the main way for Cisco employees to complete tasks. The company rewards employees based on customer satisfaction, which is a manifestation of the spirit of teamwork. Since the bonus is based on customer satisfaction, any employee will pay attention to improving customer satisfaction. In addition, Cisco has created CAP awards to honor individuals or teams that accomplish outstanding tasks. A Cisco employee who has made outstanding contributions can be nominated by other employees, customers or suppliers and will receive the award and cash award within 48 h after being reviewed and approved by a manager.

Open communication. Open channels of communication are an effective way to keep everyone united. Chambers wanted everyone he spoke with to be forthright about Cisco's status and problems. He often asks, "How can we do better?" In order to keep abreast of changes in the company, he regularly appears in front of employees and has frank conversations with them, encouraging them to ask various work-related questions. As a result, employees have many opportunities to report any opportunities or problems they find to their bosses. In addition, Chambers has a weekly lunch with the company's vice President for one-on-one communication. Not only is there a good open communication atmosphere within the company, but this habit is also reflected in the relationship between the company and customers, which directly affects the company's ability to predict market transformation.

No technology worship. Technology is an especially important factor in Cisco's success, but it cannot be the dominant factor in the enterprise, because it is easy to lose sight of the market and deviate from it. The determination of this principle has to do not only with Chambers' own background as a salesperson rather than a technical talent, but also with the fact that he has seen Wang's company's technology mania lead to failure. "We also have a culture of technological unknowability," he once said. "Whatever we think, or the market says, we create and provide whatever our customers want."

Trust, fairness, integrity. Trust is to give employees the opportunity to create the value and interests of the enterprise, which is a concept and system recognized by every employee in the enterprise culture. A good corporate culture maximizes the energy and responsibility of employees.[3] Fairness applies to everything inside and outside the company. Inside, for example, Mr. Chambers' office is as big as any analyst's; in the process of communicating with customers, employees should always maintain an equal and respectful attitude. Integrity refers to using an honest and conservative financial strategy that is truly transparent and does not allow unprofessional issues to arise.

Culture. At the heart of Cisco's culture is a high adaptability to environmental and competitive challenges. According to Chambers, one of Cisco's competitive advantages is a corporate culture that is receptive to change. Over the past three decades, Cisco has transformed its technology and product systems from routers, switches, packets, mobile, virtualization, video, smart grids, and the Internet to the interconnection of everything. In this process, Cisco constantly changes itself with the development of technology, experiencing five generations of competitors and never stopping the pace of self-innovation.

Mr. Ricci, Cisco's chief cultural officer, sums up Cisco's core competencies with three elements: Process, culture and technology. How do you maintain the flexibility of a small business in a highly competitive industry while still having the scale advantages of a large business and being culturally compatible? In Cisco's view, culture is reflected in people's behavior, while the real culture is the conscious behavior of employees in the absence of leaders. Culture determines the operational efficiency and results of the organization and determines the adaptability of the organization. The slow pace of change in many large organizations may be due to the following reasons: People do not know which decisions they are responsible for, all decisions are not final decisions, it is difficult to obtain useful information when making decisions, and they cannot accurately and objectively evaluate the work quality of team members. To solve these problems, in the top-down leadership system of Cisco, the superiors are required to clearly explain to the subordinates: (1) who is responsible for the decision-making of the team; (2) how decisions are made; (3) clear words to avoid ambiguity; (4) create a common language system; (5) reach a consensus quickly and as a whole. In the communication from the bottom up, the boss should let the subordinates clear their own decision-making style. According to the way leaders think and communicate, Cisco divides decision-making styles into four types: Conceptual (who like ideas and ideas) and analytical (who like facts and data); deductive (starting with answers and conclusions) and inductive (focusing on the analytical process). In'terms of communication, there are extroversion (listening to everyone's opinions) and introversion (thinking independently). Linear narrators (step by step) and non-linear narrators (focus on telling process). By making the decision-making

[3] Xiaoli Shen. Cisco's corporate culture is the driving force for high-speed trains [J]. Research on Material Circulation, 2000, (7).

and decision-making process transparent, making the discourse system consistent in the decision-making, and letting employees clearly understand the company's strategy, implementation details and successful milestones before taking actions, Cisco ensures its high adaptability by improving the communication efficiency of the organization.

Enjoy it. Find pleasure in demanding work, learn to enjoy, love work, enjoy life.

Thrifty. Cisco has always emphasized the virtues of frugality and practiced them from top to bottom. Mr. Chambers spends an extra half-hour parking his car in a long-term parking lot instead of a nearby temporary space, so the company can save $2 a day on parking expenses. When every Cisco employee checks his or her email at the beginning of the month, the system automatically generates a letter that reads, "your phone bill last month was × ×, and your current rank in the company is × ×." It suggests that employees should save their phone bills, and there is usually a link at the bottom of such emails telling employees how to reduce their phone bills. All Cisco computers come from the same brand, because centralized procurement helps reduce the cost of individual products and the same standard configuration is used to complete the installation of computers, saving maintenance costs. In order to save paper, the company stipulated that the paper should be printed on both sides. When traveling on business, the standard from top to bottom is economy class. If you want to upgrade the cabin, you need to pay by yourself.[4]

Perhaps Cisco's all-employee options scheme explains some of the phenomenon of employees calling the company home. At Cisco, all employees are entitled to options, and 40% of the options are in the hands of ordinary employees, who earn an average of $30,000 in equity gains if they have worked for 12 months. The lower the company's costs, the higher the employee's benefits, so everyone is naturally willing to take the initiative to save the company a dime and eliminate any waste.

3 Build Innovation Culture

Culture plays the most significant role in innovation. Corporate culture is hard to describe in words, but it guides employees' behavior all the time. Cisco places immense importance on the construction of innovation culture. For example, in the R&D team, there is an "innovation day" every quarter. During the day, employees do not have to do their daily work. Instead, they go back to the office to think about their innovative ideas for products, problems with the process, market research, etc. During an innovation day, teams from China and the United States produced more than 500 ideas. Cisco then selected the ten best ideas from more than 500 ideas and incorporated them into their daily work, and employees who came up with the ten best ideas were rewarded.

The formation of innovation culture is not achieved overnight but is gradually cultivated. There are several elements involved. One is process and structure. Some

[4] Cisco review http://www.fenzhi.com/gsr3277.html 2011-3-31.

companies' innovations are short-lived, once or twice, and unsustainable because they lack a proper process and structure, which is especially important for large companies. The second is to clarify their core technology and competitiveness. Before innovation, it is necessary to clarify the core competitiveness and core technology of the enterprise. For example, it is not feasible for Cisco to create a business to make electric cars, because this is not Cisco's core technology and would not allow Cisco to capitalize on its most advantageous network. In the process of innovation, if we do not know what our core technology and core competition is, we will blindly innovate. Third, the evaluation of innovation results. Innovation involves the investment of capital and personnel, and enterprises need to constantly evaluate whether the innovation project meets the needs of users. User needs change over time, so assessments are ongoing. When many enterprises innovate, once they have an idea, they will move forward with it. However, it is very likely that after the product is made, the market demand will change, and the innovation will fail. Therefore, the evaluation needs to keep track of the market and customers. The fourth is to reward and commend innovative behaviors. The Cisco China team did a better job of rewarding and honoring, which is divided into spiritual and material rewards. Due to the cultural relationship, the American team does not do well in terms of spiritual rewards, only offering cash, stocks and other material rewards. Generally speaking, Cisco does not punish innovation exploration by cracking down. When innovation fails, it is the top who feel the pressure, because it shows that the top has made poor decisions.

4 Use Culture to Build Sustainable Competitiveness

Harmony and cooperation between culture and other elements. Sustainable competitive advantages of an enterprise are not made up of just a single element of culture. According to Cisco, sustainable competitive advantage comes from three pillars: Technology, process and culture. Culture can bring lasting competitive advantage to enterprises and maximize the value of enterprise culture only when it is coordinated with enterprise strategic process and technology.

The harmony of corporate culture will make employees feel at home. They will be more resolute, willing to devote more time and energy to the company, and more willing to accept challenging work. Just like the relationship between parents and children, respected parents create a harmonious family environment and atmosphere, and children are willing to pay more for their parents and family and do more things without complaining.

Integration of information technology application and culture. Cisco itself is a high-tech enterprise. Many technology applications start from within Cisco, which enterprises find valuable after using, and then convert them to products to recommend to customers. In this process, Cisco strives to achieve the integration of technology and culture, and through the combination of the two to create enterprise competitiveness. Here are some examples of Cisco's use of information technology to develop its sales force.

For engineers and salespeople in high-tech companies, the most important ability is to recognize early changes in the environment and customers and figure out what products should be sold to customers. Cisco continuously trains its salespeople to update their knowledge of technology and products. At first, the staff thought of using technical means to complete the timely training of the sales staff, so they tried to carve the training information of the recent technology and new products into a CD and send it to each sales staff, so that they could go home to briefly study. It turned out that this did not work, and the sales force's performance declined because the technology didn't mix well with the corporate culture. Here are the problems: First, the sales staff do not need to know all technical details, they only need to know the product information in order to sell it; second, after the sales staff return home to accompany their families, people may be tired, and it is difficult to spare a full hour to concentrate on study. With the above two factors in mind, Cisco transformed the training course into an Internet video courseware, customized according to the diverse needs of the sales staff, who only need to surf the Internet for 7–8 min to quickly understand the core contents of new technologies and new products. In practice, the new method has improved the efficiency and learning speed of Cisco's sales staff.

In this case for Cisco, the management of the high-tech enterprises must get technical application methods combined with the company's culture, corporate management only in the deep understanding of the relationship between technology and culture, and creatively apply technology to solve the problem of management, to achieve differentiation with competitors, and to achieve success in the market competition.

5 Shaping Highly Adaptable Enterprises Through Culture

As a global enterprise, Cisco has to adapt to different social, political, economic and cultural environments in different countries. The dynamic changes and complexity of the environment require the enterprise to have good adaptability and learning ability. The adaptability of enterprises is reflected in their ability to quickly adjust their decisions and actions according to the changes of consumer groups and markets, so as to seize the new opportunities of market development. Instead of sticking to existing strategies, companies adjust their business goals and strategies through rapid learning of external environment and market. For its enterprises, high adaptability is more important. Enterprises with poor adaptability usually show three main characteristics: First, low efficiency, organizational redundancy and serious waste. Second, companies often make bad decisions. Because of top-down, bottom-up, parallel departments and trans-regional poor exchange of information, there are a lot of information, make decisions did not master the accurate and timely the necessary information, thus making the wrong judgment or delay, failed to optimize enterprise's decision-making and operating system, and enterprise operation and resource allocation problems. Third, weak execution or delayed action. Because the enterprise fails to reach a consensus, the information dissemination is not timely, the process and operation system design bottleneck, resulting in the enterprise slow action, slow response.

For Mr. Ricci, Cisco's chief cultural officer, it is not easy to build a highly adaptable corporate culture. Procter & gamble's crest, for example, has long been number one in the toothpaste market in America, and it took Colgate 45 years to find a strategy to beat Crest. And the development speed of information technology is extremely fast, in the fierce competition, technology enterprises will not have such a long time to defeat the opponent. Enterprises must learn to surpass sprinting, which puts forward higher requirements for culture.

Companies usually look for one or two strategies to enhance their adaptability. One strategy adopted by Cisco is to pursue operational excellence, expand sales scale, expand product distribution channels to the world and build a global brand. In this case, large enterprises may choose other strategies, such as enhancing innovation, decentralizing decision-making mechanisms, and focusing on innovation speed and marketization efficiency of innovation results. Such enterprises need younger, more motivated and passionate employees. Which is more effective for the enterprise, operation excellence or innovation? Some research suggests that companies with operational excellence often outperform innovative ones overall.

True, companies with two strategies are more likely to succeed, but why do most companies have to choose between innovation and operational excellence rather than both? This is because the corporate culture behind these two strategies is not the same. Large companies with excellent operations usually have the advantages of scale and efficiency, but the dependence on path and the pursuit of efficiency may make them lack the flexibility and quick response ability that small companies have. Therefore, for Cisco to compete quickly in the high-tech industry, it needs to develop and build the flexibility and quick response capacity of small businesses. In order to achieve this goal, Cisco needs to undergo cultural innovation and transformation.

6 Five Levers for Establishing a Highly Adaptable Corporate Culture

Before 2000, the internal competition in Cisco was very fierce. Different teams competed with each other to win more customers. Sometimes teams sold the same products to different people at different prices and provided different services. Such internal competition not only wastes a number of resources, but also forces Cisco to focus on resolving internal disputes rather than customer satisfaction. In this context, Chambers decided to change Cisco's culture from one that focused on internal competition to one that shared purpose—a cultural shift that allowed all parts of the organization to work together around a common purpose and mission.

After several organizational changes and strategic transformations, Cisco also experienced cultural changes and innovation, striving to realize the transformation from a competitive culture to a common goal culture. The internal competitive culture is characterized in decision-making, leadership, resource allocation and responsibility by low corporate transparency, passive participation of employees, vertical adjustment of business units, and fighting alone. At the core of the common goal culture are higher corporate transparency, the provision of true and reliable information, the enhancement of execution through portfolio management and teamwork, and cross-departmental collaboration. In the process of cultural transformation and innovation, leaders play a key role in achieving the goals of cultural transformation through resource allocation, performance appraisal and responsibility arrangement.

Cultural transformation is a demanding thing, so Cisco first needs to figure out which levers can effectively promote cultural transformation. In Cisco's experience, there are five levers that are critical to cultural transformation in building a highly adaptable business: Transparent decision-making, creating a common language for the organization, honest leadership, horizontal allocation of resources, and clear accountability.

Transparent decision-making process. The first lever is to design a sound decision-making process, the key to which is to make non-public decision-making transparent. Transparent decision-making processes ensure that companies move faster than their competitors in three areas: First, people within the organization know exactly how decisions are made, so they don't spend time speculating and gossiping in private, which improves the effectiveness of organizational communication; second, the transparent decision-making process allows all team members to clearly understand their positions and responsibilities, so that the shared accountability system can improve the efficiency of execution. Third, the transparent decision-making process fully considers the opinions of all aspects and has a preset plan and thinking for the problems and obstacles that may be encountered in the action, which will also increase the efficiency of the enterprise action. If these three conditions exist at the same time, the team will have to adapt to more elasticity and flexibility, and not spend a great deal of speculation towards members of the decision-making process, because there may be false information and ideas in the organization, more than a few processes that will slow down productivity; as a result, decisions have to be transparent.

Create a common language for the organization. The second lever is to create a unified language for the organization. Another problem that may arise in the decision-making process is that misunderstandings between people often result from inconsistent understanding of some concepts and issues, making it more difficult for enterprises to reach consensus. As a global company, if people cannot clearly describe the core strategy of headquarters, it is less likely to implement it quickly and flexibly. To address this problem, Cisco's approach is to create a common vocabulary and framework for understanding and making decisions about important concepts. For example, when each team reports, they adopt the unified template of vision, strategy, implementation and measurement, and express themselves according to their respective specialties within a unified vocabulary and framework. This unified representation system plays a normative role in ensuring the consistency of the decision-making process. By understanding the principles, rules, procedures, and vocabulary of the enterprise, the efficiency of team decision-making and consensus building can be improved.

The leadership is sincere and credible. The third lever is for the leadership to have a clear set of values. The leader may be negative or positive, in which the negative action is to face to face and behind the back, and not to express himself truly. According to Cisco, leaders must demonstrate two characteristics: One is that they are consistent in their actions and actions, which is a crucial factor in creating a sincere and trusting relationship between people; second, when there are different opinions within the enterprise, it is right for things and opinions but not for people. When the leader and the employee have different opinions, the employee will worry about the personal enmity caused by the difference of opinion with the leader. Only when it is clear that people only express their opinions on different opinions, will people speak freely.

Horizontal allocation of enterprise resources. The fourth lever of cultural transformation is to clarify the principle of enterprise resource allocation. Many enterprises organize assessment and performance evaluation with profit at the center, across different businesses, products, regions and customers. This approach emphasizes vertical integration and emphasizes investment and development at the island level. Cisco takes a horizontal view of enterprise investment and resource allocation, so that the enterprise's expenditure will form a variety of investment portfolios. Cisco, for example, spends about $6 billion a year on R&D, of which 70% goes into core product development, 20% into extended and innovative product development, and 10% into cybersecurity product innovation. Cisco is very transparent about this. It looks laterally at the future direction of the business, not just at today's or tomorrow's profits. Cisco needs to make sure that its investments are investments in the future, and that it can create sustainable advantages for the company by making a horizontal portfolio of future developments.

Establish clear accountability. The final lever is accountability, the belief that there are sufficient incentives and accountability for the consequences of decisions. In some enterprises, internal responsibilities are taken by themselves, which are similar to islands. Some enterprises have their own incentive mechanism to strengthen the islands, which further weakens the cooperation mechanism between enterprise teams and departments. Cisco believes that accountability should be holistic, that institutions should be designed with the best interests of the whole in mind, and that accountability should be clear from the start of decision-making.

7 Principles for Promoting the Implementation of Culture

The leader introduces his decision-making style to the team. The leader should clearly tell the team members their preferred style of making decisions and how the decisions will be made. Different leaders may have diverse ways of making decisions. Some may prefer concepts and need others to provide ideas and input. For example, Chambers makes decisions based on others' ideas. Some leaders are analytical and make decisions based on data and facts. Therefore, the decision support team needs to prepare a great deal of data and information. If team members do not know how the leader makes decisions, how to get information and how to analyze them, the pace of decision making slows down. In addition, the senior management should make the team members clear about the decision-making process, procedures and principles. In this way, when participating in the decision-making process or reporting to the leader, the team members will make corresponding adjustments according to the decision-making style and way of the leader and choose effective communication and cooperation ways to ensure the smoothness and efficiency of the decision-making channel.

Develop transparent measures of success. A second factor in promoting culture is that measures of success must be transparent. Within Cisco, there are six process criteria, which correspond to growth, profitability/efficiency, time to market/innovation, customer experience, partner experience and employee experience. Under these big metrics, there are 29 key performance indicators (kpis) that anyone working at Cisco can use to measure their work no matter which part of the company or business unit they are responsible for. By making these metrics publicly available, the company gives employees a clear picture of what success should look like for the team. Once employees have a clear definition of success, they have something to strive for, are more engaged in their work, and understand the growth and rewards of their efforts.

Build a culture of common purpose. If the enterprise has a common goal and culture, its development speed, adaptability and flexibility can be improved. The only person who can create this environment in the enterprise is the top leader. The talents of business leaders define the corporate culture, and they are the most important people to promote it.

8 Summary

The head of an enterprise plays a key role in shaping culture. In Cisco's view, culture is built on the success and failure experiences of leaders, who, after witnessing the rise and fall of an enterprise, have a deep understanding of the important characteristics that an enterprise must possess in order to achieve sustainable development. After the painful experience of the bankruptcy of Wang and company, Chambers realized that technology enterprises should not only focus on technology, but also focus on customers, pursue customers' needs and expand the development direction of enterprises. Customers, rather than the guidance of technology, will certainly give the enterprise the opportunity and space to survive. Therefore, Cisco's customer-demand-oriented code of conduct and incentive mechanism are deeply embedded in the thinking and behavior of all levels of the enterprise and become a primary law for employees to follow consciously. At the same time, in the face of pressure and failure, enterprise leaders can lead the enterprise out of the predicament, create miracles, develop in doubt, promote transformation in pressure and resistance, adhere to the vision and strategy of the enterprise, patience and persistence, perseverance, proactivity is crucial to shaping the enterprise's cultural genes.

The establishment of a highly adaptive culture in Cisco is to define the basic principles and methods of the interaction between the enterprise and the external environment. For high-tech enterprises, market transformation and technological innovation put forward higher and higher requirements for enterprises to respond to the speed of market changes. Highly adaptable enterprises should pay close attention to the changes of various stakeholders, products and market structures, political and economic relations, human behavior and technological functions in the market environment, and establish a flexible, efficient, and constantly changing organization to respond to various changes. In order to build a highly adaptable organization, Cisco focuses on improving the transparency of decision-making system and communication process. In other words, at the core is the drive to solve people's problems. A transparent decision-making process allows employees to avoid suspicions and hearsay and allows opinions to be fully expressed. The common language tries to avoid the deviation in the definition of basic concepts, which reduces the efficiency of communication. Leaders should explain their decision-making style to employees, match words with deeds and speak frankly, which will reduce unnecessary misunderstandings and trouble in communication, improve the efficiency of reaching consensus between superiors and subordinates, and thus improve the organization's execution ability and response speed to the external environment.

In today's world, the development speed of information technology has exceeded the development speed of business. If we combine technological change with business change, it will bring innovation in the business model and management. The challenge for companies is how quickly we will change and integrate modern technologies and businesses and to what extent. Usually, people have a sense of distance and fear towards technologies and businesses they are not familiar with. The first reaction to new technologies may be to question or reject them. The more traditional, mainstream and successful enterprises are, the less they attach importance to opportunities brought by new technologies. Marginal, young, struggling companies are likely to see innovative technologies as new business opportunities. Therefore, for both old and leading enterprises, how to make technological changes and innovations happen faster requires cultural construction to facilitate the process. In order to accelerate the construction of highly adaptive culture, enterprises need to be full of curiosity, openness and exploration spirit to external changes, so that people with exploration spirit, dare to take risks and try new things can get opportunities. Enterprises need to systematically and continuously invest and support forward-looking technologies to reduce technology and market risks through appropriate portfolio investments; through brainstorming, integrating internal and external information and resources, new ideas and methods can be obtained so that mature enterprises still maintain the mentality of entrepreneurial enterprises, which is also an important part of cultural construction.

Chapter 8
Corporate Governance and Risk Management

1 Introduction

Corporate governance refers to the company's guidance and control system, which balances the relationship between internal stakeholders (boards, investors, executives, employees, etc.) and external stakeholders (shareholders, creditors, trade creditors, suppliers, customers, and communities) through the governance structure and coordination mechanism of the rights and responsibilities of different interest groups of the company. Corporate governance sets out the principles and procedures of corporate decision-making, instructing enterprises to balance the relationship between social, legal, market and environmental factors in order to achieve their goals. At the same time, corporate governance is also a mechanism for monitoring corporate actions, policies and decision-making. In recent years, due to some large enterprises have financial fraud, integrity crisis and other issues, corporate governance focused more attention on compliance management issues, while governments have also issued new laws and regulations. The governance behavior of enterprises remains at the top of higher requirements. According to the Cadbury Report (1992), OECD Principles of Corporate Governance (OECD, 1998, 2004) and Sarbanes–Oxley Act (2002), the principles of corporate governance include shareholder rights and fair treatment. The rights and interests of other stakeholders, the roles and responsibilities of the Board of Directors, honesty and ethical conduct, disclosure and transparency.

The risk management system of an enterprise refers to the methods and processes of evaluating and managing the risk and seizing the opportunity in order to achieve the development goal of the enterprise, at the same time, the system is also the integrated concept of internal control, Sarbanes Act and strategic planning, and makes plans in advance to ensure the safe development of the enterprise through the prediction of risks and opportunities. At home and abroad, there are a variety of enterprise risk control frameworks, each of which shows the enterprise identification, analysis, response, monitoring of internal and external risks and opportunities, while developing risk response strategy, including risk avoidance, risk reduction,

X. Dong et al., *Cisco*,
https://doi.org/10.1007/978-981-19-7870-8_8

optional actions, risk sharing and risk acceptance. In general, the risks that companies should deal with include sudden risk, financial risk, operational risk, ethical risk and strategic risk. Risk monitoring is part of internal control activities, including the management committee's analytical report evaluation, understanding the implementation of the risk response strategy and the achievement of objectives. The process of risk management includes background analysis of risk generation, risk identification, risk analysis and quantification, risk assessment of the likelihood of integration of risk occurrence (correlation effects between risks, combined and linked effects), risk assessment and risk prioritization, risk management and risk utilization, risk monitoring and response assessment.

2 Corporate Governance Structure and Wind Control System

Cisco's goal is to equip Cisco with industry-leading governance, risk management, and control mechanisms that create efficient, effective, ethical governance, risk management, and control processes to optimize shareholder value. Cisco is improving its risk management and control capabilities in five ways: continuously improving the company's operational capabilities, ensuring that it develops its own people, strengthening fiduciary responsibilities, promoting awareness of risk management, and promoting an ethical culture. For each dimension, there are corresponding implementation strategies and evaluation criteria for performance.

In terms of corporate governance policy, Cisco defines the responsibilities of each control department: (1) the Board of Directors has a clear and unambiguous governance policy; (2) the Board's charter clearly sets out the responsibilities; (3) a clear code of conduct for business conduct, overseen by the Ethics Office, which is confirmed annually by employees; (4) the establishment of an Ethics Office hotline, audit committee e-mail domain name and audit committee mailbox for anonymous complaints; (5) ethics standards for all members of the CEO and financial department, including the Chief Financial Officer and Chief Accounting Officer, and report directly to the Audit Committee of the Board of Directors, (7) the CEO and CFO sign the SEC certification, and (8) develop specific guidelines and regulations for compensation, equity, and stock trading.

As a global company, Cisco operates in more than 100 countries and is an expanding offshore business, with increasingly complex market environments, competitive environmental and political laws, and ensuring efficient and smooth operations in more than 100 countries. As a high-tech company, Cisco makes 6–10 acquisitions per year, while keeping an eye on innovation, investment innovation, risk management and auditing that are critical to the healthy development of the business. Audit and risk control seem to have put a brake on a high-speed car, which is not installed to stop the car, but to make it faster and safer. If companies have the right and effective processes for governance and risk control, they can avoid unnecessary risks and pitfalls and take full advantage of business opportunities.

Board. Cisco's Board of Directors consists of the Chairman, independent directors and 12 members. The chairman and CEO are Chambers, and 80% of the 12 members are independent. The selection of independent directors is subject to independent investigation by a nominating committee or consulting firm. When nominating independent directors, consider that they can bring diverse backgrounds and knowledge to the company, and the list is determined and submitted to the shareholders' meeting for approval. Current board members include Dr. Hennessy, President of Stanford University, and Mr. Bartz, former CEO of Yahoo. Board members are invited to join because they are respected and are therefore a social honor to take responsibility for the general policy of the enterprise. The board of directors meets five times a year, many of whom are present. The core issue is the overall control of the enterprise, for major decision-making control and control of risk to ensure the success of the enterprise investment.

Committee system. There are five committees on the Board: the Audit Committee (members of the Audit Committee are not paid and must be independent), the Remuneration and Development Committee, the Nomination and Management Committee (all three members of the committee above have independent status), the Acquisitions Committee and the Finance Committee. Cisco establishes the Ethics Office, whose members are elected by employees. The various contact details of the Ethics Office and the Audit Committee are public to facilitate employee oversight and anonymous complaints. The Ethics Office's code of ethics applies to everyone in the business. The job of internal audit is to monitor the financial process and submit audit reports directly to the Board of Directors.

Corporate Governance and Risk Control. Cisco's Corporate Governance and Risk Control division has three divisions: Audit, Risk Management Control, and Ethics Investigations. Cisco's Corporate Governance and Risk Control division is in parallel with the Finance Division, which has more than 100 employees reporting directly to the Finance Committee and the Audit Committee. These units are managed directly by Mr. Phil Roush, Vice President of Risk Management at Cisco. Audit and Risk Control is a global team with more than 50 members: 22 at headquarters in San Jose, 8 in North Carolina, 8 in Europe, 8 in India and 5 in China. The core competencies of the audit are primarily reflected in accounting workflows, process/control assessments, IT systems (architecture and infrastructure) and business knowledge. The team reports directly to the Controller and the Audit Committee and represents this relationship in a dotted line in the organization's structure. Corporate Governance and Risk Control need to work closely with business units to evaluate the company's 120 risk types, each of which is negotiated with the relevant business units to define and jointly develop risk assessment criteria, and EY and Deloitte help Cisco identify risk models that apply to them. Consider where the risks may occur and who is responsible for decision-making and management during the development process. For example, Mr. Chambers, the president, is at risk in terms of which team is responsible, which finance team is responsible for the exchange rate risk, which department is responsible for communicating with the finance department over the European debt crisis, assessing whether management is out of authority, and so on.

In order to ensure the independence of the company's wind control department, the wind control department can report directly to the board of directors. On major issues such as acquisitions, investments and equity stakes, it is primarily determined by shareholders' meetings. Significant issues are also discussed at regular board meetings, and Mr. Chambers, of course, has some decision-making power. For major decisions, the company has a noticeably clear definition, in the company's strategy also has a strict management charter to provide decision-making authority, for which Cisco has a very careful system design. Some stock traders on Wall Street have made unauthorized trading because they overstepped their authority, resulting in large losses for customers, and the lessons learned are painful.

The head of corporate governance and risk control department deals with the audit committee every month, in the process, the corporate governance and risk control department must maintain a certain degree of independence, but also for the benefit of the company, so the boundary is blurred. The Finance Department and the Audit Committee are responsible for assessing the work of corporate governance and risk control. Corporate governance and risk control department of the role of the company is to apply the brakes, here, the brake specifically refers to the enterprise process to set control levels, so that enterprises cannot run quickly, but to go through an evaluation process, the use of certain standards for self-measurement, so as to control both risks, but also seize business opportunities. Cisco has 30,000 engineers, and the process is designed to manage the engineer's work effectively without making it feel like he is being handcuffed and restrained. The vital role of corporate governance and risk control is not to handcuff companies, but to help them effectively use opportunities.

The core responsibility of Corporate Governance and Risk Control is to identify issues and submit audit reports to the CFO and all the senior management associated with them each year. At the six annual audit committee meetings, department heads report significant issues identified during the audit process to the board and summarize the audit results if there are no significant problems with the audit. At the meeting, the Audit Committee approves a plan that endorses the department's work. For projects not approved by the Board of Auditors, the Wind Control Department will continue to provide current information to ensure that all minor changes are communicated in a timely manner.

Corporate Governance and Risk Control often acts as a consultant when servicing business units. Because risks are primarily present in the business unit, wind control provides risk prevention advice, such as merger and acquisition activities, looking at the risks in the merger integration process from a holistic perspective, as well as the history and process records of mergers and acquisitions transactions. Corporate governance and risk control departments and other business units of the monitoring responsibility, engineering departments are responsible for solving engineering risks, supply chain departments are responsible for addressing supply chain risks, each function is responsible for their own risks, corporate governance and risk control department's responsibility is to coordinate other departments to effectively address risk. The finance department's role is to review the details of each transaction, the small number of transactions are automatically approved, and large amounts of transactions require special approval. In this process, the finance department is responsible for the overall financial aspect of risk control, while the corporate governance and risk control department sits in the process to ensure that there are certain metrics, assessed, and clearly measured by the size of the profit.

Wind control departments are also involved in the monitoring of research and development risks, but the team's responsibility is not to inform the research and development department of the direction of innovation, how the product is developed, but to audit the research and development team's processes, to see whether they are ready for the new technological revolution, how the product portfolio and management, whether the product and market have been carefully analyzed, who is responsible, and so on. In short, wind control is responsible for auditing risks in the research and development process, not their decisions.

3 How to Manage Risks Facing Global Markets?

Risk management is easier when business operations are concentrated in a geographical area, but when companies operate in global markets, there is a high degree of interdependence, with manufacturing, customer service and back-office services in different countries and regions (e.g. manufacturing bases in China, customer service in India, when background services may be in Brazil), the complexity of management increases significantly. At the same time, the political, economic and social situations in emerging market countries is very different. Global enterprises operating in all regions of the world must ensure that the flow of information is fast, so what happens in a region, in a matter of seconds, can inform headquarters. There must be strong information sharing mechanisms between regions, especially within the supply chain management system of enterprises who need to have a rapid risk response mechanism, Because disruption slots anywhere in the world can affect overall operations, such as the floods in Thailand and the tsunami in Japan, risk management and response mechanisms can directly affect the efficiency of a company's global supply chain.

As a global company, Cisco inevitably experiences risks as it grows its business around the world. Before entering a country, Cisco does a comprehensive assessment to see what the primary risks are, and then asks the board's two senior managers to provide feedback on the risk assessment to ensure that someone can address such risks, and that those responsible for risk management develop an action plan to ensure that the action plan is transparent. There may also be various political risks when entering different countries, and the company employs two teams to manage political risk: one country team and the other company team. Before entering a country, Cisco also investigates and evaluates potential risks in areas such as government and currency, and then discusses with the senior team in charge of the country's business to analyze whether the risks in the area are of legal regulation or employee policy. The marketing department has a dedicated team focused on competitive risk, and people in the engineering department focus on the risk of product transformation.

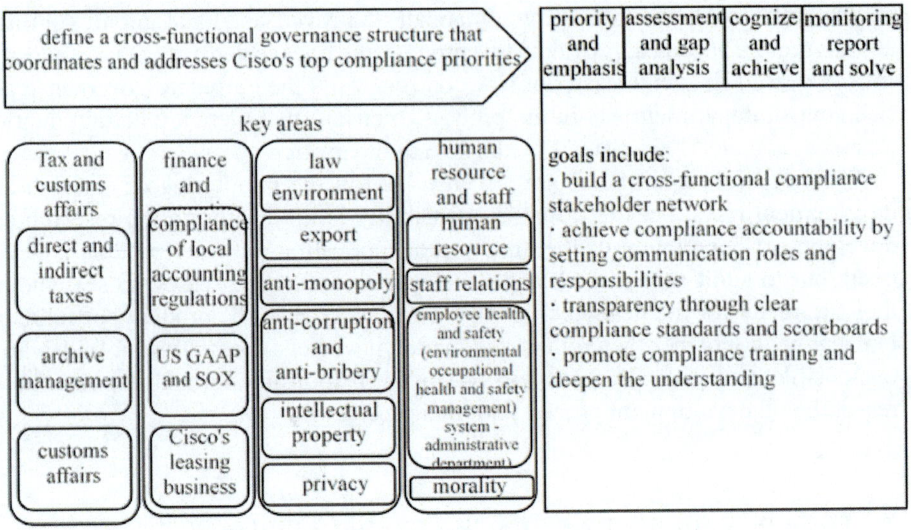

Fig. 8.1 Cisco's global compliance governance framework

"The core responsibility of the wind control department at the corporate level is to ensure good coordination between the departments, which observes market share, product comparison, price comparison and customer feedback through an analytical matrix." If there is a notable change in the competitor, all the data will be centralized and submitted to Chambers, and the wind control department will ensure that the data submitted is unfiltered, accurate and true, and that the presentation of the problem is as clear and transparent as possible, without complicating the situation.

Special attention to compliance issues is also paid to risk management at branches around the world, with the close cooperation of the heads of Cisco headquarters and national compliance governance committees who understand the compliance requirements and risks of local development operators, as no one wants to face the local justice system if someone encounters legal problems regardless of who is responsible. Once accountability is clear, people know where they need to take responsibility, while also ensuring transparency in the business, with a matrix for each team and a risk-awareness training program. Cisco's global compliance governance framework looks like Fig. 8.1.

4 Framework and Process of Risk Management

Some companies respond to risks as if they were flying defenses and respond immediately when a crisis arises. In contrast to Cisco's approach, Cisco's board of directors provides direct support to the wind control department, which reports and reviews the potential risks to the company's functions. There is also a Risk and Continuity

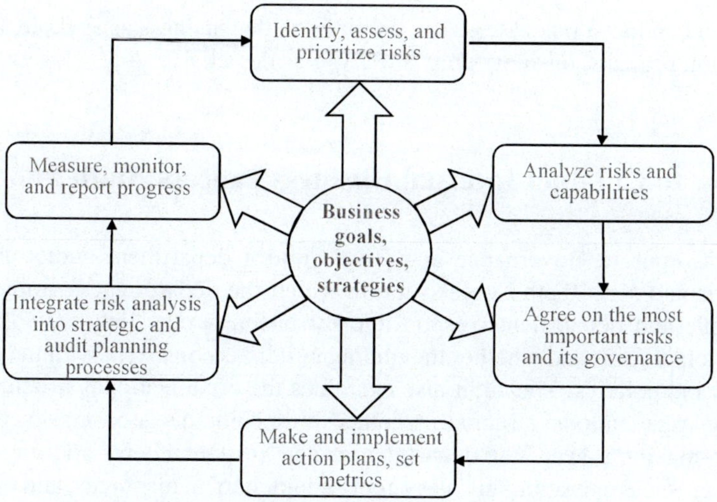

Fig. 8.2 Cisco's risk management framework

Operations Council, which includes eight vice presidents of Cisco, whose function is to enable Cisco departments to work together to address the different risks they face. Cisco also has risk review working groups, risk assessments and action plans to conduct risk management.

Risk management has a complete set of process models. First, Cisco identifies and evaluates risks, prioritizes risks, and analyzes risks and capabilities. Second, reach consensus on the most important risks and their governance, develop action plans and set metrics, and then integrate risk analysis into the strategic and audit planning processes, and measure, monitor, and report on progress. Finally, such a closed process returns to the risk identification assessment phase, as shown in Fig. 8.2.

Cisco's risk management process is closely focused on the goals and strategies of the enterprise, and in the process of combining corporate strategy with risk monitoring, senior managers at all levels should consider three issues: First, how to minimize risk in order to protect the effective development of the enterprise business. In the process, executives answer questions that include analyzing and assessing the risks they face and how to ensure business continuity. Second, how to optimize risk management and response capabilities. In this process, executives should answer how to effectively monitor business risk, how to deal with risk, how to bear risk, and how to distinguish between controllable risk and uncontrollable risk. Third, how to actively face and take risks, rather than negative response. In this process, senior management should be clear how to make serious decisions, effectively grasp the opportunity to deal with risks, and actively conduct business and technological innovation.

Risk management enables Cisco to examine risks and identify catalysts for change, as well as to manage risk through alignment of plans and resources, while evaluating management effectiveness and driving risk action through objective assessments.

Cisco can conduct a risk assessment not only on the business as a whole, but also on acquisition projects, business units and large-scale activities.

5 How to Conduct Internal Business Process Audit?

Cisco's Corporate Governance and Risk Control department audits all business processes and sorts them by risk, during which the department examines whether the people and departments responsible for business decisions are following the transaction process and whether the trading system is consistent with the company's strategy and policies. The audit also examines the organizational structure, such as from the organizational structure, whether the specific decision-makers are granted decision-making power. The department is also responsible for auditing functional departments and operations such as supply chain, human resources, and even professional conduct to see if its operations in the business are legitimate, dependable and efficient.

Often, business units in many enterprises are concerned that audit oversight will affect the efficiency and benefits of their business, and Cisco's corporate governance and risk control departments will try to consider and communicate in advance from the needs of the business units to clarify how long the entire audit process will take. Temporary employees are also assigned to conduct data research to assess the time required, which is not typically wasted by business personnel. The department conducts routine day-to-day audits of projects, and many businesses and functions welcome audits because they feel that they can help business processes add value and ensure the security of their businesses by identifying potential risks while continuously optimizing and controlling their processes.

6 Use of Information-Based Tools to Quantify Risk

Risk assessment is an especially important and complex task, often with many layers of risk, sometimes at the enterprise level, sometimes at the time of acquisition, sometimes in major events and activities. For example, at the Olympics, sponsors assess the impact of supporting the Games on the brand and operations of the company.

Cisco uses information tools to provide a comprehensive picture of quantitative metrics and correlations for risk assessment and risk response, using a tool called the Enterprise Risk Management Dashboard to chart and compass the enterprise's risk record tables and risk charts, as shown in Fig. 8.3. In the risk record table, a single data source (SSOT) repository of risk data is presented on the basis of a comprehensive analysis of each data, the management system presents a comprehensive view of all risks, factors that exacerbate them, the severity of the risk, the plan to reduce risk, and their associated relationships. Helps management dynamically monitor and

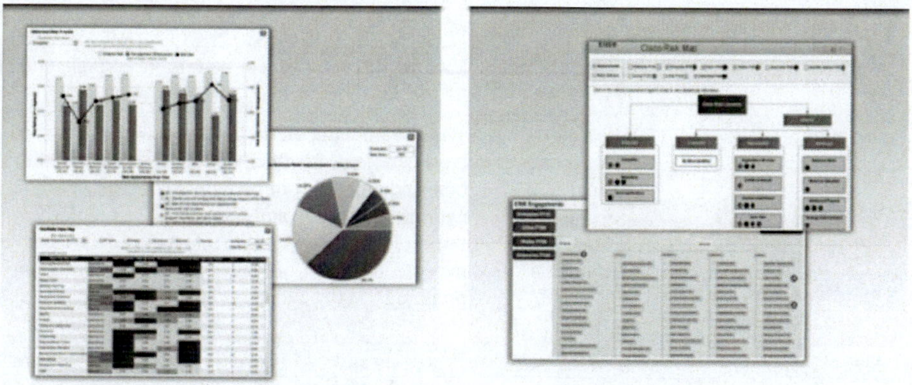

Fig. 8.3 Risk record table and risk chart

comprehensively assess the risks faced by the enterprise, as well as comprehensively evaluate the current state of risk management.

Cisco discovers where the primary risk is based on the Enterprise Risk Management Dashboard. Cisco defines approximately 120 risks. For each of the 120 risks, there is a separate chart showing what the risk is, what measure was used, who is responsible for it, what has already occurred, and the risk management process is documented in detail. It is important for a large company to sometimes have no way of letting all executives know where the 120 risks are, but it is important to break down this responsibility and identify 20 to 30 risks from 120 risks and present them to the board of directors for focus, which can have a significant impact on the business, which the board must discuss regularly.

Cisco also has a risk management maturity model (see Table 8.1), which defines the ability of an enterprise to manage risk and divides the pressure of enterprise risk management from weak to strong in four levels. By comparing this model, Cisco can see its own level of risk management.

The lowest stage in the risk management maturity model is the improvisation level, which means that the enterprise does not have sufficient awareness of risk management, and when the risk is encountered, the enterprise will "improvise" to deal with it. At this level, there is no formal documentation for risk management, nor are the roles and responsibilities of departments and responsible persons in the enterprise defined by risk management. When the enterprise evolves to a higher level of "formation", the enterprise has already defined the risk management process. If important documents related to risk management already exist, the company is able to use them to manage the requirements, resources and capabilities of the enterprise to deal with risk. However, this stage does not institutionalize the enterprise's risk management process. There is no continual learning from every risk management endeavor in the enterprise. The third level of enterprise risk management is the "clearly defined" level, where the enterprise has a clear definition of the risk management process, acts on the process that is in place when the enterprise is at

Table 8.1 Risk management maturity model

Activity	Improvisation (1)	Forming (2)	Clear definition (3)	Management (4)
Definition	Lack of process; no formal documents or limited formal documents	The stream name has been (is being) defined, and the files of important fields have been prepared	The process has been defined, implemented and tracked; documents for all areas have been prepared	Review and update the process regularly; documents in all areas are prepared and monitored
Assess	Lack of process; no formal documents or limited formal documents; undefined roles and responsibilities	Processes and reports have been (are being) defined, documents in key areas have been prepared, and resource and capability requirements have been understood	Processes and reports are defined, implemented and complied with; documents are available for all areas; resources and capabilities are defined and funded	Review and update processes and reports on a regular basis; all areas are documented and monitored; resources and capabilities are in place and in use
Response/mitigation	Lack of process; no formal documents or limited formal documents; undefined roles and responsibilities	Risk action plan has been (is being) defined; resource and capability requirements have been understood; action plan status has not been reported regularly	Risk action plan is being implemented; investment funds have been determined and resources are in place; appropriate periodic reports will be made on the status of action plans	Review and update processes and reports on a regular basis; documents are in place and monitored in all areas; resources and capabilities are in place and in use

(continued)

risk, and the enterprise has a clear definition and understanding of the resources and capabilities required to deal with the risk. As a result, companies can prepare funds and other resources in advance to respond to risks in accordance with the risk action plan. The highest level of enterprise risk management is at the "management" level. At this stage, the enterprise has institutionalized risk management, the risk of the enterprise is regularly reviewed and updated, and the documentation and information required to deal with the risk are complete and monitored. Companies are always ready for the resources and capabilities needed for risk and can use those resources in a timely manner to mitigate risks.

Table 8.1 (continued)

Activity	Improvisation (1)	Forming (2)	Clear definition (3)	Management (4)
Testing/verification	Lack of test/verification process; no formal documents or limited formal documents; undefined roles and responsibilities	Test/verification roles and responsibilities have been (are being) defined; test/verification reporting frequency has been determined	Test/validation roles and responsibilities have been defined and implemented; necessary funding has been in place; formal results response process has been implemented	Review and update processes and reports on a regular basis; documents are in place and monitored in all areas; resources and capabilities are in place and in use; response to results is effective
Monitoring/improvement	Lack of formal risk monitoring and improvement process; no formal documents or limited formal documents; undefined roles and responsibilities	Formal risk monitoring and improvement processes have been (are being) defined; resource and capability requirements have been understood; no regular reporting has been conducted	Monitoring and improvement processes have been implemented; resources and capabilities have been defined and funded; appropriate indicators have been in place and reported accordingly	Review and update processes and reports on a regular basis; documents are in place and monitored in all areas; resources and capabilities are in place and in use; actions are reported an implemented

7 Process of Internal and External Audit

Cisco sees corporate governance and risk management as a whole and combines the focus on both. Cisco conducts both internal and external audits. An internal audit is primarily designed to perform the role of trustee, ensure that the internal audit and risk control processes are effective, and develop audit and risk control personnel. Internal audit reports are sent directly to the Board of Directors. An efficient audit process is important, and each audit has an external auditor who has a better understanding of Cisco's situation and practices.

The core objective of an internal audit is to ensure that all processes are monitored and reported to the Audit Committee. Each quarter, the CEO signs the Code of Conduct, and the CEO and CFO sign the certification required by the U.S. Securities and Exchange Commission, as well as develop the company's compensation, equity stock trading guidelines and norms.

When Mr. Roush answered a question from a Chinese SOE executive about what to do if the audit found a CEO problem, he replied, "It is my responsibility to raise the issue with the auditor and then report it to the board, which is a very difficult and challenging job." "This issue doesn't necessarily involve legal issues, it may be a moral issue, there is no grey area in the face of ethical and legal issues, and everyone is equal."

External audits are primarily designed to complete financial reporting. Cisco's external audits employ PricewaterhouseCoopers, which looks at Cisco's financial reports, gives opinions on the fairness of financial statements, and provides independent perspectives to investors. It is valuable for Cisco to keep their independent views and ideas. Risk assessments are conducted when external information is audited to arrive at the top ten risks, as well as the factors, probabilities, severity (including the impact of the dollar), and management risks. The Audit Committee is then asked to study with the Board of Directors to determine whether there is a management risk gap and where the risk is greater. Those responsible for responding to risk management will mention several special risks for special attention, at which point the wind control department will design a specific risk management plan. As a result of the audit team, the audit committee will give departments a pass or fail score, in order to avoid failure, the wind control department must identify the problem and solve the problem, and the audit committee approves the annual plan.

Cisco's audits are conducted globally, and Cisco has country-specific risk audits, such as China, India, and Russia, where the head of the committee is to do so in person to ensure the quality of Cisco's audits. Each year the company has an annual audit plan in three phases (see Fig. 8.4): the first phase is in February–March of each year, when Cisco identifies the key managers to interview, plans to interview, and proactively collects other recommendations. The purpose of this is primarily to obtain information, including financial information, current trends and industry trends, on previous structures and to identify changes. Then meet with the management staff of 75 companies and the information will be consolidated and analyzed. In the second phase, results of the interview are consolidated and analyzed in March–April of each year. In the third phase, reviews and validated results from all sources and lists compile a program summary in April–May of each year.

Cisco's audits, include interviews with the Finance Department and the Legal Department on the scope of the Sarbanes Act and the risk of fraud and financial statements. They also rely upon the assessment and interviews from human resources on employment risks, with management on mergers and acquisitions, with the Information Department on information technology and process changes, and with various departments on industry and emerging market risks, annual risk assessments, and business objectives.

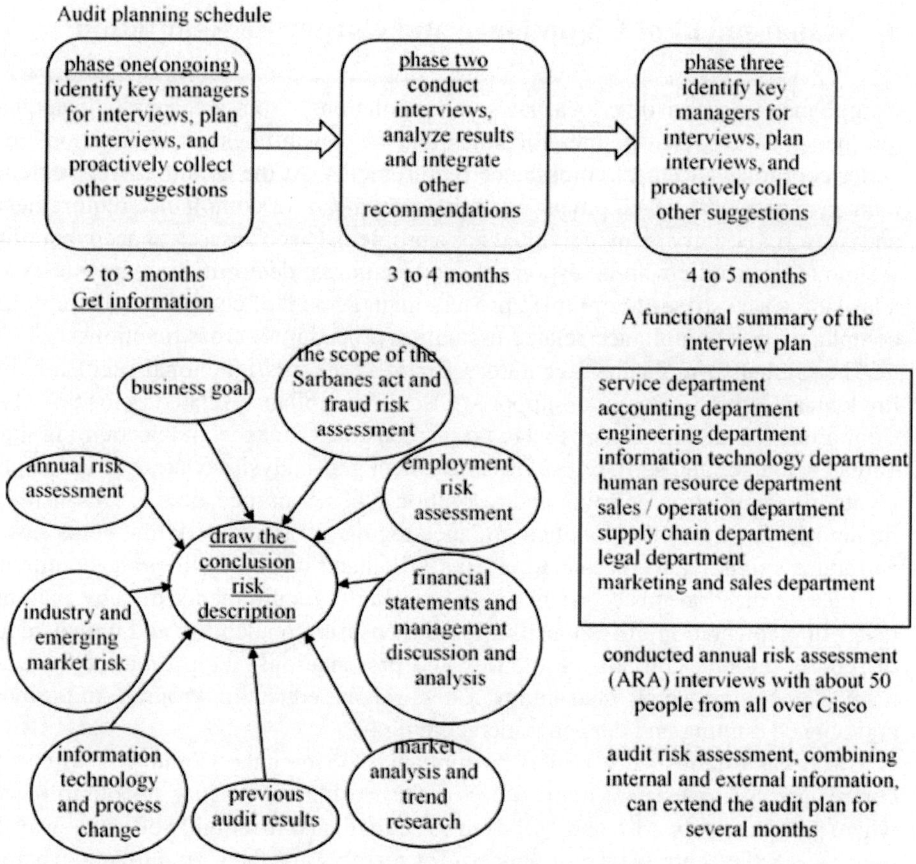

Fig. 8.4 The company's audit phase and risk management services

In its analysis, Cisco also evaluates the gap between risk and the management efficiency of risk response. Cisco first identifies the most important risks and then compares them. The size of these risks is measured by the severity of the consequences they may cause, and management efficiency is expressed on a scale of 1 to 10. The main types of risk include data security, intellectual property infringement and counterfeit products, business models and portfolios, strategic implementation, competitors, acquisition integration, resource allocation/coordination, business disruption, recruitment and retention of talent, regulation, etc. These are then compared graphically to see how far the gap between these risks and the efficiency of the company's management response is. By identifying these gaps, Cisco will find a gap between the risks it faces and the corresponding management capabilities and efficiency, and can then design special plans to improve control, with the audit department paying particular attention to the risks of particular concern at the top of the enterprise.

8 Management of Compliance and Corporate Reputation

Compliance issues involve local laws and regulations. From a corporate headquarters perspective, Cisco defines the roles and responsibilities of all functions and better coordinates to meet compliance requirements. At the country level, regional managers and local development operations are aware of compliance requirements and risks. If a country or an individual has a problem, Cisco has a clear accountability system to determine who is responsible and, with that determination, how to avoid a lawsuit. Cisco strives to optimize process management of compliance by unifying compliance and compliance-related escalation procedures across functions.

The Global Compliance Regulatory Board is a cross-functional regulator that implements, coordinates and supports Cisco's compliance-related priorities. The Committee has eight areas of focus: tax and customs, finance and accounting, law, human resources and staff, priorities, assessment gap analysis, awareness and implementation, regulatory reporting and resolution. The committee aims to establish and implement a sustainable global compliance regulatory framework that helps assess and address significant cross-sectoral risks, articulates responsibilities and communicates across the globe in accordance with compliance requirements, thereby enabling better implementation of responsibilities and ensuring readability and transparency of reports through compliance metrics and presentations, with a matrix for each team. The committee also has an awareness-raising education program to promote compliance training and deepen understanding.

Cisco has established a Global Compliance Governance Committee to ensure compliance in a consistent manner across the world, and it sends people to places where problems may arise and will need to be regulated in a highly effective way. In the process, the central issue of concern for members of the Committee is whether decision makers have the power to make decisions.

In terms of reputation management, the annual Reputation Index survey in the United States is an important measure of a company's position and image in the eyes of consumers, the most famous of which is Harris Interactive. There are 6 measured metrics: (1) emotional attractiveness that gives consumers a good sense of feeling, trust and respect; (2) products and services, including product quality, innovation, value for money and durability, (3) working environment, including good employees, fair treatment and a good workplace, (4) financial position, better than competitors' performance, low investment risk, good profitability and future growth prospects; (5) vision and leadership, excellent leaders, market opportunities and future awareness of the community, and 6 The index ranks the top 100 companies based on sales revenue, sorts them according to a survey of 8,000 audiences, then surveys 20,000 people and selects six companies that each person knows well, and on top of that, survey on six large metrics and 20 sub-indicators. In the process of determining the social value of an enterprise, 10 years ago the tangible assets of the enterprise accounted for 90% of the reputation of the enterprise, but now intangible assets accounted for 80% of the enterprise's reputation. Cisco's Corporate Social Responsibility division has 100 full-time employees and 100 contractors. Chambers' former spokesperson is in charge of the job, with an annual social responsibility budget of $295 million and a 3% increase in net profit of $9 billion. The work of the social responsibility department is to analyze the demands of the stakeholders of the enterprise, to feed their opinions back to the enterprise, to engage in dialogue with the stakeholders, and at the same time, to target competitors at the social responsibility level. Cisco's Social Responsibility Division works closely with various functions, such as developing green supply chains, focusing on greenhouse gas emissions, clean energy, cooling equipment, increasing energy usage, and building data centers where clean energy is purchased. The purpose of paying attention to corporate social responsibility is to ensure the commercial value and stock value of the enterprise, to maintain the sustainable development of the enterprise, so that the value of the enterprise is not seriously affected in bad economic times. Cisco recognizes that every employee is an ambassador for the company, and that its annual social responsibility report is published in conjunction with corporate financial reports.

At Cisco, each year all employees must sign off on the company's conduct and ethics guidelines and agree to follow the specifications, which is one of the requirements for working at Cisco. Cisco's ethics training for employees also uses videos, guides, animations, among others, as seen on the first day of work for new employees to remind them of the importance of ethical issues.

Chambers' message to business executives and all employees is that ethics is especially important to Cisco, that ethics is the cornerstone of its corporate culture and policy development, and that it is a key element to consider when making any decision. Employees can express their ethical concerns or report in six ways: hotlines (available in 150 different languages, 24 h), e-mail, fax, and more. Cisco has dedicated teams that use specifically designed tools to establish management systems that document each case, report on a quarterly basis, investigate all reports, and risk audit also works closely with human resources and legal departments. Key issues identified are reported to Chambers, the Treasurer, or the Regional Sales President, depending on the severity of the issue.

9 Summary

The decline of many enterprises was not as a result of being overtaken by competitors but rather at their own hands. In a highly competitive environment, successful enterprises usually make fewer mistakes in the transition and development period. This system may invest resources or slow the pace of growth of enterprises, but from the results, it has played an important role in avoiding significant losses to businesses and ensuring their safety and stability.

In Cisco's case, its risk control has formed a systematic, data-based and institutionalized management system. In the risk identification and analysis system, the enterprise is facing 120 potential risks to fully perceive, early warning, measurement and evaluation, and risk management of the responsible person and plan have a response mechanism, from early detection to rapid response, so that enterprises can avoid the risks that may be encountered and ensure the overall development of security. Building on a comprehensive take-over of 120 risks, the Board focused on 20–30 risks that have a significant impact on the long-term and overall development of the business, avoiding "unthinkable" or surprise at decision-making levels. In this sense, risk control needs to face the truth, face the problems and challenges, do not hide, do not avoid the cultural atmosphere and institutional environment, so as to contain the risk in the bud, so that the healthy development of enterprises.

Risk control should occur sooner rather than later, before the risk has evolved into a crisis, resulting in waste of corporate resources, and a damaged reputation. Risk control is not just an audit or wind control department, but the responsibility of the entire enterprise. Of course, each person has different levels of control and responsibility, but everyone needs to play a part in risk control. Wind control departments in the methodology and framework system to support, only when every corner of the enterprise has a pair of alert eyes, the risk can be contained before it escalates. Especially in grass-roots risk, front-line employees are often the first to face the risk, and if the enterprise does not have a rapid warning and response mechanism, the grass-roots risk reported to senior management when a risk has already formed presents a gaping loophole.

Chapter 9
Informatization and Value Chain Management

1 Introduction

Since the 1950s and 1960s, enterprise informatization is a process that enterprises use computer technology to realize business process transformation, which involves computer network hardware and software, as well as people's activities of collecting, filtering, processing, creating and disseminating data. Enterprise informatization has integrated computer technology with enterprise strategy, business model and business process, realized operational innovations such as high efficiency, low cost, rapid response and customer orientation of enterprise supply chain and value chain, and has made an important contribution to improving enterprises' data-based decision-making ability. Effectively promoting the informatization process involves the informatization strategy, information systems management and the development of information technology and information organization construction, involving people's ideas, skills, behavior, and culture change. Therefore, in the organizational change process, many enterprises must set up the management jobs, including chief information officer and chief financial officer, chief operating officer and chief technology officer, and become the core of enterprise leadership team members. The economic globalization process is becoming faster, while the enterprise informatization construction and integration of the global supply chain management is achieving the ability to rapidly respond to customers and is reducing the cost of the supply chain system, which includes the suppliers, manufacturers, warehouse, distribution center and distributors who have organized together, to product manufacturing, transport, distribution and sales.

Enterprise value chain is a strategic analysis tool. American strategic management scientist Michael Porter (1985) first proposed the method of value chain analysis and incorporated it into enterprise strategic planning. The value chain framework combines large-scale interconnected enterprises into a value system that includes all relevant stakeholders, including suppliers, core enterprises, sales channels, and customers. The value chain is a high-level logistics model that starts with raw materials as input assets until they are sold to customers through different processes, in

X. Dong et al., *Cisco*,
https://doi.org/10.1007/978-981-19-7870-8_9

which all value-adding activities are part of the value chain. The scope of the value chain extends from the core enterprise forward to suppliers, and back to distributors, service providers and customers. It also formed between assignments in the value chain, enterprise internal between different departments, between companies and customers, the relationships between enterprises and suppliers, make up the value chain, core enterprise internal between departments, between the homework between core enterprise and the node enterprises as well as the interdependent relationship between the node enterprises, affecting the performance of the value chain. Therefore, it is particularly important to coordinate, manage and control the interdependent relationship between nodal enterprises in the value chain and improve the operating efficiency and performance of nodal enterprises in the value chain. The value chain emphasizes the link level of each process and each department, and emphasizes the collaboration and collaboration across processes, departments and systems. Through the optimization and innovation of links in each process, the total value of products or servers can be increased, and unnecessary costs can be reduced. Through information system and information technology and value chain and supply chain integration, the solidification, the role of optimization, improve transparency and create new value, as in a leading position in the vendor request supplier gathered in assembly enterprises or from the consumer the most close to the supply, through the realization of parallel operation of upstream and downstream enterprise information sharing, across the tradition of the intermediate links to achieve business model innovation, and so on, all is the important content of managing change in operations management. In recent years, with the uncertainty and volatility in the market is more and more big, the more customers put forward faster, more agile, more efficient and more high quality requirements, the value chain and supply chain sector is facing challenges of demand chain management, customer driven up the value chain, demand-driven supply chain and other new concepts and new system arises at the historic moment, and require companies to minimize inventory, reduce unnecessary waste, on the supply chain to minimize the bullwhip effect. At the same time, enterprises should develop marketing capabilities based on big data mining and analysis and use the Internet as a sales platform to improve enterprises' quick perception of customer needs, direct response, and optimize customer experience.

From the perspective of product and service providers, the supply chain carries out process design, construction and thinking. The main difference between supply chain and customer value chain lies in that supply chain takes process management as the core, and through continuous integration and optimization, provides enterprises with the best path, optimal architecture and optimal resource allocation for production and service. The customer value chain considers the perspective of the customer and does the right thing on behalf of the customer. In the process of providing products and services, the main responsibility of the enterprise is to optimize the customer experience. Cisco's customer value chain emphasizes the integration of the enterprise's design and production systems into or into the customer's production systems to provide end-to-end services and experiences for customers.

Cisco has approximately 60,000 employees, 96 branches and 9 functional departments in 32 countries or regions, with a total of more than 1,000 suppliers. 25,000 to 30,000 people work for Cisco. In addition, with 25,000 components and 25,000 product logos in its product portfolio, Cisco has a global production and logistics infrastructure that includes five manufacturer partners, five major original design manufacturers, more than 30 manufacturing sites, four logistics partners and 17 logistics sites.[1] Cisco's supply-chain division deals with more than 1, 000 suppliers, and for strategic reasons of focus Cisco spends 95% of its spending on a handful of suppliers, about $12 billion a year. But in the whole value chain, Cisco has ensured that its profit margin has remained between 64 and 66% for more than a decade, which indicates its leading position and core advantage in the value chain.

How does Cisco serve its customers efficiently, as a global company with a vast portfolio of products? How to achieve synergies and seamless operations with suppliers, manufacturers and partners? How to deliver products and services to customers in the shortest time, in the fastest and most convenient way? These are the key and core competitiveness of an enterprise to establish an excellent operation system.

In Cisco's view, it is important to develop innovative business models and maintain relationships with stakeholders by identifying all participants and partners in the value chain and integrating all elements of the information architecture to share information and ideas in an integrated manner. In this process, information systems help companies collaborate across departments, across enterprises, and across regions, and this architecture and network is key to enabling companies to operate effectively globally. Innovative business models supported by information systems help enterprises to quickly understand changes in the market, integrate their internal resources and get close to customers and partners.

2 Manage Global Customer Value Chain

For Cisco, the design principles of its global value chain are threefold: first, to cope with market volatility and to respond quickly to change in a volatile environment. Second, integrate global supply demand. In the global value chain planning, Cisco needs to do a unified forecast and planning, not only to predict the sales, but also to predict the business units and customer needs, so as to integrate the information of the sales, business and finance departments on a global scale. Third, establish a multi-dimensional global sector to support corporate growth. In order to achieve growth, Cisco needs to analyze and solve problems from a global perspective, including vertical and horizontal perspectives. Vertical perspective refers to the design of the operation system from the regional dimension, while horizontal perspective refers to the overall layout of the operation process. In 2011, Cisco reduced its global footprint to the Americas, Asia and Europe, allowing it to integrate in both dimensions, effectively combining its global operations with localization.

[1] Source: Internal training program in Cisco.

In strategic planning and R&D system design, Cisco has begun to consider the internalization of customer value and enhance the position of customer value in its decision-making priorities. To this end, Cisco set up customer value chain management (CVCM) team, from the department joint planning, product quality, delivery, localization, order management and so on various aspects to provide design and services, beyond the traditional supply chain management, its category by designing the end-to-end integration way for customers to provide one-stop service from order to delivery, to help customers improve their competitive advantage. The customer value chain management team adheres to the principle of the customer primarily, striving to provide the best value chain in the world and bring unparalleled experience to customers.

Since Cisco has a long customer value chain, a unified operating system and information system are critical to the effective operation of the entire system. In addition, the value chain also involves virtual factories and networked virtual supply chains. The purpose is to achieve seamless integration between enterprises and ensure the consistency of operations, so as to make their value chains continuously extended and replicable.

3 Customer-Centered Value Chain Management Mode

Cisco's customer value chain has five models, each of which actually represents a business challenge and opportunity.

(1) Mixed production mode. Cisco uses a global manufacturing framework that outsources 95% of its finished products. On the one hand, the company itself to do well, and at the same time to conduct good cooperation with partners; on the other hand, the composition of the value chain is very complicated to integrate the production model that is compatible with all parties.
(2) One-stop network service. Cisco has a wide range of products to provide customers with a unified, one-stop network services.
(3) Customized products. Cisco's production model is to first take orders from customers and break them into rows. Then feedback the corresponding supply information to the supplier and partners, produce the products required by the customer, and finally deliver them to the customer. Cisco has few products in stock and makes them on demand.
(4) Recruiting clients. Cisco welcomes customers of all types and natures and provides them with customized services. From small and medium-sized enterprises to global top 500 multinationals, from commercial enterprises to government departments, from services to manufacturing, Cisco has a wide range of customers.
(5) acquisition and integration. Cisco achieves rapid value growth by acquiring potential enterprises and integrating the value of these enterprises into its own value chain.

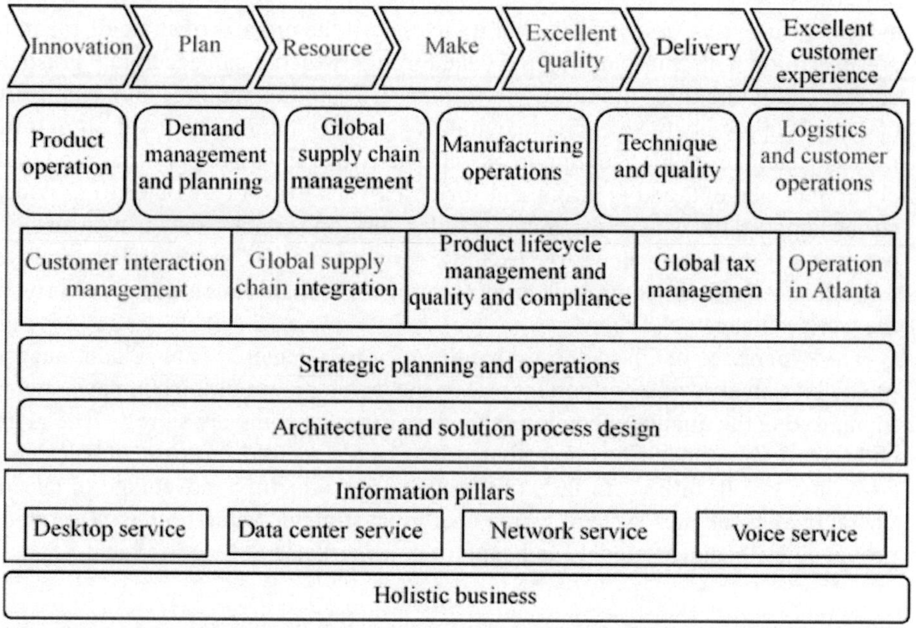

Fig. 1 End-to-end service delivery system across customer value chain

The first line in Fig. 1 is the customer value chain delivery process, the second line is the corresponding business support, for example, product operations support the innovation process, while requirements management and planning support the planning process, and all business support belongs to the scope of global business operations. If all the departments are integrated to form a dragon, then the enterprise will become more powerful. In a one-stop enterprise, each person's work results need to be responsible for others, departments are intricately linked, we jointly build a successful value chain system, this mode of operation is completely different from before.

As a one-stop enterprise, Cisco has formed a comprehensive solution integrating customer service, architecture, strategic planning, global supply chain, operations and value chain. Viewed from the top down in Fig. 1, Cisco's value chain encompasses end-to-end processes from innovation, planning, resources, manufacturing, excellence, delivery, and customer experience. The information systems applications that underpin this value chain cover six areas: product operations, demand management and planning, global supply chain management, manufacturing operations, technology and quality, and logistics and customer operations. Cisco's manufacturing is outsourced, so it needs to develop information systems to monitor the manufacturing process to ensure product quality. Supported by information systems, Cisco has built a seamless global operation system, including customer interaction management, global supply chain integration, product lifecycle management, quality, compliance, global tax management and operations in Atlanta. The global operating system ensures that Cisco has the ability to control the process of strategic planning and execution with transparency and data, through which it can accurately grasp the current and future three months of performance. To do this requires both enterprise-class and supply-chain level architectural design and solution process design. Information system in addition to support business activities and the supply chain and value chain management, and environment for employees to work together to provide a strong support, the concrete content includes desktop services, data center services, network services, and voice services, these services enable Cisco's global employee to work on a platform, communication, learning and collaboration, greatly improving the work efficiency.

The experience of Cisco shows that the customer-centered value chain management plays an especially important role in the development of the company, mainly in improving the quality experience and increasing the company's profit. The global end-to-end value chain has contributed to Cisco's tenfold increase in sales from $4 billion to $40 billion. In fact, this is the core competitive advantage of Cisco's operational excellence system, which is of great strategic value for Cisco to rapidly promote new business models and explore new markets.

4 Transformation of Value Chain Management

In 2001, after the bursting of the Internet bubble, Cisco began to think about what was most important for the further development of the company, what the company's goals were, and what kind of capabilities and development customer value chain management could bring to the company. In this process, Cisco's supply chain and value chain management has undergone several transformations.

Outsourcing is the core of value chain management. In the 1990s, as the company grew too fast to keep up with production capacity, Cisco naturally adopted outsourcing to improve manufacturing scale and level. Since then, the concept of "outsourcing" proposed by Cisco has gradually been followed and popularized throughout the industry.

Value chain management with virtual value chain as the core. Until 2005, Cisco's "outsourced" manufacturing model was just "virtual factories" and even "virtual supply chains". Cisco has a lot of great people who have been with the company for many years, but the company is not better able to benefit from their experience, and the people themselves are not able to move to a higher level of development. Cisco has embarked on a shift, first to "extend and deepen manufacturing excellence", then to "extend the supply chain" and, more recently, to "manage the customer value chain". In the process, what Cisco has to do is bring in the old leaders and employees to the new jobs, which of course is risky because people tend to be constrained by "muscle memory" when companies change. So-called "muscle memory" refers to people's behavior inertia, people are too used to the traditional way of behavior. As a result, Cisco needs to break "muscle memory" through innovation and job rotation. Everyone needs to change the way they think and act in a new learning mode.

From operation—centered to customer—centered management. After 2006, as market competition intensified and customers demanded increasingly customized services, fast delivery and high-quality services, their demands constantly hung-over Cisco, and Cisco needed to meet these demands one by one every day. In such an environment, Cisco global value chain pursues a one-stop service experience of the customer value chain, including innovation, planning, resources, manufacturing, excellent quality, delivery, excellent customer experience and many other links. This process corresponds to Cisco's specific business operations, which are product operations, demand management and planning, global supply chain management, manufacturing operations, technology and quality, logistics and customer operations. Through its customer value chain management, Cisco hopes to integrate its business operations along these "one package" processes to achieve an end-to-end user experience.

The core characteristics of a one-stop value chain are customer orientation, a shift in measurement from an operational to a customer focus, and a shift from a focus on cost, quality, delivery and speed to a focus on customer input, operational excellence, financial efficiency, and employee and organizational development. Its transformation characteristics are shown in Table 1.

After the customer-centric shift in the value chain, Cisco actually gained more power to fulfill more responsibilities and expanded the concept of traditional manufacturing management. Cisco used to think of manufacturing as making parts and combining them into finished products, but now it thinks suppliers responsible for manufacturing need to be more involved in the design of products, processes and supply chains, and even in Cisco's planning process, while helping the company's distribution partners become more profitable. Cisco's transformation is driven by clear goals, careful planning, implementation in the organization, and the actions of everyone involved—each step taking more responsibility for improving the customer experience.

Table 1 Compare operation-oriented and customer-oriented supply chain management

Project	Operation centered	Customer oriented
Focus on the core	Cost, quality, delivery and speed	Customer opinion, operational excellence, financial efficiency, employee development, organizational development
Process management	Deliver high quality products on time and in quantity/control cost	Perfect product launch
Structure management	On time delivery	Accurate delivery
Cycle management	Adhere to the delivery cycle	Track the whole cycle from order to settlement
Achievements	Limited customer feedback	Pay attention to the actual customer satisfaction index

5 How to Manage the Complexity of the Value Chain?

As volatility in global markets has increased further since the 2008 financial crisis, the focus of Cisco's value chain management has shifted to how to deal with the complexity of the environment. Previously, a good supply chain meant good margin protection and customer satisfaction; In an increasingly complex global environment, new value chains must be on demand in an uncertain and dynamic environment if they are to become "the primary drivers of enterprise growth and customer experience". The dynamics and factor complexity of the external environment are mainly reflected in the following aspects:

One is expanding growth opportunities. The impact of globalization on an enterprise's value chain is reflected in how it operates effectively in different countries and environments. Cisco inspects, manages and evaluates potential and realistic manufacturing facilities in different places, and manages customer experiences with different expectations, which is directly related to Cisco's competitiveness in different markets.

The second is the increasing complexity of the competitive environment. The diversity of customers and products determines that Cisco needs to constantly adjust the way it operates to solve complex problems.

The third is the increasing volatility and risk in the value chain. Over the past few years, Cisco has invested heavily in improving the value chain's ability to cope with risk. For example, in the 2011 earthquake in Japan, it was due to the past efforts to improve the ability to cope with risks that Cisco was able to quickly integrate multiple technologies to obtain overall intelligence and understand the affected suppliers, so as to quickly adjust suppliers and make timely responses.

Fourth, the instability of the global economy. Around the world, every day's headlines focus on unexpected events that affect the world's financial markets and businesses. Thus, Cisco's value chain management needs to develop the ability to respond dynamically to changes in the economy, which Cisco does by investing in market research, competitive intelligence, and business intelligence based on data mining.

In the context of the changing world political and economic environment, Cisco has shifted from a single-core business model to a multi-supply chain model. The so-called single core means that Cisco has a core technology and products; The multi-supply chain model combines various product lines to provide a more rapid and flexible management system with a high focus on customer experience, presenting Cisco's high degree of integration to customers.

In terms of performance measurement, Cisco has evolved from a focus on costs and the pursuit of strong gross margins to an optimized profit mix. Now Cisco needs to consider how a 10% increase in profits in one area will affect other areas. In the past, its delivery cycle focused on unfinished orders, and now it is focused on responding quickly to customer needs, with the aim of bringing Cisco as close to its customers as possible. In addition, the focus of supply chain management has evolved from focusing on local flexibility to focusing on overall flexibility and agility. The focus of geographical selection has shifted from focusing on low manufacturing costs to focusing not only on low costs, but also on whether there is room for further development in regional markets, focusing on regions with Cisco partners or close government relationships.

Cisco integrates the value chain with the supply chain to form an efficient supply chain management team. In the supply chain department, there are six teams working together:

(1) the product operation team working with the engineering team is responsible for product innovation and new product development to ensure that the technology used by the engineering team meets the company's quality standards and scale standards.
(2) global planning and execution team, sales and operation team.
(3) the global supplier management team responsible for supply, whose main task is to select professional suppliers, seize the opportunity to cooperate with suppliers, and find the best time for the next phase of technology development.
(4) the global manufacturing operation team responsible for manufacturing, mainly to find the core manufacturing partners and promote cooperation, to carry out simple testing.
(5) ensure the technical team of excellent quality, mainly responsible for testing the quality of the manufacturing process and products and testing the best time for the next generation of products to enter the market.
(6) global manufacturing and operation team responsible for delivery, logistics and transportation.

In addition, Cisco has set up a global business operations division, the nerve center of the supply chain, which reviews financial expenses, sets up processes for different functions, and also runs sustainability, risk management, acquisitions, and integration programs. Global business operations are cross-functional and follows a centralized management model. In fact, Cisco's functional teams, which have represented the company for the past five or six years with global businesses and suppliers, are highly matrix.

In order to better cope with the complexity of the value chain challenges, Cisco formulated response strategies from the following six aspects:

First, manage volatility. Cisco needs a more agile and flexible supply chain. At the strategic level, first, product flexibility, using common platforms and reusable component patterns to minimize specific components. The second is the flexibility of the network, segmenting the company's supply chain and integrating partners and manufacturing bases around the world. Cisco needs to respond quickly to change in a volatile environment without increasing costs and affecting the customer experience.

Second, optimize global value chain planning. In global value chain planning, Cisco has to do a unified forecast and planning, in addition to forecasting sales, but also forecast the business units and customer needs. To integrate supply and demand and achieve a balance, Cisco needs to integrate information from its sales, business and finance departments.

Third, build multi-dimensional global divisions to support growth. In order to achieve growth, Cisco needs to analyze and solve problems from a global perspective, in which the vertical perspective is to design the operation system from the regional dimension, while the horizontal perspective is to conduct the overall layout of the operation process. The regional dimension can list North America, Latin America, Europe, the Middle East and Africa, and the Asia–pacific region. In 2011, in order to reduce organizational redundancy, reduce unnecessary costs and improve overall efficiency, Cisco compressed its global layout into three major segments: the Americas, Asia and Europe. While it is not easy to drive the company's global integration from both horizontal and vertical dimensions, Cisco clearly recognizes that localization of its regional operations teams is essential for efficient operations.

Fourth, move from a single value chain to multiple synchronous value chains. Today, Cisco has value-chain models, including "order to order", "order to order", "stock to stock" and other types. Value chain management will continue to be the focus of corporate investment.

Fifth, simplify the way you work. Cisco simplifies business processes through extensive process reengineering, encourages employees to provide Suggestions on workflow simplification, and selects the five most important parts to execute; Meanwhile, improve the process optimization management of all functional departments, especially financial departments; optimize the service system of the supply chain and standardize the IT system in the supply chain; finally, through organizational restructuring to reduce redundancy.

Sixth, people localization. In 2010, Cisco adopted a strategy of localizing people, emphasizing delegating power to regional executives and giving more decision-making power to local management. Instead of concentrating teams in San Jose, Cisco has them train in San Jose for three to six months, focus on Cisco's business processes, and sends them out to other locations.

6 Integration of Information Construction and Value Chain Management

In Cisco's business model, there is a symbiotic relationship between the customer value chain department and the information department, but the customer value chain department takes the primary responsibility to ensure that the company can conduct product design and research and development in real time. In case of business problems, the customer value chain department takes the primary responsibility. The strategic intention of customer value chain department is reflected in the roadmap of information system construction. When customers' needs conflict with Cisco's value chain, Cisco's strategy is to try to listen and understand customers' problems, seek solutions through dialogue and try to meet customers' needs. The basic principle of Cisco is not to do things that you do not do well or that are outside of Cisco's core values.

For Cisco, information construction can effectively promote the landing and operation of its value chain. Cisco's core of customer value management in the process of informatization goal is to improve the transparency of enterprises and prediction accuracy, through the seamless value chain between the various departments, the operational optimization was achieved through the method of automated, establish easy to extend, highly flexible business model, to promote the use of business transformation and interagency collaboration technology.

The informatization construction of Cisco has gone through a dynamic evolution process. Since the 1980s, the promotion process of enterprise informatization has gone through four stages.

In the first stage, in the 1980s, Cisco's information technology application environment construction focused on the core manufacturing operation system, such as using Oracle enterprise resource planning (ERP) for inventory management, raw material procurement, printing labels and automatic testing.

In the second phase, 1990–2002, Cisco's information technology application environment was built based on outsourcing manufacturing. Based on the previous phase, partners could operate in Cisco's IT environment, such as access to Cisco's internal network and automatic detection on external network.

In the third stage, from 2003 to 2009, Cisco's information technology application environment construction was dominated by lean manufacturing. In this stage, the newly added functions realized the business-to-business docking between Cisco and partner information systems.

The fourth phase, after 2010, Cisco's information technology application environment construction in end-to-end value chain is given priority to, with particular emphasis on collaboration of this phase, Cisco hope to build the partner ecosystem, integrate the resources of the value chain, set up unified standard integration platform, use of high-tech means such as cloud computing to realize resources sharing.

At this stage, the goal of Cisco's customer value chain management is to achieve end-to-end user experience, so that a seamless enterprise can be truly implemented in practice. Cisco calls this feature "end-to-end value chain performance". The impact of information technology on the performance of Cisco's value chain is directly reflected in the promotion of "end-to-end value chain performance".

Informatization supports the construction of one-stop enterprises. Information construction plays three roles in supporting one-stop enterprises. First, it promotes the interaction between Cisco and its customers. Its efficient demand response and customer feedback improve customer satisfaction. Second, improved relationships with suppliers/contract manufacturers. Cisco's information environment facilitates collaboration with supplier/contract manufacturers, enabling customers' needs to be quickly translated into supply, thus synchronizing supplier orders and demand with production delivery, saving costs and increasing efficiency. In addition, Cisco has made significant improvements in the negotiation and audit of suppliers/contract manufacturers with the support of information technology. Third, the extension of the value chain to channel partners has enabled Cisco to excel in inventory optimization, packaging improvement, delivery cycle control, and export volume.

Through the information to achieve the performance management of suppliers. Cisco has a complete supplier performance management system, including supplier strategic development, new supplier entry, long-term supplier management and continuous improvement. In the past, supplier performance was only measured based on indicators collected by Cisco. During the performance review, suppliers were dissatisfied with or disputed about these indicators, which led to the time-consuming quarterly review. To address this, Cisco introduced the WebEx Connect executive control panel, which allows vendors to view quarterly metrics and report back to Cisco. The use of this IT product has led to increased efficiency and transparency in Cisco's quarterly audits, with vendors adjusting their pace based on performance metrics.

In terms of supplier risk management, Cisco has faced three major business challenges, namely, component suppliers affected by the credit crunch, signs of financial crisis in the supplier community, and insecurity in the sole supplier/major supplier. To address these three challenges, Cisco has come up with a number of it-based solutions. First, through the cooperation of the three parties of supply chain risk management, finance and IT, the risk suppliers are identified and evaluated. Then, vendor meetings are held through WebEx/telepresence; Finally, the portal provides an instant scalable solution to integrate vendor information. Through this series of operations, Cisco effectively addressed the challenges of supplier risk management.

Information portfolio analysis and practice framework. In the information investment planning, how to establish the priority of investment, clear the direction and purpose of technology selection, is the problem that troubles many enterprises. Cisco establishes its IT portfolio from two dimensions and four quadrants. In the two dimensions, the horizontal axis represents the degree of innovation, and the vertical axis represents the impact of information technology investment on business. After dividing the level, the four quadrants are shown in Fig. 2.

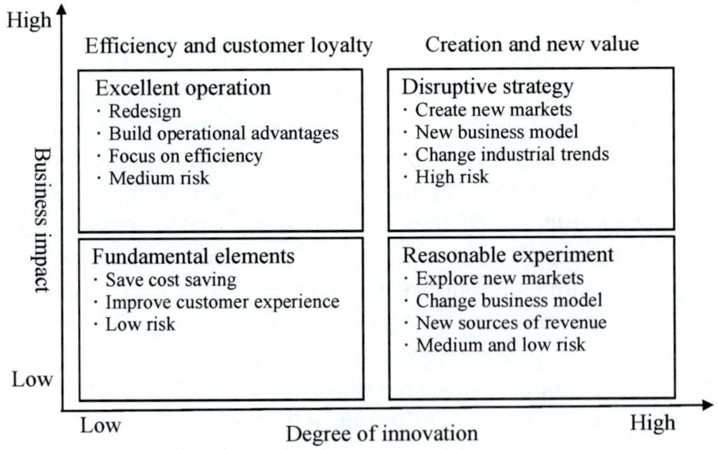

Fig. 2 IT investment analysis matrix in Cisco

(1) Fundamental elements (low level of innovation, low business impact). The purpose of IT investment in this quadrant is to save costs, improve customer experience and control risks at a relatively low level.
(2) Reasonable experiment (high degree of innovation, but low business impact). The purpose of IT investment in this quadrant is to enter new market areas, change the existing business model, and increase new revenue sources. The risk level is medium to low level.
(3) Excellent operation (low degree of innovation, but high business impact). IT investment aims to improve efficiency and customer loyalty, redesign the business process, give play to operational advantages, improve efficiency, and moderate degree of risk.
(4) Breakthrough strategy (high degree of innovation, high business impact). Its IT investment aims to open innovative markets, seek new business models and change the industry dynamics, but the risk level is relatively high.

When people make IT investments, they tend to focus on the fourth quadrant, the breakthrough strategy, which is really important, and the company that does that may be the next Google or apple. But in the real world, very few companies can really achieve disruptive innovation. Cisco's IT department is more focused on the first quadrant, the new basics—as the enterprise's information infrastructure and management application, IT's the most basic, the simplest, the least risky, but very powerful, very fast feedback. For example, through information technology to change the signature process of leaders, although it is not obvious from the innovation degree of technology application and the degree of impact on the business, but it affects the whole company, improve the management efficiency of the whole company. The risks of a breakthrough strategy are often high, so it is best to start from the dimension of sound experimentation before implementing it. The rational experimental quadrant is a strategy for products to enter the market. New products have a high degree of innovation, but they have not been widely accepted by the market and customers, so their business influence is relatively low. However, after the customer discovers and chooses this product, its business influence will gradually increase, the enterprise occupies the leading position in this new technology, with strong scarcity, rapid sales growth, high added value, the enterprise's technology will enter the breakthrough strategic quadrant. But as market influence spread, competitors followed suit, and products were quickly copied. Although the business influence of enterprises could remain high for a period of time, its scarcity and innovation degree were greatly reduced. In this period, Cisco will focus on shifting into the quadrant with operational excellence as the core. The main goal is to make mature technology products quickly reach greater market scale and bring economies of scale to the enterprise. As time went on, similar products emerged one after another. Cisco could not dominate the market with original products. Its innovation and business influence gradually declined.

The above model shows the process of value transfer in Cisco's IT investment, which is a dynamic process. In particular, it is important to note that many of Cisco's technology applications begin in the new fundamental quadrant that is most often overlooked because of its low level of innovation and low business impact, but which is key to enterprise competitiveness. It reflects the development process of new technology innovation from low to high, and also the process of execution from difficult to easy. In this process, the core element is how to transform from new basic elements quadrant to rational experiment, breakthrough strategy and excellent operation. Each transformation means that the enterprise's new technology gradually develops from "humble" to large-scale promotion process.

7 Formulation and Implementation of Information Strategy

In the formulation of Cisco's information strategy, the strategic vision of information technology application leads every wave of information technology application. The importance of the application of information technology mainly lies in: (1) constructing a new business model for the realization of virtual collaborative communication; (2) provide high-quality information services for high-level decision-making; (3) to serve the requirements of enterprises for efficient leadership in the context of economic globalization; (4) to achieve efficient intra-organizational, inter-organizational and supply chain collaboration through communication systems; (5) establishing the business model of the enterprise through information system; (6) supporting the enterprise value chain and one-stop operation system to ensure Cisco's competitive advantage and leadership position; (7) build an organizational form of borderless network through information network and information platform construction, so as to achieve seamless docking between Cisco's organizational development and the Internet era.

In the execution of information strategy, Cisco's core competitive advantage lies in technology, process and culture. The key of technology system is video technology, which has become an effective channel for internal and external communication of Cisco. Video is different from voice, when people use voice to leave messages to others, they cannot get a timely reply, nor can they see real people, and body language cannot be displayed, so the information in interpersonal communication cannot be expressed in a comprehensive and real way. Information security in technology systems provides physical and content security for Cisco's global operating systems. The data center integrates the information content of Cisco's global resources, operations and strategy execution. Through data integration, data mining and decision support, senior managers can gain insight into the current situation, problems and challenges of enterprise operation at any time, and formulate strategies for quick response.

In the process, Cisco's IT department focuses on providing practical manuals for services and virtual desktop infrastructure, so that Cisco employees can log in at any office or terminal and obtain customized information related to their work. At the same time, formulate effective system management methods and rules, and deal with emergencies. In addition, IT departments develop strategies and approaches for building a digital ecosystem.

At the cultural level, information culture is closely related to the transformation of enterprises. Many enterprises believe that informatization is a technical problem, but it is essentially a process of management transformation. In the execution system, Cisco specially arranged the IT change management team and the professional work group, so as to help enterprises effectively realize the management transformation in the process of integrating information system and business process.

In the measurement of information strategy, the evaluation index of the degree of business support of information technology is mainly reflected in eight aspects. The other is the user experience of the information system. The content of the experience includes whether the technology is easy to grasp, whether the system is easy to use and whether it is pleasant to use. This is what Cisco hopes to distinguish itself from other companies. The third is the contribution of information system to the improvement of work efficiency. The fourth is the time it took to improve Cisco's business capabilities. If the IT department in a very short period of time greatly enhance the business response to customer needs, improve the operating efficiency of the value chain, and improve the decision-making ability of senior decision makers for integrated data mining, the value brought to the enterprise by the information system will be huge. Five is replicability. The great value of the information system application is that once the initial application was proved to be successful, the application can be quickly copied to a different country, different industries and different departments, and the time cost of copy is much lower, so that we can support enterprise bigger and faster expansion planning and not bring the confusion and out of control and management to ensure the consistency of enterprise overall operating at the same time, the specification and standardization, it is very important for a global enterprise. Therefore, Cisco attaches great importance to the replication effect brought by the application of IT technology. Sixth, flexibility. With the change of market environment and competition pattern, and the adjustment of enterprise business system, the flexibility, adaptability and agility of information system become more important. The application and acceptance of new technologies and software systems also requires the ability of enterprise information systems to change as needed. The seventh is scale, that is, the coverage of information technology to enterprise business support to be broad. Eight is the speed of technology adoption.

Cisco's information strategy architecture. Cisco's information strategy consists of information architecture, business architecture, and technology architecture to improve customer satisfaction. In designing its IT architecture, Cisco considers not only the interests of its customers, but also the feelings of all its users. In other words, the design of information systems focuses on customers, partners, and Cisco employees, and on how everyone feels when they work on the IT platform every day. In complex applications, customer needs take precedence.

According to Rebecca Jacoby, Cisco's CIO at the time, CEOs and CIOs have different expectations for information technology applications. The CEO's priorities are: first, the growth and development of the business, while ensuring that operating and administrative costs remain constant. Second, process change, to make the process more efficient, convenient and rapid; In addition, to close the distance between enterprises and customers and partners. Third, new business models. The development of enterprises often needs new growth points and market opportunities, and information technology can bring new opportunities. Fourth, sustainable development and environmental protection. The green and sustainable development of the enterprise is also an especially important issue. Cisco needs to shoulder social and environmental responsibilities. The priority for CIOs is: first, to make IT the driver of strategic business. Second, make IT globally scalable. Third, ensure information security. In the IT environment, ensuring information security is not only an enterprise's capability, but also a commercial advantage. If customers understand that Cisco's information services are among the most secure in the industry, this will be an advantage for Cisco in a volatile and insecure international environment. In building this advantage, a good relationship between the IT department and the business is critical to IT success.

When Cisco establishes a connection between Business architecture and Technology architecture, its analytical thinking and overall framework should consider four aspects of Business, Operations, Systems and Technology, which are called BOST analytical framework. It can be decomposed into the following four steps: first, it should clarify the Business strategy and the core Business of the enterprise; The second step is to establish the operation process and identify the key capabilities needed in the business process. The third step is to build the system application and make clear which software applications and tools are needed to realize the business. Step 4, the underlying technologies, identify which technologies can provide these applications and tools. The BOST analysis framework helps Cisco understand the interdependencies between business and technical architectures and is widely used internally.

Cisco manufactures thousands of products. Faced with the ever-changing and increasingly complex business and technology environment, the decision-making and management model of information technology applications is divided into four steps. Second, integrate the roadmap to establish the appropriate business architecture and technical architecture; Third, planning; Fourth, test the effect, then to the market implementation. IT services and operations are the bottom layer of support, both simple and difficult to create uniform standards. The transformation of Cisco's IT division began in 2006, after Cisco's IT services were lower than other industry leaders. Cisco information goal is to improve the speed of innovation of enterprises, in order to meet the different needs of various technology and product innovation, Cisco will first keep leading position in the architecture, its architecture is not only to support the rapid running of the existing complex system, but also for the future of Cisco could reach $80 billion sales ability to lay the foundation, to meet the requirements of Cisco internal and external customers.

Cisco's IT department is positioned to integrate technology architecture, business architecture, and strategic architecture. To achieve this goal, the vision of the IT department is to leverage network information technology to lead every change. The strategy of the IT department is to integrate the technology process with the IT process in the concept of all services. IT has three main strategic goals: to build an architecture of multi-channel services, to create superior operational and decision-making processes, and to provide an impressive experience for customers, employees, and partners. At the executive level, in order to achieve Cisco's vision and strategic goals, the IT department operates on the following principles and approaches: smart people to leverage, capacity and technology roadmap, service provider accountability, talent strategy, and stakeholder support.

For the performance of the IT department, the main assessment indicators are four: growth, speed, efficiency and customer experience. IT departments meet every three months to establish the effectiveness of performance. The IT department provides information technology support for the entire innovation and operation system of Cisco mainly in four aspects: (1) supporting the transformation of the enterprise's architecture in the trinity of technology, process and culture through the matching and integration of information technology and business system; (2) support the application of video and other tools for corporate collaborative communication, so that all employees can achieve instant communication across regions or space; (3) data integration. The cloud computing system can integrate and integrate more than 150 data centers of the enterprise; (4) use mobile technology to realize dynamic interconnection of enterprises and seek market segmentation.

Rebecca, Cisco's CIO at the time, led an IT team of nearly 7,000 people who reported directly to Chambers; There are four senior vice presidents in the team responsible for global channel planning and Internet business solutions, globalization of IT, communications and collaboration, and global infrastructure. Services provided by the IT department include consulting services, Internet of everything exchange, platform services and hosting services, technical services and advanced services. The average customer satisfaction rating for services provided by IT departments rose from 3.9 to 4.6. In 2015, the company's investment in IT department accounted for 2.5–3% of the sales, among which, 2% ensured the support for the business, and 0.5–1% was the investment and research and development of new technologies. 80% of the IT investment is centrally applied by the IT department and the other 20% is left to the business units to choose. In short, Cisco has tried to make its IT department one of the best in the industry.

8 Value of Informatization and Return on Investment

Cisco's customer value chain is long and its unified operations and IT systems are complex. With virtual factories and networked virtual supply chains throughout the value chain, the goal of Cisco informatization is to achieve seamless integration between enterprises and ensure operational consistency, and to enable the continuous extension and replication of Cisco's value chain. To meet this goal, Cisco's information division employs more than 7,000 people, nearly half of whom work abroad, and the company spends 3% of its sales on it. Enterprises' input in informatization has brought rich returns to business development, and the input–output ratio has reached 1:4 for many years. In addition to driving performance growth, informatization investment also contributes to the enterprise in other aspects: technology application brings new use experience to customers and enterprise employees, and improves the enterprise's ability to respond quickly.

-- -- -- Virtual secretary in charge of over 40 buildings-- -- --

For Cisco, information services and products are quickly copied and learned from by competitors, and the only thing that gives a company a differentiated competitive advantage is the experience it creates for its customers and partners. Only by creating an unparalleled experience and continuously improving and optimizing it can an enterprise attract and retain customers, employees and partners. The user experience is inseparable from the product and determines its scalability. In the past, the user experience was mainly determined by the product, and the user's judgment criteria were relatively simple, mainly to learn about the product from the advertisement. But today, users' experience is judged by the information and word of mouth Shared by other users on social networks, and customers' expectations are getting higher and higher.

The value judgment of the top management of an enterprise on informatization is usually based on the strategic and business considerations. They want to increase the total revenue and the productivity. They want to expand the enterprise, innovate quickly, eliminate inefficient links, get closer to customers and increase the number of customers, but they do not want to increase the cost of information technology input. To achieve these goals, it leaders will need to help companies find new sources of revenue and new business opportunities that innovations and applications of information technology may provide. In fact, what business leaders expect from their

IT departments has changed. In the past, the IT department was just a cost center, used to minimize the company's costs, but after the economic recovery, business management realized that IT could both reduce costs and improve efficiency. With the development of the enterprise, IT investment in the value chain system can help the enterprise to reduce operating costs and improve the overall operating efficiency of a one-stop enterprise. Therefore, information system has become a part of Cisco's core competitiveness.

The application of information technology must be closely integrated with the business development of enterprises. To achieve this goal, CIO must keep close contact with enterprise leaders and conduct effective communication. In order to support the business, the core task of the IT department is to provide services, instead of just focusing on the technical work of developing software, developing databases, and so on. Meanwhile, high-quality and stable IT service system also needs to undergo transformation.

With the acceleration of social informatization, Cisco's view on the business value of information technology is changing constantly. The customers they serve are becoming increasingly powerful, armed with gadgets such as mobile phones, laptops and ipads. Customers are increasingly demanding more personalized service and rich experiences, and they want immediate enjoyment or a satisfying lifestyle, such as shopping at home or ordering dinner at the beach. From another perspective, information security is becoming more and more important. For example, customers attach great importance to information security and privacy protection when making electronic payments and transfers through online banking. In addition, with the acceleration of globalization, the world has become more mobile, and the application of information technology needs to be personalized, dynamic and integrated.

Cisco is very focused on innovative technologies for the next three to five years. For example, using IPV6 for unlimited connectivity: everything has its own IP address, and the number of Internet addresses will rise to 3.36 by 1039, a smart environment capable of recording everything a business does. By then, any flat object can be turned into a display, and video is everywhere; Computer—made people look so real that people can't tell the difference. Again, such as, the application of biological implants and accessories: edible sensor can be attached to each pill, when the body moisture sensor after activation, it through the body's transmission electronic signal can be reader monitoring of the outside world, used to determine drug levels and types, then the IP address of the tablets can be transmitted to the smartphone, so that a doctor or family members to monitor patients taking the pills right on time.

Another important issue in the application of information technology is how to reduce energy consumption, save money and reduce operating costs. IBM, for example, spends 50% of its money on energy. Its "green innovation initiatives" include the use of virtual servers, enabling hardware to do more with the same amount of energy, using air-conditioning only when necessary, optimizing data center ventilation through thermal engineering and 3d modeling, and so on. With the program in place, IBM doubled its data-center capacity by the end of 2010. Typical is Amazon, where 50% of the cost is information technology operating costs. To this end, they have embarked on a program to reduce energy consumption, doubling the stock of data centers by 2010 without increasing it. In other words, they use only a quarter as much energy as they used to. Similarly, Cisco has accumulated $3.3 billion in savings from green IT. As mentioned earlier, virtual cloud computing is a green practice for IT departments because IT makes more efficient use of servers and their storage space, reducing the number of devices actually running.

9 Summary

Efficient management of global value chains is one of the core competencies of global enterprises. According to the report of the OECD secretariat, in the 1990s, governments and enterprises around the world accelerated the investment in global value chains (GVCs) related to international trade. Many transnational corporations conducted the global value chain layout while carrying out the global market, resources and capacity layout: They keep the core links such as R&D, design, marketing and branding, which are high value-added and knowledge-intensive, at home, and outsource the labor-intensive links such as assembly and production of parts to developing countries, so as to maximize their own benefits by seeking cheap labor and getting close to the market. By reducing income tax and other relevant incentive mechanisms, the government encourages enterprises to invest in R&D and other core links, so as to enhance the core competitiveness of enterprises. Cisco has achieved operational leadership by integrating customer value chains, supply chains and information systems. In the process of integration, the customer value chain is the core of the whole system framework, providing the development direction of supply chain and information system. Supply chain determines the allocation of specific logistics and capital flows to improve customer experience. Information systems digitize, standardize, and transparently specific operational processes into replicable, scalable, and traceable strategic assets. The information system creates values such as efficiency, speed, transparency and accuracy, enabling customers to trace and dynamically monitor the implementation process of orders from the moment they place orders. In this way, the uncertainty and fuzziness in the order delivery process are reduced, and the process is visualized and monitored. The management of process is the management of results. With strict process management, the quality of products can be guaranteed, which greatly improves customer experience, improves customer satisfaction, and truly realizes end-to-end service. During the economic downturn, Cisco enhanced the optimization and improvement of international supply chain, making its supply chain operation and management ability rank the fifth in the us enterprise supply chain management ranking, ensuring the high value-added and sustainable development ability of enterprise process.

Business model innovation is closely related to process management and information system. As the scale of the enterprise expands and the product category increases, the number of suppliers and customers will increase, and the complexity of the enterprise will also increase. In order to simplify complexity, enterprises need to follow the principle of consistency and reproducibility in information management system.

Cisco's consistency and reproducibility have been very successful in the construction and operation of its global enterprise. The information system brings the characteristics of low reproduction cost, fast speed and strong integration to the economies of scale, which makes it become the important foundation and resource of the enterprise strategic investment. But at the same time, the construction of enterprise informatization is a long-term process, which needs to be constantly weighed and adjusted in complexity and simplification, dynamic and stability, flexibility and integration, so as to meet the requirements of customers and enterprises' own development of diversified capabilities.

For a global enterprise, its level of information-based management determines its ability to control global resources, especially customer resources, financial resources and operational processes. The western management thought and method take the process as the core, the process construction is the system construction, the process management is extensive, the system loophole is many; The continuous improvement of an enterprise is a process of continuous optimization and improvement. Once the process is controlled, the result can be controlled. Cisco's ISO series, six sigma, process reengineering, fine manufacturing, value chain management, supply chain management, and information system management all take business process as the core for management reform, and from the enterprise level, industrial level to the global value chain, e-commerce ecosystem evolution, its coverage is more and more extensive. Whether government or enterprise, its ability to control processes determines its ability to integrate resources, position and influence in the business ecosystem. Enterprises with core competence in this respect can truly become the leading enterprises with core leading role and occupy the high end of the value chain. In the future, as the Internet and the Internet of things are increasingly integrated with enterprise business, enterprises holding the big data of transactions between enterprises and between enterprises and customers will become the uncrowned king.

Chapter 10 Collaborative Organization and Knowledge Management

1 Introduction

The collaboration and cooperation of enterprises are two different concepts. Collaboration refers to the creation of a model of joint planning, co-execution, and joint evaluation between individuals or organizations, in which stakeholders share responsibilities and participate in the decision-making process. Collaboration invests more time and effort than collaboration. Cooperation refers to the work between individuals and organizations through mutual agreements, in the process, the parties concerned are independent and autonomous, working together for common goals and projects, but that is all. The research shows that collaborative organizations have three characteristics: first, they have cross-sectoral and cross-enterprise collaboration mechanisms, sharing resources with each other in different geographical or professional contexts; Conduct cross-sectoral communication, cooperation and decision-making, in order to achieve a common goal, in the planning and implementation of the formation of a joint team, the joint team has a consistent understanding of the results, delivery and assessment of the project; Transparency of information is important; fifth, at the resource level, the joint team is willing to contribute time, resources and capabilities during the planning phase, and both share the relevant systems and platforms.

To build a collaborative organization, you need to start with eight aspects. One is market-oriented, the agility and flexibility of the enterprise is reflected in its matching to market demand, only the establishment of an efficient collaboration between the various departments of the enterprise, can truly become a market and customer-oriented organization. The second is to clarify how the tasks of the enterprise are completed, how the process is, how people's rights and responsibilities. On this basis, really do the right information, in the right time to the right person, and let him make the right decision. The third is to make the necessary adjustments to the organizational structure and processes. Collaborative organizations don't just care about whether they're doing things, they're more concerned with how things are done, what are the obstacles and difficulties, so the design of structures, systems, processes, and incentives is key. Fourth, in the process of building a collaborative organization, the

X. Dong et al., *Cisco*,
https://doi.org/10.1007/978-981-19-7870-8_10

role of leaders and managers is very important, how they position themselves, how to authorize, how to design ways to do things, what kind of culture to create, can be built into a collaborative organization is very important. Fifth, grass-roots employees do not collaborate automatically, so it is necessary to design at the organizational level, encourage collaboration between employees through training, support, motivation, and guidance, and transform internal competitive relationships into collaborative relationships so that employees are given the right information to make decisions and take action at the right time. Sixth, the support system to keep up, enterprises to support front-line staff thinking and redesign ingesting methods, supplemented by a variety of incentives. Seven is to establish a collaborative culture. The main purpose of a collaborative organization is to achieve a rapid response to and response to customer and market needs, which is critical to the survival and development of the business, while a collaborative organization is full of entrepreneurship, highly sensitive to opportunities, and departments work together for the same goals. Eight is the use of information technology tools and methods that facilitate enterprise collaboration to support information flow, information sharing, and knowledge management between collaboration departments at greater efficiency and cost.

Cisco has 460 offices in 96 countries around the world, and the organizational system is structured by functional and three geographic regions, with no subsidiaries. The advantage of this organizational structure is that management costs are low, and businesses do not need to have many plant managers, finance directors, and sales staff, which can significantly reduce costs through unified procurement and scale operations. At the same time, Cisco has built a large, unified IT architecture to support the operation of the entire enterprise, ensuring the truth and integration of information, helping to flatten the management of the enterprise, reduce the level, improve decision-making efficiency, and enable talent to flow internally. At the market level, customers only need to deal with one sales representative and not with multiple different departmental representatives to ensure consistency in delivering products, and the business operates a single brand, reducing external transaction costs, and increasing collaboration between distinct functions, resulting in different revenue combinations.

"However, there are also many weaknesses in this organizational structure: management workload, strong coordination between functions, inherent complexity of the organizational system can also result in poor decision-making, slow collaboration between functions, poor internal flexibility, etc. "The size of the enterprise may lead to slow response times to market changes, poor coordination between functions, high cost of internal transactions, and the possibility that firms will spend a lot of time on internal coordination rather than customer-facing." Because of the high concentration of decision-making, to a certain extent, risk control is highly demanding.

2 Using Knowledge Platform to Build the Foundation of Enterprise Differentiation

With the rapid globalization of economy, transnational competition makes the living environment of enterprises increasingly severe, how to explore and construct the real strategic differences of an enterprise, and ensure the sustainable competitive advantage of enterprises, has become a serious problem facing business leaders.

Cisco is a knowledge- and technology-intensive enterprise, how to effectively manage knowledge as a strategic resource, how to stimulate collective intelligence and potential, and constantly explore the space for innovation and transformation, is an important basis for Cisco's differentiation with other enterprises.

In designing an organizational structure and culture that is appropriate for the post-80s and post-90s, Cisco's leadership is acutely aware that good organizational design and management requires observing the character and needs of each generation and developing the appropriate organizational approach based on their characteristics. In the United States, for example, people living in different eras have very different personal qualities and characteristics. Most of the people born between 1925 and 1945 were hard-working and diligent, but most of them had retired. People in their post-50s and post-60s have experienced a boom ingress economy. For the post-80s and post-90s generation, they are characterized by strong learning ability, independence, friendship, openness, freedom, high turnover, and willingness to work in any place in the world that is more recognized and respected for their values and talents. In this context, Cisco believes it is important to create a work environment and working mechanism that adapts to the flow of talent and therefore designs an information platform that meets the needs and characteristics of this generation to meet their desires and needs for career development and job competition. This is important to improve the level of human resources, productivity and productivity of global companies.

For knowledge-based and innovative enterprises, three things must be done to ensure a leading position in the fierce international competition:

(1) Continue to attract innovative talent to work at Cisco. Cisco is very focused on how to attract truly talented people to work and stay at Cisco, so organizations need to understand the metrics of the best talent and how they can attract them. Cisco has also built a complete talent pool that focuses on the demand for talent at different times and achieves better talent management.

(2) When the talented people come to the enterprise, can they meet the challenges of various customers' needs from all over the world, anytime, anywhere, quickly and efficiently, and realize effective collaboration and cooperation? At this point, the construction of the information platform creates good conditions for cross-border, cross-time zone, and cross-cultural collaboration among employees, and Cisco has achieved support and recognition from employees.

(3) Knowledge-based enterprises need the right leadership, the right people, and the right timing. At Cisco, the right employees have engagement, and the definition of engagement is that employees are willing to put in extra effort at work, which

makes sense for improving the competitiveness of the business. We find that a good job of developing talent in an enterprise will have a positive impact on the improvement of performance. Therefore, fostering employee engagement is one of Cisco's key strategies and the foundation of Cisco's differentiated competitive advantage, and how to create a good working environment and collaboration platform for employees is seen as an important part of Cisco's organizational capabilities.

3 Use of Information Technology to Create Different Working Environments

Over the course of 34 years, Cisco will shape new work environments and approaches based on different information technologies of different eras. In the 1990s, Cisco used primarily individual and computer, as well as the way in which endpoints were connected and interacting; With the creation of social networks and network platforms, Cisco has seized the opportunity to build a global, collaborative network platform that is critical to building a collaborative organization, investing and building as an important strategic asset that differentiates it from other businesses in order to engage in interaction and communication between multiple people and multiple people through a collaborative network.

The results show that by 2016, more than 60% of employees will be working in a mobile state. The constant travel of employees on business trips poses challenges to the traditional office-based approach, and if managers continue to organize and design according to the way the office works, it can result in a huge waste of space and time, as well as difficulties in responding to customer needs and working together. In a mobile state, employees need to connect and collaborate with each other anytime, anywhere, which is the most effective way to work, and new collaborative technologies and tools can effectively help businesses solve these problems.

4 Use of Information Technology to Build a Collaborative Organization

Collaborative organizations are able to quickly adapt themselves to changes in the market and seize new opportunities in the market. Collaborative organizations can break down barriers between departments, businesses, and functions, and organizational design is designed to combine people, information, and resources within the organization based on customer needs and market changes, rather than designing and managing with the internal needs of the organization at its core. As a result, collaborative organizations are more adaptable, agile, and responsive, and more resilient to new environments.

As international competition becomes more intense, speed becomes more important. Procter and Gamble's Christie's toothpaste has consistently led the u.S. toothpaste market share, and it took Colgate 45 years to find a way to beat Christie's. But with the rapid development of information technology today, the market will not give companies so long to beat their competitors. As a result, collaboration efficiency within the enterprise is critical to speed.

Information technology can build a borderless network for enterprises, help enterprises to break down barriers inside and outside the organization, break the boundaries with customers, suppliers and even competitors, so that all departments, regions and links can be seamlessly integrated, efficient operation, the organization's knowledge and platform to employees and customers to provide strong support and collaboration, help them do their job better. Information technology also helps companies expand their virtual boundaries and extend their reach to a wider range of markets and customers.

Build a new work ecosystem. The financial crisis and recession have forced employees to change their way of working. The advent of Web 2.0, such as social networking, makes technology easier to use, more pervasive, and more influential. This has an impact on the work ecosystem of employees, customers, and technical support. In this work ecosystem, employees want to use new technologies in their businesses, preferably the same technology they use in their daily lives. For businesses, it is hoped that the application of technology will promote more effective collaboration between employees, departments and geographies, and while many have recognized the importance of new technology tools, few enterprises have the ability to integrate these technologies with enterprise collaboration. For customers, they have the right to share information, compare prices, write and read comments, and the information and opinions provided by people of the same needs or around them are helpful in making important decisions. The client also wants to participate in the buying and selling process and take control of the transaction process. For Cisco, being able to provide a perfect experience for its customers is critical, otherwise, once a customer is dissatisfied with a product or service posted online, it is the equivalent of instantly telling thousands of friends around the bad experience, the consequences are unimaginable.

Build a collaborative work environment. For a healthy business, listening and communicating candidly are important, and the work environment and work platform it creates should be aligned with its value proposition and culture. In Silicon Valley, different high-tech companies' pride themselves on providing different cultural and working environments. Google, for example, is known for providing employees with a wide range of services and benefits, such as carefully cooking delicious and free food, and helping employees wash their clothes for free, in the hope that employees will stay in the workplace for as long as possible, which is the value of Google's value proposition to employees. For Cisco, the emphasis is placed on employees with greater flexibility and provides them with a very convenient remote collaboration work environment. Cisco has 40% of its employees who work on the move regularly, and they call themselves mobile employees.

It is not fixed to work in the office, but for 60% of engineers, the office is more efficient. There are also some employees who prefer to work from home, about twice a week, and for this reason, Cisco has introduced and developed a number of information technology tools to support employees working remotely, and making them as productive as working in the office, which is an important practice for Cisco to experience collaboration technology, and employees also believe that flexible work models are more efficient. At the same time improve their quality of life and time management capacity, but also can be work and family balance.

---------------Cisco's remote video management system-----------------

The contribution of telepresence to face-to-face communication. Telepresence technology is a remote video conferencing technology that can integrate video communication and communication experience in recent years, with the characteristics of real-life size, ultra-high clear, low latency, its focus on real face-to-face communication, the realization of the process involving network, communication, conference environment, functional applications and other aspects, The final presentation to the participants is an integrated and real communication experience combined with the transaction application. Telepresence is easy to use, realistic, interactive parties as if in person to carry out face-to-face exchanges, to solve the general remote conference video system screen dull, small images of personnel, difficult to conduct the speaker and audience interaction. Telepresence technology makes distance barriers no longer exist, employees around the world can easily exchange experiences with each other, virtual speakers can teach guests very realistically, and the latest technology also allows people not only to know what the two sides of the conversation are talking about, but also to allow the interviewer to look the other eye and observe each other's body movements. It's like face-to-face communication. Telepresence technology has increased Cisco's customer base by 2–3 times, reduced travel costs and costs (17%), reduced spending by $1.5 billion, and reduced resources by $1 billion to reallocate, low-carbon, environmentally friendly, and better communication. Cisco also uses virtual conferencing systems to operate globally and to reach its customers in emerging economies. Cisco has two headquarters: one in San Jose, California, and one in Bangalore, India. The two centers are closely linked. Much of this connection is achieved by Cisco's telepresence and unified communications. Heads of the regions also install telepresence at home, sometimes in the middle of the night to attend the company's global video executive meetings. For Cisco, telepresence is the best way to meet and meet face-to-face across borders. To date, Cisco Systems has deployed 223 telepresence conference rooms around the world, and the technology has won several awards for best high-tech innovation.

In addition to having the function of meeting and communicating, Net-a-Porter can also be used for interviews with new employees, recruitment discussions (which are very efficient), and can also be used for personnel training. Cisco has a program called e-coaching, where employees can choose their own mentors, and many times employees and selected mentors don't even work in the same city or country and collaborate tools to provide distance training for mentors and employees to compensate for the inconvenience of distance. In 2015, Cisco developed language automatic translation technology, which eliminates language barriers in communication and brings people closer together.

Real-time conversations between front-line employees and headquarters executives. In addition to telepresence, Cisco has developed a new technology called Jabber, whose main function is to communicate with Jabber during executive meetings. This communication is efficient, and remote executives can immediately know what their employees care about, thus greatly increasing employee engagement in business matters. In the case of Cisco headquarters and employee dialogue and communication around the world, Chambers usually stands in the middle of a large room to speak to employees around the world, and the big screens placed nearby are Cisco employees who are participating in real-time meetings around the world, who can ask and express their opinions through Jabber, a way for global businesses to communicate. For Cisco executives, meetings, we'd love to hear feedback, comments, and suggestions from Cisco employees working in other countries, and there's no situation where geographic isolation creates a lack of opportunities to report directly to their superiors, which is positive and effective, allowing employees to voice their voices anytime, anywhere.

The impact of social networks on businesses. Social networks that are popular with young people around the world are gaining popularity, and the impact of social media on employees is unknown in the future. At a 2011 gathering of America's chief human resources officer, everyone talked about the impact of Internet social media on the way employees work and behave. Young people have a sense of being connected and connected to these networks, so how do they connect to the workplace while contributing to the development and advancement of human resources? In the face of more and more young people joining social networks, are companies also incorporating or developing their own social networks? Human resources executives in the industry have different views and arguments about this type of issue, and many industry executives are reluctant to involve their employees in open social networks, fearing that important information could be leaked and unwittingly shared, leading to an outflow of trade secrets and affecting the competitive advantage of the company. For Cisco's human resource managers, they see the positive impact of social networking. From the current performance management system of many enterprises, performance management is recorded and evaluated through paper text, many goals are set at the beginning of the year, and then by the end of the year according to the target performance evaluation. Looking ahead, we envision creating a virtual space around the world through social networking where people can work together while evaluating the work of others. For this vision, the industry was still in a state of exploration, the value of social networks to the enterprise needs to be further explored.

Cisco has reaped significant benefits through collaborative technology. Traditional management techniques and hierarchical structures have a management span of about 10, Cisco's management span in 2005 was about 40 through collaborative technology, and by 2009 Cisco's collaborative management span had grown to 500–3000 people. In fiscal 2009, Cisco invested $116 million in Web 2.0 collaboration solutions, generating a net income of $1.1 billion in less than nine months. Cisco's people-related costs account for about 84% of the total cost, which shows that the more you invest in collaboration tools, the greater the return.

5 Inter-organizational Collaboration

In addition to supporting internal collaboration, collaborative organizations support external collaboration, including collaboration with customers, partners, suppliers, and partners. Building a shared value network and business ecosystem through a collaborative platform creates obstacles to competitors' catch-up, while collaboration between enterprises not only reduces transaction costs, but also improves common efficiency, which is important for sustainable development. Wikipedia, Firefox and Linux, YouTube and Flickr are all examples of co-creations. In this respect, Apple is doing better than Sony, the music industry leader. Sony's Walkman, which has generated 200 million units in sales, has $62 billion in online music sales and its products can be connected to many brands of computers. By contrast, Apple's iPod was only connected to the Mac, and sales were only a tenth of Sony's, not to mention that the iPod's battery was made by Sony. In this industry, if everyone chooses the winner, perhaps everyone will choose Sony. However, through business model innovation, Apple has created a greater space for innovation, it will be its own design industrialization, with different companies, through crowdsourcing, a large number of app applications integrated into Apple's platform, the industry chain of parties to form a community of interests. Focus ingenuity and power on a platform that can share resources on its Mac, iPhone and iPad, creating a huge appeal to customers, making it the most innovative and valuable company in the world today. But Sony is closed, and suppliers have no expansion of cooperative relations, the company's many departments operate independently, the computer and music departments do not interfere with each other, the emergence of comprehensive problems cannot be resolved in a timely manner. As a result, Sony was eventually defeated by Apple in the heat of international competition, and its corporate culture did not even allow inter-department collaboration, so when Sony began to try to collaborate, sales plummeted. Thus, bad cooperation is worse than no cooperation.

The application of telepresence systems not only addresses Cisco's cross-sectoral, cross-regional, and cross-border communication and collaboration issues, but also has a positive impact on the management of its customer value chain. According to Cisco's official statistics, as many as 2,932 telepresence meetings were held in 2009 alone. The use of telepresence in customer value chain management resulted in an estimated 1,681 reductions in travel costs, savings in travel costs estimated at $1,866.3 million, and reduced carbon emissions estimated at 544.76 tons, resulting in an increase in production efficiency of several million dollars. Among them, reduce travel costs by 30%, increase employee interaction by 23%, increase employee knowledge sharing by 19%, increase employee productivity by 18%, improve customer issues by 3%, accelerate new product time to market 3%, mitigate the crisis, maintain business growth by 2%, increase Cisco executive face-to-face interaction with customers 1% and present 1% of Cisco products face-to-face to customers.

6 Collaboration Technology Used in the Sales Work

Sales enhancement. Collaboration technologies can have a positive impact on sales, and Cisco has made virtualization and mobility technology applications a development priority. Cisco Headquarters has a Comprehensive Technology Product Display Center to reflect Cisco's comprehensive solutions and technical capabilities, and it is not practical to have the same display center in all 500 Cisco offices worldwide because it is expensive, but customers around the world are interested in looking at Cisco products first. To solve this problem, Cisco uses virtualization technology that allows salespeople to virtually demonstrate Cisco's existing products and their applications to customers around the world in a virtual way. Now that Cisco has established the Cisco Sales Information Center, all applications used by the sales services team are centralized in a knowledge base where all salespeople can share the results of their knowledge.

Dynamic mobile payments. In 2011, Cisco embedded collaboration technology into iPads and iPhones for cost calculations. When account managers and sales managers travel, they can open the app and report travel expenses online. If you drive from your home to your customers, automatically start the application, mark the starting point and destination, and connect it to Google Maps, you can calculate the distance and fuel cost of this section of the trip. When the sales staff travel abroad, stay in a hotel, they can directly enter the hotel information into this application system, and it will automatically calculate the cost of accommodation based on the immediate price, and these reimbursement costs will be included in the personal account. Through these technologies, Cisco helps employees significantly reduce the time and effort they spend on tedious work, devote these valuable resources to more valuable and important things, and help sales teams increase productivity and productivity.

Telepresence sales conferences. In the past two to three years, one of the most innovative technologies Cisco has explored is virtual sales meetings through telepresence, bringing together salespeople from Las Vegas and San Francisco to meet, greatly reducing travel costs, and winning industry awards. To that end, Cisco invested $20 million in design concepts, implementation plans, and technical solutions that enable salespeople around the world to participate in global conferences through telepresence video. Some universities in the United States also build virtual classrooms through telepresence systems to provide EMBA program training.

Expert knowledge sharing. As a global company, Cisco needs to visit customers around the world, especially in the newly industrialized countries, but experienced experts are scarce in any business, constrained by this resource, and sales teams often feel stretched, and companies struggle to scale up sales. To effectively address this issue, Cisco has set up a 7-by-24 virtual technical support team of engineers to help sales teams quickly address complex issues such as bidding projects and technical solutions. For example, when a sales team sees a large customer at noon, the customer asks the salesperson to complete a business plan at 3 p.m., a job that would otherwise seem impossible to do efficiently with the help of a virtual team. Any time you assign a task to this 7×24 virtual technical support team, they can do it quickly. This is how it's great to use information technology to accelerate the response and increase productivity.

7 Knowledge Management and Knowledge Value-Added Chain

The new challenge and challenge for Cisco today is how to manage substantial amounts of data. In 2012, home broadband generated more data traffic than the entire Internet in 2008. By the end of 2010, the entire Internet will be transmitting 0.5 gigabytes of data. The rapid growth of data is based on three main reasons:

The widespread use of video. "Video is a new voice," says Cisco CEO Michael Chambers. Because video is a richer way of communicating, it contains more data than traditional text communication. With most handheld devices having cameras, audio and video capabilities, this popularity and convenience will dramatically increase the number of videos viewed on the Internet.

The fast-growing Internet. The Internet is still expanding rapidly. The next generation will have 1 billion people connected to the Internet via wireless devices. The number of nodes and devices on the Internet doubles every 5.32 years, and if a person has multiple devices connected to the Internet, it means that by 2020, the number of devices connected to the Internet will exceed the number of humans on the planet.

The ubiquitous cameras. Almost all devices are now equipped with cameras, which have turned ordinary people into part-time photographers and videographers. Televisions are also gradually equipped with in-line cameras. With the spread of these cheap, high-quality, easy-to-use cameras, the amount of data generated through multimedia will continue to increase significantly.

Big data presents many challenges. The rapid increase in data volume has created a big data problem for mankind. So-called big data refers to the collection of data sets that are quite large and complex, thus stretching the database management tools now in use. These tools are hard to capture, store, retrieve, share, analyze, and visualize these data resources. According to Gartner expert Doug Laney, the problems posed by copious amounts of data are both a challenge and an opportunity for humans on three levels (known as 3 V by Laney): an increase in data volume and an increase in velocity. Third, data diversification. How to deal with these information assets and how to find value from them is both a problem for Cisco and a problem for its customers as an Internet device provider.

In addition to the large number of general data problems, large amounts of data also bring about data pollution problems. Pollution usually refers to the instability, disorder, destruction or ecosystem chaos that comes with the introduction of pollutants into the natural environment. Today's massive amounts of data often pollute the environment and cause "instability, disorder, destruction, or discomfort" to business. This phenomenon is called data pollution, or data rapidly increasing the pollution of the information environment, making decision-making and problem-solving more complex. For example, it is difficult to find the needed information and knowledge, as real and fake data is mixed, data is difficult to create new value, and useless data storage takes up storage space and technical resources.

Data pollution increases the operating costs of businesses, which can measure these losses by spending money on storing excess data. Cisco, for example, spent $77 million in 2010 on data that has not been used for more than a year. Cisco is not the only one. According to Gartner, more than 70% of the data in traditional businesses has not been used.

Faced with such a large amount of data, for enterprises, a central problem is how to turn large amounts of data into valuable information and knowledge. The data itself is useless, it can only be added to the value of information after it is marked, organized, integrated, and classified. Information can be turned into knowledge only when it is processed to help improve people's decision-making speed and efficiency. In other words, knowledge generation is based on correct and reliable data, from which useful information is generated and used by people, from data to knowledge is a continuous process of added value. In addition to the challenges of dealing with large amounts of data, Cisco has also found it challenging to handle the rapidly growing amount of video information for the enterprise. So far, people still lack effective methods of classification, labeling and retrieval of video information. Video contains more and more data and information, but it is difficult for businesses to find valuable and important information from stored video libraries.

How should businesses turn data into information? The answer may come from the human brain. People are good at filtering noise and focusing on what's more important to them, and companies process data by imitating the human brain to ensure that employees are always able to find the information they need. Cisco's approach is to develop a professional interest information classification system (e.g. finance, marketing, product design, etc.), employees, according to their own interests in the information classification system, through interest groups in the enterprise to form a large number of virtual community, in the community, through the exchange and sharing of information related to their own professional interests and to recognize peers, learn from each other, grow together, and access at anytime, anywhere when employees need relevant information and peer support.

Once the data is translated into information, the next step is to turn information into knowledge. This step is important because knowledge is essential for managers to make important business decisions.

Businesses also need to create an environment where knowledge-sharing is easy to share. Employees need an environment that facilitates collaboration, free sharing of knowledge and resources, quickly and effectively discovering, utilizing, and sharing data, and quickly finding and communicating with target experts within the enterprise, which is best done on a single platform that needs to be supported by appropriate technology, processes, and culture. When established, this environment creates a culture of knowledge innovation that supports the free sharing of new ideas among groups within the enterprise and the free discussion of ideas and solutions, an open, borderless, transparent atmosphere of organizational communication that transcends the limitations of position, geography, language and time and space. It is conducive to the improvement of enterprise productivity and the acceleration of innovation.

8 Integrated Work Experience Platform and Knowledge Sharing

Cisco has a clear vision of knowledge management, which connects every step of its development with networked information technology and moves toward a service-oriented organization through technology and business integration. To achieve this, Cisco's employees and users make it easy to connect people, information, and business processes so that people can work efficiently.

Employees and users alike need to collaborate easily, freely share knowledge and resources, effectively find, organize, and analyze information, enable users to find experts efficiently, and communicate efficiently with experts within the enterprise, relying on the right technology, processes, and culture. Ultimately, Cisco's information technology will develop and foster an open, borderless, and transparent work environment that enables people in different sectors and regions to work efficiently and increase productivity.

Cisco Knowledge Management focuses on building integrated work experience (IWE) platforms. The core issues to be addressed by the IWE platform are: first, the knowledge and information caused by the rotation of employees in different functions or regions as a result of economic globalization is difficult to detect, and thus cannot be effectively organized and managed, and the loss of knowledge resulting from the departure of employees; there are a large number of information silos within the enterprise; third, knowledge is static and not shared and reused; fourth, it is difficult for users to share or add value to knowledge; fifth, knowledge is rarely retrieved and used when it is stored; sixth, experts are not necessarily willing to show up; and seventh, many personal insights and know-how exist only in people's private interactions; information between platforms is difficult to exchange and integrate, greatly reducing productivity; the IWE platform will replace other platforms and create more convenience for employees to communicate and collaborate. For example, when an employee attends a meeting, the platform can provide background information for other attendees, including the participant's expertise, projects and areas of expertise, as well as literature related to the topic of the day's meeting and links to external information related to it.

The IWE platform consists of three parts:

(1) People. New information has been added to the human section of the IWE platform, including skills, previously created files, and communities, interests, and more.
(2) Information. The information section of the IWE platform is a knowledge base of information created by all Cisco employees. When an employee looks for a specific topic, the IWE platform provides a series of relevant literature. In addition to the document name and abstract information, users can also see other information completed by the author of the document.
(3) Community. The community is the most effective part of the IWE platform because it makes it easy for employees to find people who need to work together and easily access the information they need.

These three parts of the IWE platform are highly integrated, ensuring that employees have easy access to the information they need, no matter where they are on the system. The IWE platform is supported by CiscoQuad. CiscoQuad is an enterprise platform that integrates the capabilities of social networks with the capabilities of communication systems, business information, and content management systems. CiscoQuad enhances business by first, maximizing employee skills and encouraging knowledge sharing and knowledge transfer to increase productivity; promoting growth by tailoring content in specific contexts to make it easier for experts in a field and employees who need them to get close, sharing best practices and lessons learned, and creating a collaborative culture.

Through the IWE platform, Cisco has a centralized information channel that enables the purposeful delivery of information. Its benefits include the easy discovery of internal information and expert background information, the organization of information in a personalized manner, the creation, release, organization and sharing of information, participation in ongoing meetings and discussions, the discovery and exchange of experts in various fields through a variety of technologies, and the integration and balance of collective wisdom.

The IWE platform brings a new way of completing day-to-day work. To centralize and deliver relevant information to employees and allow employees to collaborate globally, Cisco's IT department helps organizations address the issues of decentralized information and knowledge in global operations, difficult to share and use, when using new technologies for collaboration within the organization.

In order to effectively evaluate the effectiveness of the IWE platform, Cisco also quantitatively evaluates the use of the platform. Metrics include which teams and departments provide valuable information, number of platform visits, clicks, internal web pages, cross-sectoral and cross-regional engagement, discussion area, number of documents uploaded, blogs, terms on Wikipedia, user-provided comments, ratings, and more. Of course, Cisco's IT department is still in its infancy in collecting platform usage metrics, and its final value is not yet fully demonstrated. But as more IT business processes are integrated and more users utilize the platform, its true value will be more easily measured. Future metrics for Cisco to focus on evaluating its key value include time-to-market, productivity increases, increased productivity, and lower communication costs. The IWE platform is of great business value to Cisco. First, by sharing knowledge, Cisco's knowledge management system has a positive impact on the business of the enterprise, with a positive impact on investment returns, costs, risks, and market share for Cisco or customers. Second, increase the influence of enterprises. Through an open and transparent environment, Cisco's connections with partners and customers can be easily expanded and enhanced. Third, improve the innovation efficiency of enterprises. Increase Cisco's partners, users, and their own innovation capabilities through the sharing of knowledge and experience. Fourth, strengthen the management capacity of change. The new work atmosphere and culture created by the platform is a new organizational change caused by the use of technology, and the platform will become the basis for brainstorming and consensus as enterprises push for new changes.

In the future, Cisco will build a "knowledge cloud" based on the IWE platform. "Cloud" is a common name for knowledge integration and knowledge-sharing storage environments, "private cloud" is proprietary to enterprises or specific organizations, "public cloud" is used by the general public, and the enterprise knowledge cloud is an example of a knowledge virtualization storage environment, often using a private cloud. Within Cisco, there is a "virtual cloud" technology that enables employees to log on to the network and share information in any network environment, wherever they are. The application of this technology can provide a favorable condition for further expanding Cisco's working boundaries and effectively leveraging the organization's strategic knowledge assets.

9 Summary

Efficient collaborative organization is an important condition for enterprises to ensure the speed of competition in a competitive environment, and this large-span collaboration is like an enterprise-wide barrier-free race, removing barriers from multiple dimensions, such as top-down, bottom-up, horizontal, cross-sectoral and internal and external to the enterprise. This kind of collaboration involves the full communication of ideas, networked collaboration between departments, teams and projects, the free flow and sharing of knowledge, the interaction between the inside and outside of the enterprise, the integration and resource allocation between headquarters and offices, and so on, the information island of the enterprise is constantly broken through, people need to communicate, no matter when and where can be carried out. Only in the information age, the popularity and widespread use of information and communication technology can make the barriers between hierarchies, departments, and regions are removed, so it is an important infrastructure for global enterprise operations.

The benefits of a collaborative organization are:

(1) The full sharing and utilization of the resources of the organization, especially knowledge and information. Because of the high cost of first-time access to knowledge and information resources, and the low cost of sharing and reuse, enterprises need to create a cultural, institutional and technological environment that ensures maximum use of knowledge and information from people and enterprises.
(2) Break down the internal barriers and information silos between the organizations, prevent the focus of departmental interests, and ensure the maximization of the overall interests of the organization.
(3) Expand the space for knowledge innovation, develop new thinking and generate new ideas through dynamic collaboration within the organization through the combination of different professional backgrounds.
(4) Continuously stimulate the internal motivation and energy of enterprise personnel, form collaborative creativity, and break organizational inertia through dynamic cross-border relationships and deep collaboration between people, departments and project teams.

Cisco has taken collaboration as its core goal in the organization's information-based construction and knowledge management practice and has realized the three-dimensional communication system of text, image, voice, video, and workflow, which brings the following benefits to the enterprise:

(1) Ensures that enterprises to customer-centric, to meet customer needs, to achieve the combination and deployment of internal resources.
(2) Ensures flexibility in organizational change. Collaborative organizations break the fixed boundaries of individuals, departments, and businesses. Each person or team works in a multi-network environment, forming a dynamic collaboration system, according to the needs of the task, the network pattern will change at

any time, the inertia and curing of the organization is difficult to form, change becomes the norm of the organization.

(3) Ensures the flow and sharing of new knowledge. For high-tech enterprises, the external market is fast, technology innovation occurs every day, the need for enterprises to build a dynamic flow of knowledge, skills, information environment, especially the hidden knowledge owned by professionals is the most important core resources of enterprises, collaborative network to different backgrounds, and different professions. People in different regions provide convenient conditions for communication, and video and dialogue are the most important way to share implicit knowledge. Cisco's collaboration environment maximizes this knowledge.

Of course, like other high-tech enterprises, Cisco's knowledge management is facing great challenges, including the network information dissemination speed and lower costs, all enterprises are faced with data redundancy and information overload caused by the problem. This information environment pollution will result in more video information moving into the network in the future and pose serious problems. The global general spread of big data also illustrates the magnitude of the problem. Cisco uses a range of information technology techniques to achieve the organization's information exchange, knowledge sharing, knowledge dissemination and knowledge integration of the order, visualization and platform, to solve the information deluge and distortion issues through valuable exploration.

Appendix

Leaders' wisdom is reflected in their insight and response to changes, their understanding and learning of new things, their balance and attention to the big picture, their appreciation and use of talents, their identification and avoidance of risks, and their management and attention to details.

This appendix lists the questions that the author participated in the group visit in Cisco and recorded the interviewing questions and dialogues with Cisco.

Question list

1 Strategic Leadership

1. What are the advantages and disadvantages of Cisco's incentive system for senior management?
2. How do managers communicate with the most basic employees?
3. How do you evaluate the departure of Cisco's founders?
4. Which is more important, the leader or the system?
5. Do entrepreneurs need the qualities of politicians?
6. What are the CEO's main responsibilities in the global expansion of the company?
7. How to balance the choice between the present and the future?
8. What's the Saturday staff meeting at Wal-Mart?
9. What are the biggest surprises and mistakes of being a CEO?
10. What is the most important reason for CEO success?
11. How can CEOs know themselves?
12. Where does the courage come from to make difficult decisions?
13. Where does the CEO get the passion and motivation to work long term?
14. What are the characteristics of the deputies they most like and intend to replace?
15. How is Cisco's leadership training system structured?
16. How is leadership specifically measured?

X. Dong et al., *Cisco*,
https://doi.org/10.1007/978-981-19-7870-8

17. Can you give us some details about the nomination process in the leadership development framework?
18. What is the chief operating officer (COO) of Cisco?
19. What are the main responsibilities of COO?
20. How can COO be recognized by superiors and colleagues?
21. Can Cisco's internal communication really solve problems?
22. Is there a phase to Cisco's operational excellence and innovation?
23. Do leaders value the opinions of front-line workers?
24. How do CTO and CFO communicate and cooperate?
25. What advice do you (Chambers) have for Chinese state-owned enterprises?

2 Enterprise Transformation and Change Management

1. What are the possible crises in the market transformation of Cisco in the next 3–5 years?
2. What's the difference between Cisco and apple?
3. How can traditional successful enterprises foresee the direction of transformation?
4. What kind of culture should a leader adopt to meet the challenge of change while maximizing benefits?
5. Young people are more receptive to new technology and adapt to change than older people. Who is driving the change at Cisco?
6. Will the pace of change and transformation slow down and stabilize in the future?
7. How to promote the transformation of Cisco?
8. How do you view the development of Cisco products in China?
9. Focusing on the core business means abandoning some other businesses. How do you handle this relationship?
10. How to deal with disagreements among the top team?
11. How to ensure the quality of products when enterprises need to reduce costs and improve organizational efficiency?
12. How does Cisco control risk for product innovation through acquisition?
13. How are the philosophies of leaders in transition different from those of ordinary people?
14. How to solve the organizational turbulence caused by too much change?
15. How do transition leaders feel about different positions?
16. How should leaders handle the relationship between innovation and operational excellence?
17. What is the difference between progressive and radical reform?
18. How to solve the negative problems brought by the transformation?
19. What if employees don't like change?
20. What is the market transformation direction of Cisco after 2012?
21. Who is Cisco's biggest global competitor? What is its competitive advantage?

3 Innovation System

1. How to deal with the input and output of innovation, as well as the relationship between present and future?
2. How to deal with the relationship between innovation and inertia?
3. Does the management team need to constantly update and adjust during the innovation process?
4. Does the organizational structure need to be adjusted simultaneously during innovation?
5. Where does innovative foresight come from?
6. Where does CEO innovation come from?
7. What kind of internal structure and organizational mode does enterprise innovation need?
8. How to promote enterprise innovation?
9. How to balance the relationship between user demand and technological innovation?
10. How to grasp the pace of innovation?
11. How to determine the R&D input in the budget?
12. Is the R&D team focused or divided into five core areas?
13. How does Cisco make institutional arrangements to promote a culture of innovation?
14. What is Cisco's regional strategy in China?
15. How does Cisco's innovation strategy contribute to technological differentiation?
16. How to evaluate the performance of the R&D team?
17. What is the difference between innovation in large and small companies?
18. What is the ratio of continuous innovation to disruptive innovation?
19. Apart from innovation, what factors can affect the longevity of a company?
20. Will Cisco's focus on indigenous research and development change?
21. Will there be a change in the direction of innovative enterprises to excellent operating enterprises?

4 Merger Strategy and Merger Management

1. What are the reasons for the merger?
2. What is the relationship between merger and acquisition and core competitiveness?
3. Will Cisco adjust the personnel in key positions of the target?
4. How to determine operating indicators after acquisition and integration?
5. How to deal with the acquired company's brand?
6. Have you considered acquiring Huawei?
7. What is the biggest difficulty Cisco has encountered in acquiring and merging Chinese enterprises?

8. In the process of merger and integration, is there a replacement for the head of the merged company?
9. What makes Cisco attractive to M&A companies?
10. How to deal well with mergers and acquisitions?
11. The greater the core differentiation, the greater the investment risk. How to treat this issue?
12. How to solve the integration problem of culture and management in enterprise acquisition?
13. How to evaluate the performance of M&A? Are there any failures?
14. Does the acquisition require an intermediary?
15. How to achieve risk management and control in the acquisition process?
16. What is the acquisition of Netcom like?
17. What are the key ingredients for the success or failure of an acquisition?
18. How do you ensure success when you meet a competitor in an acquisition?
19. What are the earnings criteria for acquisitions?
20. How to retain talents in the acquisition process? How does the acquired company fit into Cisco better?
21. Why are Cisco acquisitions always faster than they are?
22. Can you give an example of how Cisco's acquisition strategy changed from one-way technology to platform to overall strategy?
23. How can Cisco achieve the integration of corporate culture during acquisition?
24. What is the process from proposal to implementation?
25. Does the acquisition need to be approved by the general meeting when it reaches a certain amount?
26. What is the architecture of Cisco's integrated team? What role does it play? What expertise do you have?
27. Who will manage the integration team members at Cisco during the integration?
28. How many public companies has Cisco bought? Will the listed company continue to go public after it is acquired?
29. Will Cisco buy a company and then sell it?
30. What is the process of integration?
31. What is the relationship between acquisition and integration?
32. How to integrate the culture of the acquired company with that of Cisco?
33. Does too much acquisition make a company less focused?
34. How does Cisco measure the culture of the target company during the acquisition process?
35. Will Cisco make targeted acquisitions of rival companies?
36. How long does it take from Cisco to acquisition?
37. Does Cisco value products, technology, or technicians more in acquisitions?
38. What are the main reasons for Cisco's acquisition failure?
39. How to solve the problems of customer retention, employee retention and cultural integration in the acquisition process?
40. After targeting the acquisition, should we take measures to facilitate the acquisition conditions, or wait for the natural opportunity?
41. What if the acquired party does not accept the time and price proposed by Cisco?

42. Will Cisco make related acquisitions around its main business or will it also make related acquisitions?
43. What percentage and structure of employees of the acquired company will stay at Cisco? What are the main contributions of the three pillars of innovation?
44. Will employees be appointed as managers of the acquired company after the acquisition?
45. Differentiated technology acquisition means that the technology of the acquired company is different from the original market, or is it higher than the market level?
46. What if the experts have different opinions in the acquisition decision? What are the biggest obstacles to a takeover?
47. What are the meanings and differences between active investment and passive investment?
48. How are active and passive investments determined?
49. In which sector are investment opportunities usually identified?
50. How are investment or acquisition decisions made?
51. What are the pros and cons of Cisco's cooperation with other companies?
52. What is the role of the finance department in acquisition activities?
53. What is the optimal profit level for a business acquisition?
54. Stock or cash? How do you balance short-term goals with long-term goals?

5 Strategic Alliance and Partnership Management

1. What kind of partners is Cisco looking for in China? Will you choose Huawei?
2. When and under what circumstances?
3. What are the criteria by which Cisco chooses its partners?
4. How does Cisco work with its partners in three stages?
5. Is Cisco's relationship with its partners long-term and strategic? Will there be constant adjustments to the partners?
6. Does Cisco have a fixed business model, or does it have a new business model for each collaboration?
7. Will Cisco pursue joint ventures with its partners as a long-term strategy?
8. How to understand the three modes of cooperation between Cisco and its partners?
9. If Cisco loses market share to its partners, what will it do to make up for it?
10. How to avoid cooperation failure?
11. Who decides on the process of choosing different partners for different products?
12. What is the difference between customer-led cooperation and partner-led cooperation in customer service?
13. What is the difference in emphasis between the sales department and the service department?
14. What is the division of labor between headquarters and regions in global customer management? What is the customer management mechanism?

15. Does Cisco have a dedicated team to study its competitors?
16. How does Cisco's one-stop sales strategy compete with a company like IBM that sells concepts?
17. How can Cisco achieve global replication of best practices for the application of new technologies?
18. What are the criteria for direct selling and distribution strategies?

6 Establish a Highly Adaptable Corporate Culture

1. What is the difference between the culture of Chinese state-owned enterprises and that of American state-owned enterprises?
2. How to expand the role and influence of corporate culture?
3. How does customer-centric approach behave in practice?
4. How can employees understand the company's vision?
5. What is the relationship between vision and strategy?
6. How do employees align with Cisco's vision and strategy?
7. How does Cisco attract and retain talent?
8. Cisco emphasizes teamwork, but why is there a "personal contribution" in the compensation system?
9. What is Cisco's strategy? How does corporate culture affect corporate strategy?
10. How does Cisco manage from vertical resource management to portfolio management?
11. Does the CEO play a major role in building corporate culture, or does the employee build it?
12. From personal commitment to overall responsibility, will it lead to unclear responsibility?
13. From the competitive culture to the Shared target culture, is it only for the internal enterprise or including external competition?
14. How to understand "to the thing, not the person"?
15. Can the culture of operational excellence and innovation strategy be integrated?
16. Does Cisco's corporate culture need to be improved and optimized?

7 Corporate Governance and Risk Management

1. What is the communication mechanism of the board of directors?
2. How do boards control risk in major decisions?
3. Will government regulation and restrictions on executive compensation affect the competitiveness of the U.S. market environment?
4. In the process of development, why do some big companies fail while Cisco can stand alone?
5. How to evaluate R&D risks in the R&D process?

6. In terms of finance, what are the roles of the risk control department and the finance department?
7. Cisco has many business units, so is the financial model a unified management model?
8. Is the risk control department completely independent of the company and other departments?
9. Risk control functions as a racing car brake. Does this process limit the company's activities?
10. Do all business processes need to be audited and how should this be done?
11. In the process of supervision, how to solve the problem?
12. Will the complexity of the audit affect the efficiency of the business department?
13. What is the mix of people in the risk control department? How to complete the risk management process?
14. Does the board have a veto?
15. What is the relationship between the risk control department and the business units? What are their roles?
16. If an audit of the CEO reveals a problem, what happens?
17. Internal risks can be controlled in advance, so how to deal with external risks?
18. Will risk control affect innovation?
19. Is there an informal audit process outside the normal audit process?
20. What to do if the risk cannot be resolved with the business alone?
21. To whom and how is the corporate risk management committee accountable?
22. How to manage political risk?
23. What should be the best practice in risk management?
24. Could there be problems with the audit or risk management process?
25. How is responsibility distributed in the conduct of audits and risk management?

8 Information and Value Chain Management

1. When expanding new business, does the enterprise need to create new processes, develop new information systems and technologies?
2. How much did Cisco spend on its information systems? How does the BOST model affect the information system?
3. Who are Cisco's successful customers in using telepresence in China?
4. How to ensure high profits while controlling IT costs?
5. How much has IT helped Cisco expand its business and reduce costs?
6. What are the key elements of successful information system construction? What are the biggest problems and challenges?
7. When there is a conflict between the business and IT, does the business lead the technology or does the technology lead the business?
8. How often do you update the old system? Under what circumstances will it be replaced?
9. Do you take risks with new technology when it's working?

10. Does Cisco adopt a unified standard for its global architecture or consider regional differences?
11. What are the biggest challenges facing Cisco's information technology systems compared to U.S. best practices?
12. How does IT control business risk for the whole company?
13. How are the IT systems of the acquired enterprise integrated into Cisco systems?
14. Does Cisco keep the paper version after processing?
15. Are all the processes and technical architectures of the Cisco innovation team supported by the IT department?
16. Why is the cost of a Dallas data center lower?
17. In the process of resource automation and virtualization, how does the IT department allocate resources?
18. Will Cisco merge the acquired company into UCS systems or let it continue to use its own systems?
19. What is the role of the IT department in the company's transformation?
20. How to transform the IT department after the acquisition?
21. How to ensure the security and integrity of data?
22. What type of enterprise will be better served by enterprise-class cloud technology?
23. Can you introduce Cisco's security business?
24. How does Cisco choose suppliers and what are its criteria?
25. In the case of outsourcing, how to ensure the quality, cost and lead time of products?
26. How long is the supply cycle of Cisco?
27. What is the role of supply chain members in matrix management?
28. What is Cisco's product data management process?
29. What is the process of Cisco's software supply chain?
30. What are the core principles of Cisco's simplified supply chain system?
31. Does the rapid recovery of Cisco's supply chain depend on the system or the team?

9 Collaborative Organization and Knowledge Management

1. How to motivate employees?
2. How to measure employee engagement?
3. How to fire employees?
4. How to evaluate the performance of the department, especially the human resources department?
5. Do evaluations of employees focus on competence, or also on ethics?
6. What are the external recruitment channels for senior leaders?
7. What is the main job of the human resources department?
8. Why is the human resources department's strategy generally 3–5 years?
9. Can you introduce the equity incentive method of Cisco in detail?

10. How to train "star employees"?
11. Why is equity incentive reduced?
12. What are the benefits for retired employees?
13. Which industry has a higher salary level, energy industry or high-tech industry?
14. Who will determine the indicators for performance evaluation and assessment?
15. What is Cisco's view on talent flow? What is the proportion of talent turnover?
16. What are some of Cisco's best ways to attract and retain talent?